FLEE THE WOLF

The Story of a Family's Miraculous Journey to Freedom

by
Marianne Schmeling

DONNING
NORFOLK/VIRGINIA BEACH

To My Silent Ally and Friend

Cover concept, design & illustration by
Fischbach & Edenton Virginia Beach, Va.

Copyright ©1978 by E. Marianne Schmeling

All rights reserved, including the right to reproduce this book in any form whatsoever without permission in writing from the publisher, except for brief passages in connection with a review. For information write: The Donning Company/Publishers, 5041 Admiral Wright Road, Virginia Beach, Virginia 23462.

Library of Congress Cataloging in Publication Data

Schmeling, E   Marianne.
   Flee the wolf.

   1. World War, 1939-1945—Personal narratives, German.
2. Schmeling, E. Marianne.   3. Children—Germany—Biography.   I. Title.
D811.5.S32   940.54'82'43   78-24154
ISBN 0-915442-67-1

Printed in the United States of America

TABLE OF CONTENTS

Prologue		xi
I	As A Man Soweth	1
II	Vengeance Is Mine—Saith The Lord	13
III	Brother Shall Turn Against Brother	31
IV	Hopes And Fears	47
V	War—Victorious	64
VI	Trials And Tribulations	73
VII	War—On Bended Knee	91
VIII	Flight From The Beast—Step One	112
IX	Flight From The Beast—Step Two	137
X	Save Us! For Thy Mercies' Sake	163
XI	Thy Rod And Thy Staff	184
XII	Gathering Them Together	201
XIII	A Stranger In His Own Country	231
XIV	Freed To Serve	260
Epilogue		284

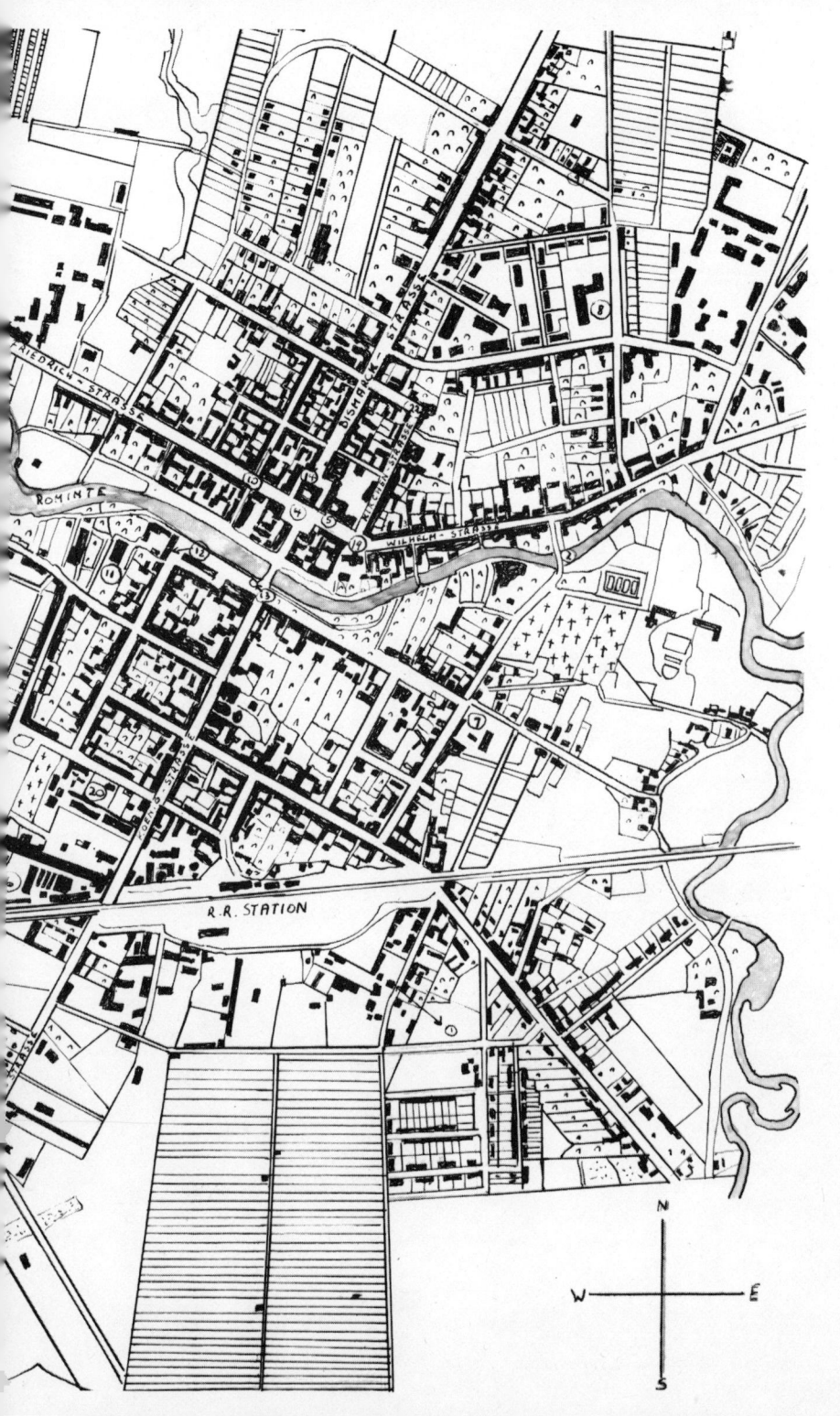

Prologue

Why should I write a book about Nazi-Germany? Haven't we read enough about the subject? Should we not rather forget such a dreadful era instead of being reminded again of this period of tyranny, horror, and death?

These questions I have asked myself when my friends urged me to write this book. If my intentions were to add a volume to the annals of history I would never have started. But my purpose for writing this book is that it may serve as a testimony, a testimony that man can overcome his ancient adversary, war, by learning to overcome the emotions of hate, resentment, and fear. As the dark clouds of war are again looming over our civilization, threatening total annihilation of man on our planet, I feel that my testimony is timely. This, then, is my hope and prayer: that those who read my story might learn the same lesson without the need to go through the same painful experience.

So many young people today speak out against war, and I agree with them. But have we really prepared our hearts for peace? As long as we still harbor feelings of hate and resentment, we will have no peace. Therefore, we must learn to love, not only our neighbor, but we must love our enemies. Only this honest outreach will free our hearts and break the cyclic and antagonistic flow of negative energy, transforming it into feelings of understanding—because love and understanding are one. Only after we have mastered this exercise will we have laid a lasting foundation for peace.

This insight I did not gain in an overnight revelation. It took twenty-five painful years of my life to come to this understanding but, today, I thank God for having tutored me in such a hard school and for having seen me through the full term.

When my mind travels back to my hometown, Gumbinnen, in East Prussia, Germany, I realize what a small, peaceful town it had been and how it changed under the nightmarish takeover of the Nazi regime. Gumbinnen was the town from which my family fled in terror of the murderous Russian armies, keeping as close as a mile on our heels, until a third and final evacuation took us far enough to the West to assure us that we had escaped the claws of the beast: Bolshevism. Only one word will express my feelings now concerning what I felt then—a miracle. It was miraculous because throughout these years of turmoil and confusion not one member of our family of eight was lost or harmed. I learned to overcome the ten years of haunting nightmares of Russians pursuing me, in one instant—by making one Russian my friend! She, also, had fled from tyranny—Bolshevik tyranny—and had come to the United States, making America her new home. From my Russian friend, I learned that Russia is not one massive, bloodthirsty monster, but that it is people. Can we imagine the fact that many of her people today still hunger for love and understanding? Are we, who consider ourselves living in freedom, willing to extend our prayers to the Urals and beyond to enfold those needy in the love of God Who created us all? We are our brother's keeper, be he on the other side of this world or standing right next to us. May I, therefore, invite you to join me in this adventurous mission to serve him in love, peace, and freedom?

More than forty years ago, I did not dare to dream that I would spend more than half of my life in God's country, America, speaking a different language than my family. Or did my soul know the path before it entered into life on earth? If I was unaware of it, I know One Who mapped out my destiny: The Author of Life, The Creator of us all. He knows every thought I think, every move I make. Time has proven this fact over and over again. He knows also the reason why I was born the third daughter of a young East Prussian couple living in Gumbinnen in 1930. Gumbinnen, at that time, was a quiet town struggling to overcome the depression of 1929, a depression which had plunged the whole western world into despair. But back then I did not dare to dream.

Chapter I

As A Man Soweth...

Since my parents were married on Christmas Day 1925, a time of rampant running inflation, the very beginning of their joint life was difficult. As a result, Mother and Father learned early to trust in God and to pray for survival. Their first five years of marriage must have been nothing but a struggle for survival. Being born into this family setting, I was introduced to God at a very young age and learned to have faith in Him, no matter what life would bring. Yet hardships neither curbed my parents' enthusiasm for life nor altered their determination to raise a large family. Within the crevices of her heart, Mother had hoped to have a son, but her firstborn was a daughter, my sister Ursula, and the next two additions were my older sister, Herta, then me. Sorry, Mother, but there we were. What could she do but accept us? When Frederick arrived in January, 1932, the whole family rejoiced with Mother. It was a boy—at last! In the meantime, our young family, demanding food at every mealtime, had forced Mother through a crash course in cooking. Father, in his dry sense of humor, often commented on the many burnt meals.

"Oh," he said, "it's Grandmother's seasoning again that makes the soup taste so strong." Mother laughingly defended herself, answering, "You must admit that I have greatly improved since our wedding day because I didn't even know how to brew coffee." Father remembered well and, in reflection, even his blue eyes were laughing as both recalled Mother's helpless attempts to scramble a hot meal together and have it ready in time to serve him when he came home from work feeling hungry and tired.

Mother greatly admired Aunt Ina as an outstanding gourmet. Aunt Ina had married Father's oldest brother, Uncle Oskar. While single, she had attended a private school for homemakers where she became an expert in cooking and baking. Aunt Ina's mother, Mrs. Kowalski, lived across the street from us on the Kasernenstrasse. Therefore, Aunt Ina visiting her mother often, stopped by frequently, tutoring Mother in cooking, often giving her step-by-step instructions, seasoned with funny, sometimes corny remarks. Aunt Ina commented that Mother was a bright pupil, and she was learning quickly. Our favorite meal was potato pancakes and Mother could not fry them fast enough while we were standing around the stove, anxiously waiting for a panful to be crisp and golden brown. I would gobble down one hot pancake after another until my stomach ached and Aunt Ina jokingly remarked that the four of us looked like hungry little sparrows.

We children were not aware that Mother and Father fed and clothed us on very limited funds. I recall, however, that on long winter evenings Aunt Ina often came, sometimes bringing a used dress or two, out of which she and Mother, by some magical way, sewed new dresses for Ursula, Herta, and me. To us, these pretty little dresses were new. How much fun the two women had, cutting a small velvet vest, or adding a ribbon and a few gold buttons to trim each dress. It had been Aunt Ina's bright idea that Herta and I wear identical dresses, like twins. Herta was very fragile for her age but I, two years younger than she, pink and fat like a marzipan piggy, wore the same size. Aunt Ina obviously loved little girls and could not understand why Mother had been so anxiously wishing for a son. Aunt Ina had only one child, my cousin Hans, who was five years older than I, and often, recounting Hans' latest tricks, she told Mother how much easier it was to raise girls.

"Soon you will agree with me," she would say with a knowing smile. Yet, Mother, proud to have Frederick, insisted that under the strict and guiding hand of Father, she would have no problem raising her son. She found out quickly, however, that Frederick had many surprises in store for her. He could move as fast as lightning and, once he knew how to walk, all doors had to be locked, especially the front and the big wooden door leading from the yard to the street. Frederick loved to run away. His aim was always for the street. One day, in his sweet manner of persuasion, he asked Mother that I take him for a stroll along the deserted Kasernenstrasse. Most children in the neighborhood played in their backyards and Mother had given me strict orders to hold Frederick's hand tightly. Yet we had not walked far when with one hard wiggle he tore loose and ran down the street toward the railroad crossing. Realizing that I was too slow and fat to follow him, I ran inside to tell Mother. Ready to spank me for letting go of Frederick, she rushed out to the street but she saw no trace of him. "Where could he have run?" Mother asked worriedly. Maybe he went to visit Mrs. Kowalski, Aunt Ina's mother, but our search across the street was fruitless. He was not with her. Mother started to panic.

"He is not old enough to say his name. How could anyone know to which family he belongs?" she worried. Mother disliked the idea of notifying the police. But unable to round up Frederick, after frantically searching the entire neighborhood, this was her last resort. So in her panic she rushed to the police station, hoping that someone had taken Frederick there. But to no avail; no one had seen a lost little boy. In the meantime, Father had arrived home and, asking the older boys of the neighborhood for help, continued the search. Mother was positive that Frederick had not walked very far, but Father swung on his bike to scan a wider area. Finally, after another hour of frenzy, Father came home with him. He told Mother that he had found Frederick standing on the Blaue Bruecke, the bridge that crossed the river Rominte connecting the old part of the city with the new, a distance of more than a kilometer away.

"I watched him for a moment," Father reported to Mother, "He was quite oblivious to anyone around him. I could see how he enjoyed picking up stones and throwing them over the iron railing into the water, watching the big splash down below." Mother was horrified. How could a young child run so far? Father gave Frederick a good thrashing, assuring himself and Mother that this discipline would serve as a good lesson. Yet Frederick either forgot quickly or did not learn at all. Only a few days later, he ran away again. This time he marched along with a brass band to the Fueselierkaserne across town. The police, alerted to him, found him and brought him home. Mother was frantic and embarrassed. How could she teach Frederick that it was wrong to run away? But Father believed in discipline and gave him another hefty thrashing, cautioning Mother not to let him out of sight.

"Who knows where he might wind up next time?" asked Father. Aunt Ina, who had dropped in on the scene, suggested that Frederick wear a name tag. Frederick, however, had his own way of reasoning and obviously ignored everyone's concern. One day Mother was talking with Aunt Ina on the opposite side of the street while Frederick was casually standing next to Mother. I was lingering on the sidewalk. The two women, engrossed in

3

conversation, paid little attention to a motorcycle racing up the street. As the machine was about to pass us, Frederick suddenly jumped in front of it, arms stretched out sideways, trying to stop the driver. The machine squealed, spun around on its axis, missing Frederick by a hair's breadth. The driver, shaking from shock and rage, shouted angrily at the two women as he grabbed Frederick and slapped him hard on his bottom. Mother turned white and was frozen in terror. Slowly, she regained her voice. She cried to Aunt Ina; "What will I do with this boy? I can't handle him. I can never relax. He is unpredictable!"

When the motorcyclist sped away, after giving Mother a lecture on watching her children, we went into the house, Mother visibly shaken. But Frederick had forgotten about his spanking and told us, grinning mischievously: "I only wanted to stop him. He was driving too fast." Aunt Ina tried to break the tension with a joke.

"Your pride and joy will give you gray hair soon. I told you that boys are not easy to raise," she laughingly said.

"When do they come to their senses; please tell me," Mother asked anxiously.

"Patience, just have patience," Aunt Ina suggested. "He might outgrow this trait, the little rascal."

When Mother had finally calmed down, Aunt Ina mentioned how much she would like to have a little girl but added that business was now picking up at the store and she was not going to take a chance on having another boy.

"I would like to borrow one of your girls," she said "You know I have always favored the little fat one, Marianne."

To emphasize her point, she seized me by my round middle and pulled me close to her.

"Would you like to come and live with us for a while?" she asked and, quite happily, I agreed, ready to leave at once, a fact which seemed to trouble Mother, because I heard her remark to Father later that she wondered where I picked up the trait of a traveler. Father smilingly reminded her that I had, at an even younger age, spent time with Oma, his own mother, and had enjoyed my stay. He recognized my venturesome, young spirit.

"Enjoy your visit, Dicke, but whenever you want to come home, let Aunt Ina know and I will come to pick you up," Father said, putting his big hand on my head.

Ready to leave, I watched Mother pack my few things and, filled with excitement about my new adventure, I grabbed Aunt Ina's hand at the door. Almost hurriedly, I waved everybody goodbye. Father's eyes rested thoughtfully on me while he reminded Aunt Ina that I always said my prayers at night. "I surely will remember to pray with her," she promised and off we went.

Aunt Ina and I arrived at the Wilhelmstrasse. I felt happy and so was Uncle Oskar. When Aunt Ina told him that she had borrowed me from Mother and Father, he picked me up and held me over his head.

"So you like to stay with us; how nice, Jannchen," he said with a smile, calling me by my nickname, Janne. It never occurred to me to wonder how Hans felt about my intrusion and I was unaware of the fact until many years later that he gladly shared the attention that should have solely been his. I loved Hans. He was five years older, going to school and, to me, so much smarter than I.

For me, two and a half years old, the move to the Wilhelmstrasse had opened a store of adventure. It offered so much to see, so many new people, and there was Uncle Oskar's store in which I could roam around. What fun! What excitement! The only territory I was not permitted to enter was Uncle Oskar's workshop located next to the store. Carrying me on his arm, Uncle Oskar had shown me around, explaining that the many wires and cables, gadgets and apparati could easily hurt me if I touched them. Therefore, he did not want me to play in the workshop. I promised Uncle Oskar to obey his request and, smiling, he took me to the kitchen where Aunt Ina busied herself at the stove.

Uncle Oskar was so much like Father. He had the same good-natured temperament, was approximately the same height, maybe a few pounds heavier, but their blue eyes were identical, emanating friendliness, honesty, and love. He had a ray of tiny wrinkles around the corner of his eyes when he smiled, and Uncle Oskar smiled often and readily. He kept his ash blond hair cut short so the thin strands would not fall into his face while he was at work. He and Aunt Ina made a perfect team. Uncle Oskar took care of all repairs at the workshop and visited customers for whom he built antennas and made radio installations.

Aunt Ina was in charge of the store. It amazed me with how much ease she dealt with people. She had a friendly and encouraging word for everyone and, for someone depressed, a quick joke at hand. Many of the customers were farmers from the numerous villages surrounding Gumbinnen, simple folks who drove down the Wilhelmstrasse with their packed horse-drawn wagons to trade their fresh produce at the open market held in town twice a week. Aunt Ina usually filled them in on the latest news that came over the radio or discussed some economic or political aspects of the time. I often heard her ask: "How is the family? What crops are you growing this year? Did the calf get better?" I could sense that she was always genuinely interested, yet she maintained a casual tone. Most of her customers were ordinary people, dressed in simple and practical clothes. During the cold and snowy winter months they wore heavy boots lined with raw lambswool, and jackets and hats made of fur to keep them warm on their long rides to town. Their movements, therefore, were slow and conversation flowed at the same pace, never wasting words, never in a hurry.

Aunt Ina, obviously in a slightly better financial position than Mother and Father and the majority of people in town, never displayed this fact. She dressed simply and modestly, favoring a cotton smock in a subdued color print over her dress to protect her clothes from stains and wear. With great care she starched and ironed them and, as a result always looked neat. She ran her household and the store in the same manner. Everything had its place. I watched her dust the shining casements of new radios with extreme care. For this job, she used a downsoft cloth, careful not to leave the slightest scratch mark. Even the hundreds of tiny boxes on the long row of shelves located against the back wall of the store had been arranged neatly like rows of soldiers standing at attention.

Aunt Ina loved order; it was visible everywhere. Her mother, Mrs. Kowalski, visited several times a week to help with the cleaning, shopping and cooking. Aunt Ina's great pride was the big floral carpet in the living room. It was immaculate, and it was my duty, getting on my hands and knees, to pick up even the smallest speck of thread after Mrs. Kowalski had beaten, brushed, and aired the carpet outside. Aunt Ina trained Hans and me to observe the same order. I learned quickly, whereas Hans used to grumble when Aunt Ina insisted on inspecting his shoes on a rainy day, sending him outside again in disapproval.

"Go and scrape the mud from your soles on the stoop or take off your shoes before you come in," she suggested firmly. Hans was a lanky boy with dark curls which Aunt Ina insisted be trimmed short. He had dimples in his cheeks, something no one in our family was endowed with, and, with fascination, I watched them deepen as he smiled. We were on friendly terms and Hans did not seem to mind that Aunt Ina had invited me to join the family. Sometimes he watched his mother when she labored over my own blond silk-like hair, cutting and brushing it often. When, after many attempts, the huge red bow did not stay in place, she complained in her typical East Prussian plattdeutsch: "I don't know what to do, Marjell, to make your hair grow thicker." No egg or beer treatment produced the desired result. With her own hair, a natural black frizz, she had trouble taming into a loose bun, keeping it pinned on the crown of her head. It contrasted with her own white skin, and her prominent Baltic features made her face unusually attractive. Aunt Ina kept herself slender. She walked erect, which gave her the appearance of being taller than the average woman.

I loved to go shopping with Aunt Ina, especially in the summer, when she went to the farmers' open market held only a short distance away across the Carl-Brand-Bruecke. But now it was the end of January and the cold weather with its icy winds and bitter frost reduced my radius of adventure to a few neighboring stores. The day Aunt Ina had taken me across the street to introduce me to Mrs. Schwartz, who owned a candy store, she had introduced me to a major attraction. I had made it my habit to visit the candy store of Mrs. Schwartz daily because the tall rows of glass jars, filled to the brim with a multitude of candies, a variety of delicious sweetness hidden in colorful wrappers, acted like a magnet on me. When Aunt Ina had bundled me up in my warm winter coat, hat, mittens, and boots, making me feel like a stuffed teddybear, I was ready for my visit to my friend, Mrs. Schwartz. Watching traffic from both sides, as Aunt Ina had taught me, I looked left and right to make sure that I would not be run over by a horsedrawn wagon or one of the new, fast-moving cars.

I was big enough now to open the door to Mrs. Schwartz's store by standing on tiptoe. Mrs. Schwartz was always smiling, taking my outstretched hand when I curtsied to her. After a brief chat, she walked over to the row of tall jars and handed me one of my favorite licorice candies for which I thanked her, curtsying again, and then ran back to Uncle Oskar's store. Once Aunt Ina apologized to Mrs. Schwartz for my daily visits, but Mrs. Schwartz had brushed Aunt Ina's embarrassment aside, saying:

"She is the one customer I can count on; please don't spoil my business." This comment settled the matter and I continued my daily visits.

But today had been a disappointment. Although it was still early in the afternoon, Mrs. Schwartz's store was crowded with people talking very excitedly to her. Therefore, I quietly slipped out, not wanting to disturb, without having received my licorice candy. Feeling depressed, I crossed the street again and took a short walk. Passing Mrs. Korn's shoe store and the big wooden doorway that led to our joint backyard, I toddled along to Borst's delicatessen store. The distinct smell of sauerkraut and pickled herring streamed through the door a customer opened but the wind, blowing from the east, was fierce and icy, forcing tears into my eyes. I gave up fighting the wind, turned around and walked back to my uncle's store. On the lower part of the big display window, the frost had artfully drawn flowers and designs of ice. They would melt, once the late afternoon sun warmed the window, and it would be fun to watch this play from the inside of the cozy store.

To add to my disappointment, I realized that even Aunt Ina did not have time for me. Several people were in the store, a stocky farmer, bundled in a sheepskin fur, and Mrs. Korn from next door. Having pulled off my coat, I quietly sat down on a footstool under the counter, wondering what their excited conversation was about. Then, to my surprise, Mother hurried in and, glad to see me, hugged me briefly. Even she had urgent matters on her mind.

The farmer was slowly drawing on his pipe and, after blowing the smoke out ceremonially, leaving a sweet aroma lingering in the air, he asked Aunt Ina with a thoughtful, almost worried look on his face:

"What do you think our lot will be under this new national socialistic government? Can we trust this man Hitler?" All three women answered at once and I sensed confusion. Mother spouted out:

"I have the feeling that this is too drastic a change, going from a monarchistic system to a leader, who is a man out of the lowest ranks of society. I think the men surrounding Hitler are too forceful, too militaristic." To emphasize her point, she added: "Fred and I did not vote for him because Fred has read Hitler's book *Mein Kampf* and is convinced that the man is a fanatic and an atheist who could only lead our country astray."

Mrs. Korn rebuffed her, saying that, although she had not read the book, it was not right to judge a man from printed pages. But Mother insisted that the book was a product of his mind and that she and Father considered Hitler a dangerous man. Uncle Oskar must have overheard their heated conversation through the open door to the workshop and commented firmly:

"Let us not criticize our new government, but let us give these men an honest chance to prove their ability, to bring Germany back on her feet. We need a strong leader especially after these discouraging times of financial and economic instability. I believe that Hitler is a very strong man."

Aunt Ina must have felt uncomfortable about the disagreement and, in her usual diplomatic manner, suggested:

"Let's leave the subject of politics to the men. I understand little about it and it does not interest me anyway."

As I sat quietly on my stool watching the late afternoon sun melt the ice on the display window, I was disturbed about their noisy conversation, their disagreement, and was wondering about the reason for such confusion. It was very unusual to have so much noise in the store and my getting no attention made matters worse. I felt miserable. Something was wrong. Only I did not know what. Soon Mother bid everybody goodbye, waving at me as she walked out the door. The farmer, after silently tapping his cold pipe out on an ashtray, left the store, and the usually friendly and jovial face of Mrs. Korn looked strangely thoughtful. Upon leaving, she said to Aunt Ina:

"If I can, I will see you later this evening."

Glad that calm had been restored, I anxiously followed Aunt Ina to the kitchen where she started to prepare the evening meal. Soon the soup was steaming in the pot, its aroma filling the kitchen, whetting my appetite and focusing my attention on food, especially on the appetizing looking sandwiches Aunt Ina prepared on a huge platter. Then she went to the front door and drew the shades as the sun had gone down. She stepped into Uncle Oskar's workshop, suggesting:

"I think it's enough for today. Why don't you call it quits? Hans will be back from his violin class shortly and will want to eat."

Uncle Oskar nodded in agreement and I followed Aunt Ina back into the adjoining living room, which also served as the dining room where she set the table quietly and with ease.

The sound of running footsteps caught my attention and I recognized them to be Hans' steps. He had stopped short at the door to the yard, either to catch his breath or to check his shoes. Nobody dared to enter the apartment with dirty shoes. Everyone observed Aunt Ina's strict rule, family and customers alike. Hans stormed into the kitchen, flung his coat on the next chair and Aunt Ina caught the violin case to stop it from falling over. He shouted his announcement:

"I'm going to watch the parade tonight!" and, in the same breath, "Why isn't dinner ready?" He was always hungry. As Aunt Ina reminded him to comb his tousled hair and wash his hands, Uncle Oskar came in and took his seat. Hans, having rushed through his clean-up, scrambled for his chair and told me to hurry as he wanted to start eating. He liked to tease me about being slow and fat, but he never called me *Dicke,* the fat one as I was called at home. Hans had coined another name for me: Jette. Sometimes when he was in an especially beneficial mood or wanted a favor, he called me Jettchen. I liked it either way because it was his original name for me and I never minded his teasing. We never had a serious fight over anything, except over a bigger or better looking sandwich but, usually, he had made his reservations in advance. To fill his hungry stomach, Hans pointed to his favorite pieces on the platter, announcing with a full mouth:

"This, this, and that piece is mine; don't dare touch it." This type of behaviour would earn him a slap from Aunt Ina but, knowingly, he had let me sit on the chair between them, thus was at a safe distance.

Tonight Hans' mind was on the parade and he gobbled down his food very fast.

"I'll leave early because I am going to meet Busch and Olle. We want to find a spot from which we can see well," he said.

From Aunt Ina's and Uncle Oskar's conversation I gathered that they also wished to see the parade but, to my dismay, both intended to put me to bed after dinner. While Aunt Ina was washing the dishes, I followed her around, fussing and crying. She asked what was troubling me.

"I don't want to go to bed," I whined.

I had the idea that the excitement of the day was linked to the parade and was anxious to find out what a parade was. When Aunt Ina told Uncle Oskar about my tears, he suggested that I be dressed warmly, wrapped in a warm blanket and, so equipped, I could come along. As a matter of fact, he offered to carry me on his arm, the dear.

After Hans' hurried departure, I watched Aunt Ina and Uncle Oskar put on their heavy winter coats. Then Aunt Ina bundled me up, wrapping a woolen blanket around me. With a big, strong sweep, Uncle Oskar picked me up on his arm.

Having turned off the lights, I could see that many people were heading in the same westward direction toward the Regierung. Mrs. Schwartz and her adult daughter had crossed the street and walked behind us. Mrs. Schwartz mentioned to Aunt Ina: "It is unusual for this time of year to have no snow." Aunt Ina confirmed her observation. Uncle Oskar, however, appreciated this fact because he was sure the crowd would have been less at this parade had it snowed heavily. He registered the big turnout as a good omen for the new national socialist party. I was happy that Uncle Oskar had taken me along and quietly hugged him for doing so. I was going to see a parade, an event that had caused so much excitement during the day.

We passed the short row of small stores adjoining Uncle Oskar's to the west until we reached the spot where the Wilhelmstrasse made that curious bend northeastward at the big drug store. We then crossed the Kirchenstrasse and passed alongside the massive structure of the "new" Regierung. Its solid Baroque style looked more artistic than the square, austere, box-like architecture of the "old" Regierung, toward which our little troupe was heading. It was familiar territory. Aunt Ina had often taken me along to the Gigelinski bakery located on the northern side of the square of the Friedrich-Wilhelm-Platz where we bought freshly baked rolls for breakfast.

As the conversation of our small group centered around the new government of the national socialist party, Mrs. Schwartz's usually happy mood changed. Her comments were subdued, worried. "I don't know how we will fare under Hitler," she mentioned addressing no one in particular.

Yet Uncle Oskar was optimistic and he tried to convince her that this new party promised better times for all of us. Mrs. Schwartz's daughter kept quiet and did not participate in the conversation as if absorbed in her own thoughts.

When we passed through the columnar archway, which connects the old with the new Regierung, I could see, despite the darkness, that a mob of people was present. The whole town seemed to have gathered. It was difficult to maneuver through the throng without losing anyone. Steadily, Uncle Oskar headed across the square toward the northwesterly corner.

"Over there we will be shielded from the bitter cold wind," he assured Aunt Ina, and the three women followed him closely. From my elevated vantage point, I could see that the sidewalks were tightly packed, about five or more people deep in places. Uncle Oskar optimistically motioned toward a spot, convinced that we would see well from it. Once our group had lined up at the edge of the sidewalk, Aunt Ina discovered that *Schuster's* tiny store was right behind us. Uncle Oskar's sister had married a shoemaker; therefore, most relatives referred to him as the *Schuster*, the shoemaker, instead of calling him by his real name.

Judging by the visible breath emanating from each person's mouth in muffled conversation, I knew it was bitter cold and snuggled close to Uncle Oskar. I felt warm and cozy in my woolen blanket, but the women soon started to stamp their feet, trying to keep the blood circulating.

Aunt Ina wondered aloud if Mrs. Korn had come to watch the parade and where Hans might be in this dark mob of people. Then I heard a strange, penetrating noise approaching from a distance. It came from the north, the Bismarckstrasse. I had never heard anything like this; it gave me an eerie feeling. The murmur of conversation stopped and the crowd fell silent as if in breathless anticipation.

The noise grew louder and louder. Then I saw what it was. They had marched down the Bismarckstrasse, momentarily flanking into the Friedrich-Wilhelm-Platz. As they passed the Gigelinkski bakery, the noise grew to a violent, metallic roar, filling the very air, the narrow street, fiercely echoing from the surrounding walls, roaring upward into the black night sky. Columns of tall men, dressed in black, with shining black jack boots marched past us. Their iron-clad heels, rhythmically hitting the cobble-stoned street in a fast step, created a violent roar, penetrating everyone and everything.

Like a huge, black, roaring monster, column after column passed. Each black-dressed figure rigidly held a lit torch at elbow level. Their eerie lights, creating fiery, flickering images on their white, stonelike faces, made them appear like grotesque grimaces—a horror parade!

The violent roar, the marching, fast-moving blackness, the swaying torches, the fierce grimaces sent panic through me. I pulled the corner of my blanket tightly over my eyes and hid against Uncle Oskar's neck. I was frightened. I was trembling.

The date was January 30, 1933. The Hitler regime had forced its way to power.

Chapter II

Vengeance Is Mine—Saith The Lord

I don't remember exactly the time when Father had taken me back to the Kasernenstrasse. Yet when I started my first day at school in the spring of 1936, I set out from there.

Mother had given me the traditional *Schultuete,* a cone-shaped container, almost as tall as I, made of colorfully decorated cardboard, and filled to the brim with candies, fruit, and other enticing goodies. To this day, I have not arrived at a conclusion as to whether the purpose for this gift was to serve as a bribe or a consolation.

Nevertheless, Mother had walked with me to the Adolf-Hitler-Schule and joined the row of other nervous parents who lined the wall of our first classroom.

Only vaguely was I aware that during the last three years many streets and buildings were re-named after new party leaders—our school, Adolf-Hitler-Schule; a newly constructed street, Hermann-Goering-Strasse. Yet, endowed with a calm, East Prussian temperament, I registered these changes as matter-of-factly as my new surroundings in school. When my homeroom teacher, Mr. Baeker, assigned me a seat at the double-seated desk near the row of tall, bare windows, I shyly smiled at the girl to my left. I liked her and wanted to be her friend.

Mr. Baeker instructed us briefly which materials to bring the next day. Then, with a friendly gesture, he dismissed his new pupils and their very nervous mothers.

On our way home, Mother again pointed out the various landmarks. Counting the blocks with me up to the railroad crossing, which led to the Kasernenstrasse, she wanted to be certain I would not get lost the next day. Having inherited her own keen sense for directions, I assured her that I would easily find my way to and from school.

Shouldering my new brown leather *Tornister* the next day, I felt as if I had grown several inches. I was not small any more, now that I attended school. With great care I had packed my slate board, *Griffel*-box, and the interesting picture book explaining the many letters of the alphabet. I looked forward to my first real lesson and gingerly I walked my way to school.

As stern looking Mr. Baeker entered the classroom, we respectfully got up from our seats and he said a brief morning prayer to open our session for the day. Telling us to get out our slate boards and griffels, he instructed us to copy the symbols he had so quickly and easily written on the blackboard. He explained to us first graders that our slate board had triple lines guiding us to write letters in their proper upper and lower proportions. Later, being more proficient, we would use single-lined boards. Our griffels were made of powdered, compressed slate, the same material as our boards.

Making our first lesson interesting, Mr. Baeker taught us a rhyme which helped us to write the letter "i" up, down, up, point on top. At this time, in 1936, all schools taught the old, pointy German script and the slow, screechy noises in class testified that we pupils put our utmost effort into our first attempts at writing. When Mr. Baeker was satisfied with several lines of the same letter, we wiped them out with the damp sponge dangling playfully from a string tied through a hole in the wooden frame. School was fun, I decided after my first day.

I recall my elated feeling when my scratchy slate board was substituted with a broad-lined paper diary in the second grade. It was a definite sign of achievement. I enjoyed most subjects. Writing, spelling, grammar, drawing, singing, and religion were fun. But I thoroughly disliked mathematics. It was a lifeless and boring subject, a total waste of my time.

One morning Mr. Baeker made an announcement in a firm voice. "Orders have been given that our opening prayer before class will be substituted with a loud and clear 'Heil Hitler!' " Immediately we had to practice several times until Mr. Baeker was satisfied with our performance. Standing at attention, heels together, we had to raise our right arm and hand, keeping it straight forward at eye level. This militaristic exercise gave me a strange feeling as if I was forced to act like a soldier. I felt stupid standing at attention, having to shout: "Heil Hitler!" But this was to be our regular morning greeting for many years until my very last day in school.

Meantime, as the economy gradually recovered, Mother and Father had scraped together enough money to obtain a low-cost mortgage to buy a small house on the outskirts of town. On March 13, 1937, still a cold spring day, we moved into our new home located in the southeastern section of town, Annahof, our new address reading: Beethovenstrasse 24.

On June 12, 1936, Maria, a new family member, had arrived and, as a result, we had outgrown the limited quarters at the Kasernenstrasse. Although our new five-room house was still a very modest abode, for us children it had uncountable advantages. We considered not only the half-acre of garden our playground but extended it to the large pond across the street and included the endless acres of farm country beyond. Another attraction was Fichtenwalde, a large wooded area with pines and birches within a fifteen-minute walking distance. These wide open spaces held promises for many exciting adventures for the five of us. During the winter months we could go skating on the pond or sledding on the big sand hill in Fichtenwalde.

Frederick could hardly wait for summer because the small island in the pond fascinated him. He kept asking Father: "How can I get over to it? I want to play Indian with the older boys." Here, Mother was sure that Frederick would not run away, at least not farther than the pond and whenever she was looking for him, she found him at the water or in a tree. He had stopped running away.

Even for Father, who often came home tired after a hard day at the machine factory, Annahof had a place for enjoyment. At the foot of the Beethovenstrasse was an even larger pond, leased by the Angler's Club of which Father was a member. When he had a few spare hours, Father asked Mother to pack him some stale bread for the fish while he picked up his rods and gear. A few minutes later he was on his bike and, with a smile on his face, pedaled toward the pond. Mother knew he had trouble remembering the time and called after him:

"I'll send the children to get you home before supper."

For Mother, naturally the house created additional work but Ursula, now eleven years old, was eager to help her with the many household chores. As a matter of fact, Herta and I had our allotted duties. We set the small table in the kitchen, around which we children sat at mealtime, cleaned up the dishes, carried in firewood, or swept the rooms. Nevertheless, our chores still left us plenty of time for play and dreaming, the latter being one of my favorite pastimes. When homework was finished, I loved to sit on the square stone, which served as our property marker at the street corner outside the fence. Alongside the fence was the narrow zig-zag walkway leading from our street to the Franz-Schubert-Strasse.

Our street, the Beethovenstrasse, had almost no traffic except for occasional shoppers on their bikes riding to and from town. Therefore, the street belonged to us, the children. It was our playground. We referred to our street as the last street of town because only a short distance behind the pond, the village of Turen started. Turen was part of the southwesterly suburbs adjoining Gumbinnen.

During our first summer in Annahof, Father gave our family, including Mother, instructions in gardening. For this new adventure, he had bought spades, forks, rakes, and an assortment of seeds and showed us how to use this new equipment. The entire half-acre behind the house needed spading before anything could be planted. It was a backbreaking job but, little by little, we got it done. Father left one long path in the center leading from the house to the newly started compost pile. To the left and in the back, we planted potatoes and, closer to the house, Father staked out vegetable beds. I was proud of him, watching him do everything with such precision. He used a long line to stake the vegetable beds out straight.

"I can't tolerate anything crooked," he would answer to Mother's question if she was doing the job right.

To Mother and us he expertly explained how much of each type of seed had to be put into the shallow rows, allowing enough space for each small seed to sprout and grow.

"Where did you learn to garden? Who has taught you these things?" Mother wanted to know. With a wistful smile, Father told us about his grandfather who had owned a farm but had died long ago. Mother recalled that Father had mentioned having spent many of his childhood years on his grandfather's farm where he had learned not only about organic gardening, as she now realized, but also about the art of oil painting, a talent he developed by watching a traveling artist whom he had met there.

Father had very talented hands. Whatever he touched turned out perfect and beautiful. He had proved this fact with the many colorful landscapes and floral bouquets he had painted. And this early spring our garden flourished under his expert touch. At least I was convinced that ours was the most carefully tended in the Annahof area—a showpiece.

With planting finished, the weather gradually warmed up.

Mother had been anxious to invite her two married brothers and their families from Koenigsberg for a visit. Enthusiastically, they had accepted her invitation. Although Mother never showed this, we knew she was proud of her achievements. She had five healthy children, a modest house, a big, expertly-tended garden, had learned to cook and take care of us. Father was having a brick stable built because he was determined to raise several small animals. He intended to leave them under Mother's care, knowing she would appreciate the savings in food cost. To a city girl, thoroughly spoiled by her own mother, this new life was an achievement. Mother, remembering her own difficulties in early marriage, promised us that we would never have to go through such a rough school, having to learn in a hurry. She would teach us while we were young to cook and care for a family. And Father had just finished giving us our basic training in gardening.

The day our visitors arrived was sunny and it was warm enough to sit outside. Mother, with Ursula's eager assistance, had baked several cakes to serve her guests for the traditional afternoon coffee. Uncle Wilhelm with Aunt Marie and Uncle Anton with Aunt Tina arrived before noontime. Aunt Tina explained that she had left her children, Christa, Trude, and Juergen, with Uncle Gustav in the city, fearing the long walk to Annahof would tire them. But, seeing our spacious surroundings, she regretted not having brought them as she was certain they would have loved to roam in the open fields. Mother served a three-course meal at noontime, drawing a hearty compliment from Uncle Wilhelm. He topped his praise with a piece of poetry which he recited with great pathos and good humor. The living room in which they had crowded around the dining room table was bursting with laughter. Uncle Wilhelm was always in grand spirits and, wherever he was, he caused laughter. I liked him and so did Mother. He was her oldest and favorite brother.

When the conversation of the men shifted to the topic of politics, Aunt Tina had forebodings because she knew the subject would cause friction. Father and Uncle Wilhelm did not favor the new militaristic trend of the Hitler regime, whereas Uncle Anton very excitedly defended Hitler's policies. Father, trying to keep the conversation at a discussion level, coolly stated that he was against the regime because it showed a definite trend toward atheism.

"If a Government looks upon me suspiciously because I am a Christian and attend Sunday worship services, I know our country is heading for trouble. Once a people allow some other authority instead of God to rule their lives, they will fall into tyranny. This is the reason I oppose our regime," said Father calmly but determinedly. Uncle Anton interpreted Father's statement as a personal affront and, raising his voice, fired at him:

"Is this your attitude toward Hitler? Shouldn't you rather thank him for your comfortable new house instead of criticizing him? Only Hitler's new policy of granting low-cost mortgages to large families enabled you to buy this house!" But Father calmly defended his point, stating that only through great sacrifices and a lot of hard saving had he scraped up the money for the required down payment. By signing a contract with the bank, he did not feel obligated to sign away his soul to Hitler. Recognizing their differences and trying to calm his excited brother, Uncle Wilhelm, in a jovial sweep, got the subject back on safer ground.

"As long as Hitler does not restrict fishing to party members, I will always find a place to enjoy myself," he said. Father, understanding his hint, suggested a walk around the pond. The three men quickly got up and left. Aunt Tina breathed a sigh of relief.

"I'm glad they agree on one subject, fishing. It worries me when Anton gets so excited about politics. Since he has joined the printers, he is convinced that national socialism is the best thing for our country." She expressed her suspicion that the men on the job were radicals and, in their ignorance, potentially dangerous, but she could not persuade Uncle Anton to recognize this fact. She wished he would stop meeting them, playing cards and drinking a lot and, instead, would buy a little house for them. Their three children were growing and would enjoy a natural playground like ours.

During the conversation the dishes were washed and stacked away. Hanging up her wet towel, Mother invited Aunt Tina and Aunt Marie for an inspection tour around the house and garden. It was funny to watch slender and fragile Aunt Marie climb over bricks and planks of wood, building materials piled in the backyard for our animal stable. Yet she managed to struggle across without uttering a word of complaint. She listened intently as Mother went along the path describing the variety of vegetables Father had planted. With a tinge of pride in her voice, Mother pointed to the newly planted trees.

"Fred is so knowledgeable about trees." Mother had watched him study various catalogues before he decided which fruit trees to buy. They had to be hardy to withstand our cold winters and of a hybrid variety to bear choice fruit. Aunt Marie obviously found Father's knowledge and ambition and Mother's interest very amiable, but we knew she was a typical city person and could never run a household with a lot of everything—children, animals, garden, or house. Nevertheless, Aunt Tina was delighting with Mother in her new adventure and hoped that some day she would own a small house like ours.

Soon the men returned from their walk around the pond and joined the women on the garden tour. Uncle Wilhelm showed his enthusiasm.

"What a lovely little paradise! The pond is filled with lots of fish. How the kids must enjoy it here!" he exclaimed. It was true. Yet this fact had never penetrated our minds as we were too busy after school exploring the many miles of open territory behind the pond.

When our four visitors bade us goodbye late in the evening, Uncle Wilhelm complimented Mother.

"Hats off to you; you've learned a lot since you were my little sister," he said, then heartily kissed her goodbye.

Much as we children enjoyed visitors, we felt more at ease and unrestricted roaming around the open country, which we considered our own playground. Summer had moved into town and we watched the boys build floats from reeds on which they paddled across the water to play Indian on the swampy island in the pond. The terrifying howls and groans indicated they took their play seriously. From the water's edge, we could see they had started a fire from which they sent smoke signals. Using amply available chicken and goose feathers, they made their own headbands, decorated them skillfully, and were proud to resemble the American Indian, a continent and an era away. Although Frederick was not old enough to join the teenage boys for play, he often asked father in the evening to draw an Indian for him.

"Draw me a chief with feathers," he prodded until Father got out his sketch pad and pencil. Then we sat around and watched him create a real Indian with a few artistic strokes of his pencil—headdress, fringed leggings, moccasins, tomahawk and all. Father was a genius and I hoped that some day when he did not have to work so hard to feed us he would be an artist. So far, we had only very few of Father's oil paintings because he had given them away. Our relatives had received them as gifts. Always determined to give something nice, but not having the money to buy expensive presents, he bought a canvas and a pretty postcard instead. The picture on the postcard served him as a theme. Within a few weeks, absorbed in working with his brushes and oils, he finished another beautiful painting in his spare time after work. To me, Father's paintings were masterpieces and I did not like them to be given away, but Father always promised that he would paint some for us. Mother would get enough to decorate the rooms.

In his sketch pad, Father had several pages with profiles of each member of our family and I loved to leaf through it. He had drawn Mother one day while she was taking a nap, leaning her head against the tiled brown *Kachelofen* in the living room. How accurately he had drawn the garnet earrings she wore and her straight dark hair swept back into a bun at the nape of her neck! Then we children followed, one after the other. Ursula's face was at attention, showing a sweet-sour smile, so typical of her when she was posing. Her dark hair, parted in the middle, was kept neat in two flimsy braids. Herta and I were on the next page, clearly showing why she was called the thin one and I the fat one. Herta smiled faintly and her thin blond hair was trimmed short because Mother hoped that frequent cutting would improve the thickness of the hair. She and I wore the same striped dresses with round white collars which Mother and Aunt Ina had sewn for us, the two unlike-looking twins. The sketch of me did my nickname justice: "Dicke." Yes, I did have a friendly, round face.

"Who ever gave you the idea for that peculiar braided bun on the crown of my head?" I asked Mother as she glanced at the sketch. She shrugged her shoulder, smiling. The rest of my hair was cut short, home-style fashion, and uneven, evidently with the hope of improving its growth. Father's drawing of Frederick was unique, depicting him at the age of six with a baldish looking haircut, yet very keen and sharp-looking eyes. It was true; nothing escaped Frederick's alert, fast-moving eyes. Maria still had an angelic looking baby face and Father mentioned that he would sketch her again a few years later.

I cannot remember ever seeing Father rest, even after a long hard day at the factory. He worked in the garden until dark, heaping potatoes, weeding the many vegetable beds, pruning tomatoes, or tending his growing compost pile. He prepared wooden bins for the potatoes in the cellar and built rows of sturdy shelving for Mother where she could store her glass jars filled with canned fruits and vegetables during winter.

After the stable for the animals was finished, Father built a fence of wooden slats around the yard so it was shielded from the wind and curious passersby. He kept the lawn trimmed in front of the house and pruned the apple tree in the center. Along the fence of the walkway, he had planted cherry trees and did not mind that the fresh sparrows took their share in the picking. He helped Mother overcome her uneasiness in handling small animals. This entirely new activity to her, having spent all her childhood years in the city, brought many surprises and many laughs, especially during the year when Father had wanted to raise a turkey, in addition to the variety of chickens and the pig.

The turkey's name was Martha. Once she had matured, she decided to spend many afternoons in one of the cherry trees, much to Mother's consternation, even panic. It was very funny at feeding time when Mother called her.

"Martha! Martha!" and the huge bird came sailing down like a big eagle. Landing right in front of Mother, she caused her to back away in fright or drop the tin with grain. Once Martha was fully grown and Mother's complaints to Father became too frequent, he decided to kill the turkey. We children, seeing the roasted bird on the table, bemoaned the loss of Martha. Mother had mixed feelings.

The many advantages that our house on the Beethovenstrasse offered compensated well for the additional kilometers of walk to school and church. Despite the distance, Father insisted we attend church, although we were the only family on our end of the street to do so regularly. On our way to church Sunday mornings, we usually took a short-cut, the narrow pathway along our fence, which also bordered the Throne's property on the Franz-Schubert-Strasse. Recently Mother had made an observation and mentioned it to Father.

"Did you notice that every time we pass here, the entire family is furiously working in the garden?" But Father answered in his casual manner.

"Some people deliberately dishonor the Day of the Lord. This must be their way to demonstrate that they agree with the atheistic ideology of Hitler. It is none of my business; they may do as they please, but I will observe the statutes of God." With this firm comment, Father dropped the issue.

We loved to go to church, learn to sing new hymns, and listen to the lively sermons delivered by Pastor Preuss. He guided his flock in the ways of God, urging them to live their lives in uprightness, honesty, modesty, and godliness. When Pastor Preuss was scheduled to preach at the small Salzburger Church, only two kilometers away, it was a situation of standing room only and our family had to arrive an hour ahead of time to be sure to get in. Father listened attentively to Pastor Preuss' words and, on our way home, confirmed his belief to Mother.

"For me, the Christian way is the only way to live. I do not agree with the preaching of the party." National socialism was not for Father. I am sure that this conviction was his reason for never buying a swastika flag which lately decorated the windows of many families in our neighborhood, especially on national holidays. Father had nothing to do with this new movement and when he referred to the "brown shirts," men who were members of the party, his tone of voice indicated that he detested and distrusted these men.

I found out in school, however, that several fathers of my classmates owned a brown S. A. uniform and a few even a black one. These men were members of the S. S. We were taught, as part of our *Deutsch* lesson, that Hitler's bodyguard was comprised of a large staff of the S. S. What we were not taught though was that troops of the S. S. were policing every city and were operating under civilian cover, guaranteeing that no opposition to Hitler's ideas could root anywhere. This fact we learned from cautiously whispered rumors in the street. A mysterious fear centered around the S. S., those men wearing an all-black uniform. Yet I don't recall that Mother and Father ever openly discussed the reasons for this mystery, this fear.

Evidently Uncle Oskar was a member of the party, a prerequisite for anyone who intended to get ahead in business or a profession. But I never saw Uncle Oskar wear his uniform. I had the feeling that his membership was more or less a pro forma function. It would not have agreed with his calm, quiet personality to ram Nazi convictions down anybody's throat, which many active and fanatic members tried to do. I loved and trusted Uncle Oskar and, I am sure Father did also, despite their different views in regard to politics. Although now and then he cautioned Mother.

"I don't trust these Nazi brothers. Especially at work I have to watch every word I say. I have the feeling that they listen in on my conversations," he would say.

Some days when work had been hard and trying, Father would come home and tell Mother that he would go fishing to the large pond before dinner. Fishing was relaxation for him and the thought alone seemed to revivify his spirit. About half an hour before sunset, Mother sent the three of us to the pond, located at the most southern end of the Beethovenstrasse, to bring Father home before dark. Quickly we ran down the street and walked across the meadow to the pond, fenced in with high reeds and cut grass. It was a game among Herta, Frederick, and me to see who would find Father first. He had taught us to walk noiselessly and, like Indians, we circled the pond. Hidden behind seven-foot tall reeds, he appeared small. His favorite dark green and much worn linen jacket blended in with the deep green of the reeds and grass. He stood holding the rod in his strong hands with his eyes fixed on the water, watching.

"Sh, sh," Herta whispered, pointing to the motion of Father's hand. He gave us a sign to be quiet for fear we might scare the big fish away, the one he had been trying to catch for hours. Realizing that the sun was close to setting, he tied the line carefully to the rod and then showed us the fish he caught. He had four in the bag, the big carp still frantically gasping for air, trying to jump out. Father killed him quickly, tied the bag securely and picked up his bike. He took a long last glance at the water, like a silent parting gesture, then the three of us accompanied our hero back home.

Judging by the broad smile on Father's face, Mother knew that he had a successful evening. According to an early agreement she had made with him, he cleaned and scaled his catch outside. Soon the aroma of freshly fried fish filled the kitchen as Mother carefully watched and turned them in the skillet until they had a golden brown, crunchy crust. Our hungry mouths could hardly wait to dig in heartily. To us, a supper of freshly caught fish was a feast, and we left only the bones.

Whenever Father brought home an especially large catch of fish, Mother invited Lisa Gander, my girlfriend from next door, for dinner. Lisa was a year younger than I and Mother had observed that of the five Gander children, she was treated like a stepchild, her mother punishing her often or pushing her around. Therefore, Mother considered Lisa part of our family and made her feel welcome whenever she came to visit. Lisa's father had a job with the army and worked in the barracks located in nearby Fichtenwalde. Favoring the bottle, he frequently arrived home tipsy or drunk, especially on pay days. Mrs. Gander, in her attempts to stop or curb his habit, would usually lock the door after dark.

"Rosa, Rosa, my sweetheart, please let me in," he would sing. Yet neither Mr. Gander's insistent knocks with a long wooden pole at the upstairs window nor his sweet serenading could change Mrs. Gander's mind; she kept her husband locked out. Father, getting up before sunrise the next morning, could see Mr. Gander crumpled up in his dark green uniform on the stoop to his own house, sound asleep. Yet we children were not permitted to laugh about such occasions, funny as they were, because neither Father nor Mother thought the situation to be a laughing matter.

During the warm summer months Lisa, Frederick, and I often volunteered to go on the three-kilometer walk to the Bennert farm in the nearby village of Turen. Father had arranged with Mr. Bennert for us to pick up two liters of fresh milk daily. The trip was always an adventure because the village of Turen was located west of our Annahof district, past the pond and beyond hundreds of acres of wheat and rye fields. We strolled along an ocean of pink-blossomed clover and, getting closer to the farm, we passed the fenced-in pastures for the numerous grazing black and white Holstein cattle. To short-cut our way, we carefully climbed over the barbed wire fences.

"Watch out!" I cried to Frederick, because a ripped triangle in his shorts would bear witness against him and guarantee a hefty spanking from Mother. However, we did not dare to cross the fenced-in area where the Bennerts kept the huge breeding bull. His furious stamping and snorting, as if to defend his domain, kept us at a respectful distance. Having safely slipped past him, we darted toward the house like arrows as if the spirit of the beast was still pursuing us.

Arriving at the farm out of breath, Frederick cautioned us to stay away from the doghouse and that very minute the big, brown setter announced our arrival, tearing at his chain, barking furiously. Frederick tried to calm him by calling: "Rex, Rex, it's only us." But the dog stopped his wild announcements only when Mrs. Bennert appeared in the low doorway to the kitchen. Dressed in black, from the big fringed kerchief to the long gathered skirts of her dress, covered with an apron, right down to her black shoes and rough black stockings, she should have looked mysterious. Yet, contrary to her black clothes, her broad, warm, welcoming smile made us feel at home.

While Mrs. Bennert generously filled our milk can, we played with the two big tiger cats who had sneaked into the kitchen with us. The red and white cat, the bigger of the two, climbed up the pail, begging for milk and let go only after Mrs. Bennert filled a big dish for them. It fascinated Lisa how fast they lapped up the milk with their pink tongues. She watched the contest closely.

We would have loved to linger on the big farm with its four buildings framing the huge two-acre yard. Nevertheless, our long hike back required more time and care as we could not afford to spill the milk, an accident which would have brought Mother's wrath down upon us.

When we arrived home, Mother had dinner ready and suggested that Lisa eat with us, an invitation she gladly accepted. Hurrying through our meal, we intended to join a group of neighborhood children for singing. In one of the four-family houses up the street lived the Rosses, and Herbert Ross was an expert harmonica player. On long, balmy summer evenings a dozen or more of us crowded around him to sing folk songs and ballads, usually ending our session with our favorite lullaby, "Guten Abend, gut' Nacht...." Herbert knew hundreds of songs by heart, down to the last verse, but he claimed that he could not read any notes. It was unbelievable because his fast fingers never missed a key. Herta, Lisa, and I loved these warm evenings of singing and if our parents had not called us home, we would have stayed and sung all night.

But the music did not stop then. Through the open windows of our upstairs bedrooms, we listened to the night-time chorus of croaking frogs from the pond across the street, lulling us into a fast, deep sleep.

* * * * *

In East Prussia the seasons changed quickly. After an early fall had dried up the green leaves, winter was on its way. November often surprised us with a two-foot blanket of fluffy snow. The icy winds, blowing from the northeastern plains of Russia, brought sub-zero weather, holding a tight grip over our province for weeks. It was not unusual for the temperature to drop minus 20° Celsius, yet it never occurred to any of us to stay home from school. Bundled up tightly, a woolen shawl covering our mouths, we filed one behind the other, letting the tallest and oldest boy of the neighborhood lead the way. The rest, stepping into his footmarks, walked closely behind him. Father had alerted us to watch for white spots on our faces, urging us to rub them with snow until they turned pink again.

"Force yourself to do this. It will prevent you from getting serious frost bites," he told us. The only problem we had was restraining the flow of tears which the cutting, sharp wind forced into our eyes, freezing them as they trickled down our cheeks.

Miraculously, no one in our family ever had pneumonia although, after a march like that, it took a long time to warm up after arriving either in school or at home. By mid-February, we could count on the snow in our street measuring three feet, with drifts often reaching above our kitchen window. One morning Father literally had to shovel his way out of the door. A huge snow drift had closed it entirely. It was great fun to help him clear the entrance and shovel the sidewalk after school. Traffic to Annahof was halted during winter. Everyone walked. The Beethovenstrasse, buried under deep snow, belonged to us children and we used it as our playground, for sleigh riding and fierce snowball battles. We also tended to our very private skating rink, the pond. In fair teamwork, we shoveled and swept it clean, sectioning it off into three areas. The largest area was for teenagers and expert skaters; the second for those still uneasy on their skates; and the rest of it for all other children. Although these rules were set by the older boys of our street, they had merely established them to keep the small fry at a safe distance, away from under their feet. Yet if any one of the boys from the Franz-Schubert-Strasse dared to skate on our pond, he was flatly and coldly turned down; the pond belonged to us, the children living on the Beethovenstrasse. One boy went home with a bloody nose, one who had been brave enough to challenge their "law."

On weekends I enjoyed venturing out to Fichtenwalde with a troop of children. We considered it a special privilege to leave the first footprints in the pure, white, untouched snow. Shaking the powdery fluff off the low hanging pine branches, we were afraid that their heavy load might break them. Our destination was the big "Sandberg," a major attraction for children. Herta and I shared our sled and loved to ride down the long slope, usually taking on as many children as would fit. It was a contest to see if we would all manage to stay on or whom we would lose on the way down. Frederick, usually more daring, made his slides down on his belly. After our legs were tired out from climbing back up to the top, we crowded on our sled to sit and watch some courageous men practice ski jumping. Captivated, Frederick watched their every move, the motioning of their arms as if in flight, and he held his breath until the skier gracefully touched the bottom of the hill. With gleaming eyes, he wondered out loud:

"Could I ever do this, fly through the air as he did?" Neither Herta nor I encouraged him; it looked too daring, too dangerous.

On our slow walk home, Herta discovered deer tracks. This made us examine all others and we counted numerous rabbit tracks. The dainty prints of birds' feet made Frederick wonder where the animals found food in such harsh winter weather. From our previous expeditions with Father, we knew that the forestry department tended several roof-covered open deer feeders to keep them alive.

"But who cares for the other animals and the birds?" Frederick asked. Herta suggested that we save our breadcrumbs and feed the birds in front of our house. "I'm curious to find out what types of birds would come to visit," she said.

One crystal clear night Father wakened us from our sleep.

"Come, get up and get dressed warmly. There is a huge display of Northern Light in the sky; something like this you might see only once in your lifetime." He urged us to get up. Wearily, we rubbed the sleep out of our eyes, then fumbled clumsily into our clothes. Too tired to talk, I followed the others outside where it was eerily bright and the sky a deep greenish-blue. It was bitter cold and Father set Herta, Frederick, and me on the sled, wrapping a blanket around us. Explaining the phenomenon to us, he mentioned that it was similar to a mirage, a fata morgana, reflecting the sun in the south on a certain layer of our cold atmosphere. Father's scientific explanation was most interesting, but I was not satisfied.

"What does this mean?" I asked curiously. He seemed to take a long time to answer my question. A huge circle of light covered almost the entire northern sky through which went a horizontal line, cutting the circle in two equal halves. A thinner line ran in a direct south-north direction, forming a cross at the center of the circle, truly a fantastic phenomenon. Whatever it was, it seemed to have life as it jerked in quick motion as if shivering in the cold night sky, dimming slightly in places, but then shining in its eerie fullness again. With great excitement I brought the great number of "falling stars" to Father's attention. "Make a wish, it will come true," he suggested. But I saw so many falling or shooting across the sky, I forgot about making wishes and instead I counted falling stars.

"I have the feeling that this is a sign from heaven; that God is conveying something important to man," Father said thoughtfully. What His message was, we did not know. Could it be a warning, I wondered. Mother mentioned that in Lapland, the northern tip of Norway, people would be able to read the newspaper at night, as we could right now, because in their region the Northern Light would be visible very brightly. The thought of living in a dark, cold northern place made me appreciate East Prussia. In Gumbinnen the sun shone even during January, the very coldest month of winter.

When we were frozen like icicles, Father urged us to go back to bed. Although my teeth were chattering, I was glad we had sacrificed a night's sleep to watch this incredible display of nature. The next day Father read the headlines in the paper:

"Aurora borealis visible over Europe and northern hemisphere."

Before going to bed, I glanced out the small upstairs window facing north to get another glimpse of this spectacle. But the circle of the Northern Light, God's message, was only faintly visible and the following night it had faded out entirely.

Back in school the next day, only one girl in class had seen the spectacular display of nature, when Mr. Baeker questioned us about it. Father knew which things were important in life, and I was happy not to have missed this incredible event.

Although at times it felt like it, winter did not last forever. Toward the end of March the sun had melted away the accumulated white mass and only patches of wet snow remained on the totally saturated ground. Around Easter we peeked over the neighborhood fences to count the first croci poking their yellow and purple heads into the air, evidently enjoying to be first on the flowery spring scene.

Once the soil had dried out sufficiently, Father made an announcement:

"Time to turn over the garden. I need volunteers." When his request interfered with my schedule of play or daydreaming, I picked up my spade with a bit of reluctance. But he was right, quoting the old saying: "With many hands a job soon ends." Only a few weeks after planting, the results were visible. A variety of tiny green sprouts covered the garden. It seemed as if an invisible force blessed every effort Father made with his hands. The yield of his garden was outstanding.

In late summer I had changed residences again and had moved to Aunt Ina and Uncle Oskar's. Now my walks to school were shorter, approximately a mile only in comparison to the three I had walked from Annahof. Aunt Ina was pleased with her third grader's eagerness to learn. Mrs. Kowalski, her mother, keeping busy with cooking, cleaning, and shopping, found time to teach me to knit, embroider, and to mend socks. Aunt Ina considered it fashionable for me to wear a stiffly starched, pure white pinafore embroidered with small flowers. For several weeks I struggled to stitch them with my own pudgy little hands. Finally, one day, proud of my first achievement, I wore it to school. No one took notice, it was too bad.

There was another, much greater disappointment. Mrs. Schwartz's candy store across the street had disappeared. Questioning Aunt Ina as to where they had moved, she gave me a vague answer.

"Oh, they left. I don't know where they live now." This amazed me because I knew Aunt Ina had been on friendly terms with Mrs. Schwartz and her daughter. Taught not to question an adult's statement, I quietly wondered what had happened to them.

Occasionally I overheard conversations in the store about Jews, customers exchanging opinions with Aunt Ina. But I had not paid close attention to the subject, my mind being caught up in my own world, until I had a strange experience on my way home from school. It had been a beautiful day outside and I took the long route home, enjoying my stroll along the Promenade, between the river and the open market place. Turning toward the Koenigs-Bruecke, I noticed a tall, dark-haired man standing near the monument. He was clad in a pair of worn, blue overalls on which was sewn the bright yellow sign of a five-pointed star with the word "Jude," Jew, printed inside.

"Why does he wear such a sign?" I wondered. No one in Gumbinnen had ever been labeled before. The man did not look queer enough to have done this to attract attention. Only people traveling with a circus dressed oddly. He must have noticed my wide-eyed astonishment and, with his gaze fixed into the distance, pretended not to see me. Embarrassed for him, I turned away trying to understand why this man was labeled like this, obviously a degradation. Telling my disturbing experience to Aunt Ina later, she told me that it was the latest government ruling requiring all Jews and gypsies to wear the five-pointed star. Visible to everybody, it had to be sewn to their outer clothing. This experience deeply disturbed me and I asked myself quietly:

"Was there a connection between this fact and the mysterious disappearance of the Schwartzes?" I could only guess. But where could they be? People did not leave Gumbinnen without a reason.

School, homework, and my duties around the store demanded close attention and kept my mind occupied. Now eight and a half years old, I volunteered to walk to the Gigelinski Bakery to pick up rolls for breakfast. Aunt Ina also trusted me with the daily dusting of radios and phonographs in the big display window. She had taught me how to use the special downlike cloth, careful not to scratch the shiny surfaces with my fingernails or a tiny grain of dust.

One day we had run out of bread. In the early evening, Aunt Ina urged me to run over to the Tiefenbach Bakery close to the store to buy a fresh loaf of pumpernickel bread for supper. Quickly grabbing the shopping bag and money from her, I jumped down the two steps, rushed to the slight bend in the Wilhelmsstrasse, and turned into the Kirchenstrasse, running in a northerly direction. The crowd in the store was in an uproar. People were shouting and talking very excitedly. From the fragments of their heated conversation I gathered that the Synagogue up the street at the Lange Reihe was on fire. The smell of burning wood crept up the street. One woman, angry and indignant, poured out the story to Mr. Tiefenbach that her neighbor had detected the fire and had called the fire engine. Yet it had taken much too long for the howling engines to arrive. It infuriated her that, once on the scene, the firemen had not directed their hoses on the burning Temple as expected.

"No, they protected the neighboring houses from catching fire and let the Synagogue burn to the ground," she shouted. Another woman cut into the conversation:

29

"This fire was started deliberately. I live opposite the Temple. I saw a uniformed S. S. man break a window and throw in a lit torch. He set it on fire."

The shoppers were raging about the fact that someone in Gumbinnen, someone of our own home town had the nerve to destroy a house of worship. Such a crime had never happened before in history. Mr. Tiefenbach, in a very slow but emphatic voice, made a statement.

"No matter how different the Jews are, it is a crime to burn their Temple, to touch the House of God."

Stunned by this fact, I almost forgot to buy the bread. As I was running up the street, anxious to tell Aunt Ina about the dreadful news, I spotted Father at the corner of the Kirchenstrasse. He got off his bike as he recognized me. He had heard about the fire and quickly jumped on his bike to see if the unbelievable rumor was true. When I finished pouring out the story his face took on a woeful look and, as if addressing an invisible audience, he said:

"We will pay for this beastly deed some day; destroying the house of the Lord will surely bring His wrath upon us." Then, almost as if talking to himself, he murmured:

"The revenge is Mine, saith the Lord—remember these words, my child." With this comment, he swung on his bike and pedaled homeward.

It was November 8, 1938, the night that the Nazis had ordered all synagogues to be burned. Crystal night. It was the beginning of the nightmare—for the Jews, and for those Germans who regarded God's Law as superior to Hitler's.

Chapter III

Brother Shall Turn Against Brother

Winter once more moved into town and school demanded all my attention. It was puzzling during geography class to see how often the German map was revised. With each broadcast announcing that Austria, the Saar, and the Sudentenland had returned to their "homeland" Germany, a new map was issued showing these areas now as part of our country.

Maybe I was too young, but I never knew that so many unhappy Germans lived on "foreign" soil and had only one burning desire in their hearts: to be united with Germany. This view was emphasized in our geography lessons and the newspapers voiced the same opinion. Visiting my family in Annahof occasionally, I learned that Father opposed this view and read another fact between the lines.

"It is outrageous how these Nazi-brothers justify their wrongdoing," he commented to Mother.

Although in school I learned a substantial number of traditional folk songs, the music played over the radio, to which I often listened at Uncle Oskar's, was quite different. Especially before and after newscasts and frequent political speeches, it blasted away with snappy melodies, intoning phrases as: "Today Germany belongs to us and tomorrow the whole world." Were these words merely an exaggeration? Or did the song writer mean every word he used? Was this a threat to the world? At least Father was convinced that our country was heading toward a dangerous future. Uncle Oskar never seemed to share his view. To me, the idea of our German government desiring to rule the world

31

sounded unbelievable and I did not take those party songs seriously. What I regarded seriously, though, were my prospects of having to join the Hitlerjugend, Hitler's organized youth. Although not yet ten, the thought of it filled me with resentment. I hated the idea of being ordered around by girls only one or two years older than I. I did not want to sacrifice my limited spare time. Yet, above all, I hated the prospects of being forced to join a herd of singing and marching children. Marching was a soldier's duty.

"Why did children, especially girls, have to march?" I demanded to know from Aunt Ina. It was ridiculous to order girls the age of ten to march up the Koenigstrasse on political or national holidays. Everybody had seen those marches. At the head of the first column were the older boys dressed in their black and brown uniforms; then followed the older girls, also in uniforms, frantically trying to keep step and orderly ranks with the boys. The younger ones, however, marching at the end looked like a hopeless mass of confusion. No one was going to force me to be part of that confusion, I had promised myself.

My cousin, Hans, belonged to the Hitlerjugend and had to wear his uniform for such marches. The stark colors of the black suit contrasted crassly against the brown shirt. Dressed in his uniform, he looked like a miniature S.A. man, a "brown shirt," from whom I rather kept a respectful distance. When he wore his old shorts and blue shirt after school, I admired him and we were friends, but his uniform seemed to put a rift between us. Therefore, I was glad that he did not wear it often.

Our homework usually wound up to be a competition. In a challenging tone, Hans would ask:

"Jette, I wonder who will finish first?" Yet, over the months, he developed a trick. While he was quickly working on his own studies, he talked to me, distracting me, so that as a result, I was often the loser. Packing up his books, a big grin on his face, he went off to meet his friends, leaving me behind to finish my work. Evidently he did not want his young cousin to get the idea of joining him, although this thought had never occurred to me.

What I enjoyed doing, however, and very much to Hans' distraction, was to sneak quietly into the upstairs bedroom and listen to his violin practice. As long as I stayed quiet and did not move, he tolerated my presence but, when he tuned his instrument, it triggered me into hysterical laughter. He could never understand that I compared those screechy sounds to the whining and whimpering of an ailing cat and, unfailingly, he ran after me, trying to hit me with his bow. Jumping down two steps at a time, I was faster than he and he never caught me.

Hans was fourteen now and attended confirmation class at the Evangelical Lutheran Church, to be confirmed the following spring after having passed his test on catechism and questions regarding his future life as a Christian. Although I don't recall seeing him study toward this event, nevertheless, he was confirmed on Palm Sunday in 1939. His new black suit with long trousers, white shirt, and his first tie made him look like a young man, an adult. The ceremony at church passed before me hazily and close relatives gathered at Uncle Oskar's apartment in the afternoon for a small celebration. Oma, Father's mother; Uncle Gustav; Aunt Frieda, with my bratty cousin, Suzanne; Aunt Minna; Mrs. Lucht, a friend of Aunt Ina; and Mother and Father had visited for the occasion.

After the lengthy, traditional session of coffee and an assortment of home-baked cakes, conversation grew loud and the air in the dining room was filled with a cloud of blue cigar smoke. Uncle Oskar's part-time mechanic, Mr. Urbis, evidently had sipped too much of the old wine. The corny jokes he told drew laughter from most of the crowd but Mother and Father reacted in sheer consternation. Then Oma casually asked me how things were going in school, to which I replied grinningly:

"Still on two feet." This smart remark, just learned in school, blew the lid. Mother demanded that I return home immediately, asking for their hats, coats, and my clothes, ending Hans' confirmation party abruptly.

Neither Aunt Ina's apologetic pleas nor my sorrowful tears could persuade Mother, and Father silently agreed with her. I was going back to the Beethovenstrasse with them this very moment. The guests dispersed quickly and silently while Uncle Oskar packed us into his small Opel, bidding his departing visitors a thin goodbye. Hans climbed into the back seat next to me, consoling me. It was a sad trip home to Annahof. Since the adults kept in utter silence, the only sounds to be heard were my muffled sobs. Our trip through the darkness went too fast. When Uncle Oskar stopped at our house, Hans handed me one of his brand new gifts, a beautiful black leather wallet. Realizing that it was one of his confirmation gifts, I did not want to take it.

"I have another one," he awkwardly assured me, after which I tearfully accepted his offering of condolence.

Uncle Oskar had turned the car around and Aunt Ina and Hans had climbed back in. They departed, not saying a word. Quietly but reluctantly, I followed Mother and Father into the house, feeling like a black sheep. Mother had blamed Aunt Ina for my bad behavior, although it had not been her fault. It was I who, at the wrong moment, had acted like my bratty cousin Suzanne. I was angry at myself.

Registering the whole sad experience as my first major defeat, it took me a long time to reconcile this problem within myself. Too upset and embarrassed to discuss this incident with anyone, I buried myself in quiet homework. Finished with it, I either took a long walk with Lisa Gander or sat on the square stone marker on the sidewalk, sending my mind daydreaming. I enjoyed this luxury, especially as it was my own private territory, the territory of mind that no one could trespass. I envisioned exploratory trips as far away as our neighboring planets.

While daydreaming one day, I had a very exciting experience. It was a partly cloudy day with the sun breaking through those big gray puffs occasionally. In the southern direction of the pond, a mighty shaft of light streamed through a small opening in a cloud and reflected as a large sunny spot on the ground. What fascinated me about this ray was that slowly moving downward as if in soft rotation, discs of light floated down to the ground, growing in size as did the ray of light and then vanished as they touched the green grass. With great concentration, I had watched this play of lights until the ray disappeared as the cloud had closed the opening. This fascinating experience made me very happy. I thanked God silently for this unique sign of love. He understood me! He loved me! He did not consider me a black sheep. At least I interpreted my experience this way and guarded it as top secret between God and myself.

During summer, Mother was preparing the crib and clothes for another baby. This new member of the family was due to arrive by the end of August.

Another quite different observation I had made on my adventure trips with Lisa to Fichtenwalde. On several occasions we had noticed that around the fenced-in area of the large army camp, feverish and extensive maneuvers were held. If we were on our way to pick wild raspberries, we had to be cautious to clear the shooting ranges, because getting hit by a bullet by accident would have been no fun. From a safe distance, we lingered to watch columns of soldiers being drilled to attack or practice to dive for cover.

Mother registered my excited announcement regarding the new maneuvers in Fichtenwalde calmly.

"Our city Gumbinnen has served as a garrison over hundreds of years. Drilling soldiers is part of the scene," she explained. Dismissing the subject, she opened the lid of the milk can and exclaimed in delight, "Oh, those raspberries will be lovely for a jam."

This year Ursula, Herta, and I helped Mother with many household chores while she prepared the clothes for the baby. When I arrived home from school on August 28, 1939, a tiny brother, Andreas, had been born. Ursula's response to our new arrival was rather cool.

"But we are five children already," she complained. Yet when Mother jokingly asked what she suggested we do with Andreas, she grumbled her consent. "Since he is already here, he might just as well stay," I heard her say. I was rather fond of Andreas. He seldom cried; he was a loveable baby with a sunny disposition. While our family was absorbed in caring for its brand new member, it came as a sobering shock to us when at daybreak on September 1, only three days after Andreas was born, the surprise announcement was broadcast that war had broken out against Poland. German armies were marching victoriously toward Warsaw. Mrs. Gander came running to bring us the news, emphasizing that the announcer had sounded very peppy, almost cheerful. The worried look on Father's face, however, expressed a different attitude. Solemnly he said to Mrs. Gander as she was about to leave:

"I have the uneasy feeling that this war will take a bad end."

How horrible—a war! Mother and Father had often recounted their experiences of World War I. It sounded as if it had been a fearful experience for them.

But today was Friday and we children had to get ready for school, the rush leaving us no time to think or to worry. At the moment, not really comprehending the full impact of a war, I was not concerned about my safety. Poland was very far away. In school, however, we had to participate in our first drill. Hurried instructions were given how to act in case of a surprise bombing attack. If the school bell rang at an odd time, it was to be considered a warning signal. If bombs fell without advance notice, we were to throw ourselves down flat on the ground, face down. Hurriedly, sandbags were packed against the outside wall to barricade each basement window. The basement of the school was to serve as a bomb shelter in an emergency.

When I arrived home from school I found Mother talking with our neighbor, Mrs. Bergdoerfer, who had rushed over to share the latest news. Listening to their conversation, I heard that several men on our street had already received their draft notices.

"I would like to know if my husband has to go to the front," Mrs. Bergdoerfer worried.

Later in the day I met my classmate Elsa in the street.

Something was wrong. The subdued expression on her usually sunny looking face gave it away. I kept prodding until, reluctantly, she admitted why she had left the apartment.

"My mother was crying. She had to pack a duffle bag for my father. He has to report to the barracks tomorrow," Elsa told me, a sad and disturbed look on her face. So far, the rumor claimed, men with more than three small children were deferred from draft. Yet the four Beinert children were almost adult age except for Elsa, the youngest. Immediately a thought rushed through my mind. With Andreas' recent arrival, we were now six children in the family. Father would not be drafted, I was very certain. I appreciated Andreas' arrival even more.

At school Mr. Baeker voiced the opinion that the war would be over soon. Hitler's blitz attack on Poland was to assure a fast victory. Yet only two days later, on September 3, Father read the glaring headline in the paper: "Great Britain declares war against Germany!" His usually calm face looked troubled and he addressed his forecast of doom to Mother:

"We will have the whole world in arms against us if Hitler continues in his outrageous acts of aggression." But that was not all. Mrs. Gander came running over later announcing that France, pledging alliance with Britain, had also declared war against Germany. Although Mrs. Gander had tried to convey the same optimism with which the newscaster evidently had presented the news, Father knew better.

"I don't believe that our country's situation could be considered a rosy one while we have three nations at war against us. Where does Hitler's mouthpiece, Dr. Goebbels, take the nerve to guarantee the people victory?" he retorted. By Goebbel's screaming voice, his fanaticism for Hitler and his party, by the lack of logic in his speeches, Father could tell that the Propaganda Minister was hoodwinking the public, if not outright lying. Mrs. Gander looked puzzled. Obviously, she had taken the news on the radio to be truth. She quietly left. Mother was concerned over Father's outspokenness and his suddenly welled-up anger. Yet both knew they could trust our neighbor Mrs. Gander. At the factory, however, it obviously was a different situation. Father remarked that he had to choose his words carefully and could voice his honest opinion about our government to only one or two trusted men.

After having vented his anger over our country's critical situation due to Hitler's madness, he quietly shouldered his fishing rod and walked off to the big pond. When he returned after several hours, his face was calm, although he had caught no fish. I was glad to see him. As long as he would be with our family, I would not need to be afraid of anything. His very presence made me feel secure.

In school the subject of history included the early life of Adolf Hitler and his rise to Reichskanzler. The fact that his parents had been poor did not trouble me, but that he had a criminal record disturbed me. How could anyone be entrusted with the responsibility of ruling a nation after having served a sentence in prison? Mr. Baeker, our teacher, did not have such qualms.

"Hitler was only imprisoned for political reasons. This nullifies the crime," he explained. It was a strange logic. We were also taught the background of Hermann Goering who had been appointed to the post of Gauleiter over our province, East Prussia. Photographs in the paper depicted him as a corpulent man with a round, puffy face, and wearing a white jacket decorated with numerous medals, which Father jokingly referred to as tinsel. Whenever Goering visited the world famous stud farm, Trakehnen, located only a few kilometers east of Gumbinnen to select horses for the army or his private stable, he traveled unannounced and on a special train. With the curtains drawn, the sleek, modern train raced eastward passing the railroad crossing at Fichtenwalde and only the next day would the fact that Hermann Goering had visited Trakehnen be acknowledged in the paper. I don't recall that anyone in town ever had reported seeing him in person. I was glad that Gumbinnen was far away from Berlin, from Hitler, from Goebbels, from Goering and all those men Father despised and distrusted. Had it not been for Father's comments, logical and enlightening, I would never have known the truth about many facts.

One of these facts was that Austria, once an independent nation, was now part of the Great German Reich. In school we were taught that this was the most logical development. Austrians, German speaking, especially since Hitler considered himself a German, should be part of Germany. Although now and then I had questions in my mind, I had learned from Mother and Father not to ask them, at least not in public. It was not safe to ask questions; besides, I was of the opinion that the subject of politics belonged to men.

Father had mentioned that our new regime was training children to bear incriminating witness against their own parents. Hitler's new system encouraged them to disobey them and abandon or oppose their parents' old Christian traditions, encouraging them to trade these for the new national socialistic ideology. Some children, obsessed with this new fanatic idea, had not only embarrassed their God-fearing parents, but had caused them to be questioned by party leaders interrogating them about their political views. In some cases, parents who had children with fanatic national socialistic beliefs were arrested, especially if they dared to voice their opposition to the new regime. Therefore, it was not safe to talk or ask questions, and I kept on guard that no one of our family would possibly be endangered through any of my careless conversation with a stranger. Father was also convinced that the party was operating an undercover spy system and that many families who were not registered members were closely watched by right-wing fanatics. Living this far out of town, however, Father reasoned that we would most likely be spared the harrassment.

In the evening Father usually focused on the news in the paper, not that it held his personal interest, but he felt he needed to keep abreast with the many events on the war scene. Victory after victory flashed across the headlines, but Father's view on these achievements was reserved, if not critical. He worried, not so much about our family, but about our country's fate. How will this war end? he wondered. He now worked additional hours at the machine factory because his foreman had made the announcement that production had to be doubled.

Visiting our neighbor one afternoon, I found Mrs. Gander listening very attentively to a speech on the radio. Motioning Lisa and me to be quiet, we sat down. Dr. Goebbels was addressing the nation. In a fiery speech he alerted the German Volk to an existing threat—a threat that our western neighbors Holland, Belgium, and Luxemburg would soon launch an attack against Germany. We should be prepared for it, and for this reason a great number of men would be drafted shortly.

Telling Father this dreadful news in the evening, he laughed bitterly.

"This speech is sheer betrayal. It infuriates me to hear these brown-shirts justify their hunger for battle and power, hoodwinking the Volk. Oh, this liar Goebbels. I detest the man," he aired his anger.

Yet as a result of Dr. Goebbels' speech, many more men had to don the green army uniform and be ready for battle. A number of girls in class raised their hands when Mr. Baeker asked whose father had been drafted. Our family was still lucky. Father was home with us. Besides, the machine factory had been declared as being part of the important war industry, another reason for Father's deferment. He mentioned to Mother how Meister Weiss, Father's one trusted friend at work, had pointed out Goebbels' frequent mention of danger from the west. Something was brewing, both men were sure. Yet Mother tried to persuade Father toward more optimistic views:

"Try not to see everything in the darkest colors. The war might be won and over soon," she encouraged him. Father, however, could not be convinced, no matter how glorious the daily victories sounded. He was worried, worried about our country, worried about us.

Several days later, he brought home different news. The factory had received a number of Polish prisoners who were ordered to fill the empty spots of German men recently drafted. To shelter these prisoners, a long, low, brown, wooden barrack had been constructed hastily, close to the factory. One of these prisoners had been assigned to work with Father. His name was Alex and Father mentioned how difficult it was to converse as the man spoke only a few German words. Both used gestures, speaking with their hands and feet. Yet the faint smile on Father's face confirmed that their first day together had gone well in spite of the language limitations.

At dinner Father told Mother that his foreman had tapped him on his shoulder while he was praying before eating his lunch.

"In this day and age, prayer is obsolete," the foreman had stated. Father had answered him that he might do as he pleased but, for himself, prayer was a very important part of his life. Gruntingly, the foreman had walked away. Mother worried, but Father assured her that she had no reason for concern.

"Don't forget the greatness of God. He is in control of the whole world, including this man." This calm statement from Father reassured her.

Only a few weeks later, Father told us that he had taught Alex to speak German and, when the other men were not watching, he had lengthy conversations with him. Having noticed Father pray, Alex evidently had learned to trust him. One day he had confided to him how cruelly the German S. S. had butchered hundreds of Polish civilians in the city of Posen. With hatred flaring up in his eyes, Alex had told Father that ministers and professional people had been arrested in great numbers.

"Do you think Alex is telling the truth?" Mother wanted to know.

"Why should the man fabricate a sad story like that? I have no problem believing him. Men who turn away from God are ruled by their own animalism and regress to savagery. I pray that God may protect us from such horror," Father reasoned. Listening to him, fear crept up my spine, especially when he told us not to mention a

39

word of this story to anyone outside our family.

Yet the reports in the newspaper portrayed an entirely different view. They stated that a great number of Volksdeutsche, Polish people of German origin, had been transported back to their homeland, Germany. What was one to believe?

In late fall, all hands in the family were busy helping Mother with the canning. Enormous amounts of fruits and vegetables went into glass jars to assure us enough food for the winter months as shortages of many items, including food, were already apparent.

Around the end of November, Father read the headline in the paper: "Unsuccessful assassination attempt on Hitler." He told Mother that the men at work had discussed this rumor during the day, but no one really knew if it was true that Hitler's life had been threatened. He amazed me with his comment:

"Not that I could ever kill anyone, but our country might be better off if the attempt had been successful." Yet in stark contrast to Father's view, the reaction to the newscast in school was that of outrage. Especially our teachers, including Mr. Baeker, regarded it to be a violent criminal act to try to kill Germany's much honored and beloved Fuehrer.

Since the day war had broken out, our so quiet and peaceful city was disturbed by news, news, and more news—all bad. As soon as the assassination news about Hitler had died down, another news item flared up. Russia had attacked Finland! Father registered this fact as another bad omen. Was Hitler's ally, Stalin, acting on his own without consulting Hitler? What would the consequences be? More war? Father did not dare to think ahead.

Usually around this time of year, I was looking forward to the many joyful Christmas preparations, but this year the family spirit was dampened. One reason was that the darkness this late November was even more apparent because all street lights in the city had been turned off so the city would not attract enemy planes. In addition, strict orders had been issued to cover all windows with black shades after dark so no light would fall outside. It was eerie to see our streets in total darkness. But the third reason, the reason closest to my heart, was that gifts and cookies for Christmas would be substantially reduced.

"I cannot buy enough flour, sugar, and ingredients to bake as many cookies and gingerbread as I have in previous years," Mother announced. Yet Father consoled us. We would still have a big real tree and he promised to hunt up the traditional white candles for it. Following Mother's suggestion, Ursula, Herta, and I started to knit and embroider gifts and Mother pedaled away busily on her sewing machine. She was determined that she would have at least one practical gift under the tree for everybody.

While we kept our small hands busy, Father kept a keen eye on the news. Although he believed only half or less of it, he was amazed that by the middle of December our German fleet had sunk so many British ships. Our own battleship, the "Graf Spee," was in trouble as, undoubtedly, were many others. But one was never sure of the facts.

"Sometimes I'm inclined to believe the many wild rumors; they seem to come closer to the facts than what is being printed in the paper," Father commented to Mother. At least in one instance his assumption proved to be right. A few days before Christmas, Elsa Beinert told me good news.

"My father is home for the holidays. He has to go back the day after Christmas," she said excitedly. Elsa prodded me to stop over and say hello to him. We found that he had gone out on an important errand. Mrs. Beinert, however, whom I expected to be in a very happy mood, was upset. In confidence and in tears she told me that while her husband had been stationed in Poland, he had watched Polish civilians, kept at gunpoint, digging an enormous ditch. Using only shovels and spades, these people had been pressed on by the S. S. until some had collapsed from sheer exhaustion. When the ditch had been the depth and size of a huge building, these civilians had been ordered to line up around the edge and had been cruelly shot by the S. S.—men, women, and children. Mrs. Beinert shuddered as she continued to explain, that dead or half dead, they had quickly been buried in the ditch. Her husband, repulsed and horrified by this act of savagery, had refused to obey the S. S. man's order. He could never shoot these civilians, he explained furiously and indignantly. Mr. Beinert had shouted at the S. S. men, saying that he had a wife and children at home and couldn't do anything so bestial. He considered this killing a sin against God and humanity, an act of brutal murder, which he had stubbornly refused to commit.

Listening to Mrs. Beinert's gruesome story, I froze in terror. She sobbed bitterly.

"I'm afraid I might never see my husband again." Blowing her nose, she went on to explain. Her husband had mentioned the possibility that, because of his refusal to obey the brutal order, he ran the risk of being killed by the S. S. himself—removal of the evidence, so to speak. I did not know how to answer Mrs. Beinert except to pray that God would protect her husband. In the face of this danger, it sounded like a thin assurance; yet, deep inside myself, I knew God could and would protect Mr. Beinert, a

41

righteous man. On my way home, I thought that what should have been a happy occasion, had turned into a sad day for the Beinerts. It was horrible—war was a gruesome affair. Poor Mrs. Beinert! My heart went out to her.

Evidently Alex, the Polish prisoner, had been telling Father the truth, the truth about the S. S.

On Christmas Eve when Father took us older children to a short, subdued Christmas service, I quietly prayed for Mr. Beinert's protection, and that Father might not be drafted. Father could not shoot anyone either, I told God. He must not allow his life to be endangered in this furious war. A horrifying thought crept into my mind: What would we do without Father? I hurriedly pushed the awful idea away; it could not be; God must not permit this tragedy to happen.

On our way home on the "black road" running along the railroad tracks, Father was quiet. Maria and Frederick, the two younger ones, were anxious to get home.

"I wonder what we'll find under the Christmas tree," they said with anticipation shining in their eyes.

It had been a family tradition to observe Christmas Eve as a day of fasting. Therefore, the empty stomach was another factor to drive us children home quickly. Only after service were we permitted to eat and Mother, having stayed home with Andreas, had a simple, meatless dish of Russian eggs ready.

After the vesper, as Mother called it, Father lit the white candles on the tree and we joined in Christmas carols. We used our Sunday school books as a guide, yet Mother knew most of them by heart. With the first yawns, Father extinguished all but one candle, took out his Bible, and read the Christmas story to us, after which he knelt down to pray an earnest, simple prayer folding his hands over his beloved Bible. Closing with a soft Amen, he quietly got up. This was Mother's signal to lift the sheet covering the gifts under the tree. Calling out our names, starting not with the youngest but with the most impatient, Maria received her gift, her eyes wide in expectancy and excitement. Mother had made her a cuddly rag doll. Frederick could hardly wait to unwrap his gift. He tore off the paper. He appreciated the Karl May book about Indians more than his new trousers. Then came the surprise.

"Here are the traditional Christmas plates, one for each," Father announced as he handed them out. They were filled with candies, cookies, and apples. Mother had even rounded up some marzipan and on top of it was a big, smiling gingerbread man, a special treat from Father. He had baked and decorated them for us. Even this Christmas I had received plenty, so much that I gladly traded some marzipan for an apple with Father. He had a sweet tooth and it was a delight to see him relish his candies. Once the gifts were unwrapped, tenderly hugged, compared and chatted about, sleepiness brought the day to an end and, upstairs, we fell into our beds, dead tired.

On Christmas morning, Father wakened us by calling upstairs from the kitchen that breakfast was ready. He loved his homebaked Danish, covered with crunchy crumbs. Having been in the baker's trade in his younger years, he was an expert baker. Mother appreciated his volunteered help as we children were forever eating.

The rest of Christmas Day I visited neighbors and classmates. Lisa Gander dropped in to see our tree. Mr. Gander was evidently too old or incapacitated to be drafted, but many fathers and brothers of families in our street were away from home at war. It must have been a dreary Christmas for them. I did not dare go visit the Beinerts for fear I might cry seeing Mr. Beinert leave.

Going back to school after the holidays, my classmate Hildegard announced sadly that her father had been wounded in battle and had spent Christmas in a military hospital.

In our history lessons we were taught that Germany's rapidly expanding population needed more space and that Hitler was determined to provide this space. From my point of view, living on the outskirts of Gumbinnen, Germany appeared to have plenty of space for everyone right here in our own country. Most likely, I was too young to understand politics. Therefore, I trusted Father's convictions and opinions.

Yet even Father was puzzled at times. One evening he questioned in what way Norway could be a threat to Germany. It was too far away from our country, he reasoned. Mother had adopted Father's attitude.

"Could it be another of Dr. Goebbels' exaggerations?" she queried. A few months later, in April of 1940, when Father read that our army had landed on the southern tip of Norway, he was appalled.

"This threat from Norway mentioned earlier was a fabrication to prepare the German Volk for another of Hitler's strategically planned aggressions. Will his mania ever cease? Will he force the whole world into war against our country? What will become of us?" He worried about our future.

Contrary to Father's feelings, the newspaper and radio proclaimed victory after victory. Narvik, Stavanger, Bergen had fallen. Denmark capitulated, followed by Norway's surrender. In May, a few weeks later, German troops had marched into Holland,

Belgium, and Luxemburg. Was the Hitlerjugend song coming true? "Today Germany belongs to us and tomorrow the whole world." Father said it was madness to try to conquer the world and, for a country our size, literally impossible.

"Goebbels might be screaming 'victory' but I can only say 'God help us!' " he said bitterly. In a tone of resignation, Mother answered:

"Unfortunately, you and I can do nothing about the situation; we cannot stop Hitler from his acts of aggression." Father agreed and, with his voice rising, he vented his anger about the National Socialist party having seized total control of the country, the S. S. policing everyone. Especially innocent Christians who, usually not members of the party, were spied upon by fanatic "brown shirts." Over such a short period of time Hitler had gained a tight grip on every living person in Germany. Father reasoned that since the unsuccessful coup d'etat on Hitler, the S. S. must have received orders to watch anyone who could have had even the slightest connection with the small opposition. As Mother and Father had refused to join the National Socialist party, both evidently were on the so-called "Black List" and both felt they might be watched.

It took Mother a while to realize that she had been followed and watched by Mrs. Thorne for some time. The Thornes had been elected to the position of "Obersiedler," a totally unnecessary function, yet a function permitting them to check people's property at random in the Annahof settlement area. The reason for such freedom on their part was to assure the regime that every house sold to a family was properly maintained.

"What humbug!" Father cried. He knew that the real reason behind this enactment was to spy on families, to knock at doors unannounced, and check on family activities, to which Father rightfully objected. "It is an intrusion into my privacy," he retorted, "it is against the law!" When Mother was a teenager, she had attended the same school as Mrs. Thorne and, therefore, had no inkling of suspicion. Yet she noticed for the fourth time that, whenever she entered the small grocery store on the Franz-Schubert-Strasse Mrs. Thorne came in a few minutes later. Not being on social terms with her, Mother usually did her shopping, bid the grocer and Mrs. Thorne a good-day, and left the store. Only because Mother recognized Mrs. Thorne's appearance to be a curious coincidence did she mention it to Father. He suggested that she watch her conversation at the store for a possible trap set up by Mrs. Thorne.

A few days later when Mother came back from the grocer, I detected a spark of victory in her eyes as she told Father that not all people were as bad as one assumed. Naturally, Father wanted an explanation and Mother told him the story. She had entered the grocery store and, being the only customer, Mrs. Schneider, the proprietor's wife, looked straight at her.

"Do you realize that you are being followed?" she asked. Not waiting for Mother's reply, she added:

"Watch your conversation when Mrs. Thorne comes in." She had barely finished her sentence when the door opened and Mrs. Thorne entered, greeting Mrs. Schneider with a loud and clear "Heil Hitler," evidently testing Mother's response. Mother had trouble steadying her knees, a reaction to what she had heard, and finished her shopping quickly. Upon leaving, she had bid Mrs. Schneider an honest and heartfelt "Thank you" and left. What had surprised Mother and Father was that Mrs. Schneider had displayed such humane feelings, such concern.

"Her husband is an active member of the party. He wears his uniform to every possible occasion, he attends every party function," Father commented. Mrs. Schneider's kindness toward Mother was unusual. How could this be? Could the rumor possibly be true that the Schneiders had a crippled, deformed young son? Neighbors claimed to have seen the child in the tightly fenced-in yard, tended by Mrs. Schneider's mother, while he spent his day sitting in a wheelchair. Could this tragedy have softened Mrs. Schneider's heart, opened it to compassion and understanding? Under the new Hitler regime, it was considered a shame to have sickly or crippled children. Hitler proclaimed that Germans, the core of the Aryan race, were superior to any other race on this planet. So then, in the Hitler sense, the Schneiders were disgracing the race. While Father listened intently to the story, Mother recalled another rumor about Mrs. Schneider: that at night under the cover of darkness, she was selling groceries to Jews from the back door of her house. No one in the neighborhood was certain or dared to discuss openly whether any Jewish families lived in our Annahof area. The houses were spaced close together. How could a person go undetected? Could the rumor be true? Was it possible that some Jews lived in hiding or came from the city at night under the cover of darkness, walking at least three kilometers to Annahof to buy their food from Mrs. Schneider, a Nazi? Father, although not too anxious to discuss this rumor before us children, mentioned that God had His own mysterious ways to perform His wonders. This incident proved that not every party member could be indoctrinated by the new Hitler theory of atheism. Not every party member acted according to Hitler's strict orders. Yet, regarding Mrs. Thorne, Mother had to be on guard.

From that day on, we did not use the narrow zig-zag passage along our fence but took the long uphill street to cross over to the Franz-Schubert-Strasse.

Chapter IV

Hopes and Fears

In May of 1940 I was ten years old and had to join the Jungmaedel. Now I was part of Hitler's organized youth and the feeling of uneasiness crept into me. Knowing from Mother's latest experience that the party put tight clamps around every civilian's private life, resentment smoldered in me. I was being robbed of my already limited freedom. School and extensive homework took most of the day, but the Jungmaedel required lengthy indoctrination sessions.

"What a waste of time," I wailed to Herta. Our training required memorizing the full mysterious history of the National Socialist Party, including Hitler's shabby background and that of his associates. We were drilled the party way to remember their birth dates, their heroic acts that made the party great, and recent data about the war that were considered extremely important. Singing the party songs I minded least, although their text was often ruthless and nonsensical. What I abhorred were the scheduled marches through town. On national holidays we ten-year-olds had to line up like soldiers and march up the Koenigstrasse. At the tail end of the column and, dressed in civilian clothes, I felt like an outcast, a lost sheep in this herd of singing and yelling youngsters. I hated this exercise. It suited my rebellious mood fine to answer our leader, who questioned me about my reasons for not wearing the black, white, and brown uniform.

"My parents do not have the money for extravagances," I used to say. I would have loved to yell the truth into her face, but I did not dare to. Instead Father had suggested that we use the answer about

47

lack of money; it sounded feasible. Yet his real reason was that he would never buy a uniform for any member of his family. He did not believe in Hitler's ideology; he refused to have us wear its symbols. It amused me when other girls would sheepishly explain to their questioning leaders that their uniform was in the laundry, a statement always drawing a furious reaction from our leader.

"For goodness' sake; did it have to be washed this very day?" Ignoring the answer, she stormed away. It angered me that I had to obey girls only two years older than I. Who gave them the authority to rule over me? My young, sensitive mind reacted violently, rebelling against this force. I asked myself how much these young snips could know about politics, since they were by far not adults. Who were they? Besides, they carried their noses snobbishly high. Father taught us that being humble was a virtue, yet this theory did not seem to apply to our Hitlerjugend leaders.

Nevertheless, life also had a happy occasion in store for me. In the spring of 1940, I started middle-school. As this higher education had been inaugurated in Gumbinnen only the year before, a brand new school had been built. The complex was located on the Moltkestrasse, several kilometers from Annahof in the northern section of town. Although my leather case with books weighed heavy on those long walks, I was proud to attend, to be admitted. My grades had been good enough.

The most interesting subject to me was English. Miss Zahn, our new homeroom teacher, explained with a tinge of apology in her voice:

"Although our country is officially at war with Great Britain, to learn English correctly, you will have to think in this new language." I liked her for making this statement. It sounded as if she was trying to build a bridge of understanding in our young minds, despite the raging war. Practicing pronunciation of the vocabulary at home, I noticed how much softer the English language sounded in comparison to my own harsh German. How does one think in English, I wondered. England was so far away. Would I ever be able to speak this language, to communicate with someone born in England or someone on that faraway continent known as America? Not now, but maybe after this war was over. I was dreaming again, but it was good that at least dreams could not be restricted. Dreams could not be forced into the National Socialist straitjacket.

Father's comments on Germany's newest victories in France jerked me out of my dream world. Although I had learned in school that the famous Maginot Line had been victoriously passed, that Sedan, Boulogne, and Calais had fallen into the hands of our strong

German armies, Father was pessimistic. Even after France had surrendered and Father had listened to one of Dr. Goebbels' victory speeches at work, his reaction was negative.

"I had to walk away from the radio. These trumpet sounds of Goebbels are not realistic, bolstering up the Volk to believe him, to justify Hitler's wrongdoing." And with a sign of resignation, he added: "How long will this war last?" These contradictions were depressing. I could tell by Father's subdued mood that something was seriously wrong. But then, thank God, the front and the intensive fighting, even all those glorious victories, were on the other side of Germany. I was glad that, here in Gumbinnen, we were far away from it.

The wide open spaces behind the pond during the warm summer months were inviting and on sunny days Herta, who disliked the Jungmaedel meetings as much as I, made a suggestion.

"Let's get lost behind the pond," and she added, "Mother does not need to know. This will let her off the hook in case someone comes to the house to question her about us." Most of the time we were positive that none of the leaders would come to check our absence because Annahof was three kilometers from the center of town. One day, however, we almost got caught. Herta and I had decided to skip the meeting and were in our fenced-in yard when Herta motioned me to be silent and pointed to the street.

"Guess who's coming," she whispered. I recognized the two girls immediately by their uniforms—black skirt, white blouse, and brown jacket. They were from the Hitlerjugend searching for us. Like arrows, we darted into the woodshed and, careful not to make any noise, crept behind a huge pile of wood, ducking so our heads would not betray us. We held our breath, listening intently for someone to approach. The two girls had gone into the house, most likely questioning Mother as to where we were. They must not have seen us, we reasoned, or they would have searched for us in the yard. When we heard no footsteps approaching, Herta carefully peeked through the slats, but saw nobody. Finally, after what seemed like eternity, we heard their crunching footsteps move down the narrow zig-zag path toward the Franz-Schubert-Strasse. Giving them plenty of time to walk a safe distance, we quietly climbed out and checked with Mother about the questioning. She did not receive us in a sweet mood.

"The girls did not believe me when I said I did not know where you were, although this was true," she said. When we told her that we had been hiding in the woodshed, she was afraid about what could have happened had the two girls searched for us. As luck had been with us once, Herta suggested that the next few weeks we show our faces at the meetings. It was safer; we did not like Mother's being harassed because of our absence. When we told Ursula about our adventure, she agreed with our decision. She never encountered difficulties with the Hitlerjugend. Conscientious as she was, she attended regularly, only skipping a meeting occasionally, to which no one took offense.

Ursula, now fourteen, helped Mother with the never-ending chore of making clothes from used ones, a generous donation from our many relatives. Only on very rare occasions did I get brand new clothes, except for the years I had spent with Aunt Ina. Although aware of the many shortages, I lacked the understanding of appreciating hand-me-downs, clothes that Ursula and Herta had worn. Yet I did not dare complain about the situation, knowing what Mother's answer would be.

"This situation will end when you earn your own money." It would take a few more years until I became self-supporting, I realized. The lingering war did not help matters either as more and more articles vanished from the market.

Raw materials were used and reused. On a regular schedule horse-drawn wagons pulled along the Beethovenstrasse collecting scrap iron, discarded newspapers neatly bundled, and all sorts of clothes. Nothing was wasted and Dr. Goebbels, addressing the people, assured us that our armies, under the prominent and knowledgeable leadership of von Brauchitsch, von Rundstedt, and Halder, would win this war. Yet we, the Volk, had to make sacrifices, keeping our military fully equipped to guarantee this victory. This logic sounded reasonable and in our family nothing was wasted. Not that Father believed in supporting Dr. Goebbels, but he felt it was our duty to stand behind our soldiers fighting for our country, those relatives, those neighbors, those friends.

"Besides, wastefulness is a sin, especially a waste of food," Father affirmed. The subject of food also made headlines in the news. Hitler was planning a blockade around Britain and, by cutting off its food supply from America, starve out its people and thus conquer the British Isles. This measure, the newspaper stated, was a counteraction to Winston Churchill's speech in which he evidently had guaranteed that Germany would be wiped out, blotted out from the map.

As the weeks went on, the war gained in fury. One of the places in which the results of Churchill's speech was felt was Hamburg where Mother's sister, Aunt Erna, lived. She had written Mother a letter complaining that the British R.A.F. had bombed the center severely during the summer. As a result, she and Uncle Franz were spending many nights in the dark bunker with their neighbors, worrying if their district would be hit next. So far, the Bahrenfeld area, where they lived, had been spared.

"I'm so worried about them," Mother said and Father was amazed that Uncle Franz could work those long hours at the wharf after spending a night in the bunker. Picking up his paper, Father read the headline to Mother: "Luftwaffe bombed London." The details proclaimed a great success with our *Stuka* bombers, registering extensive damage to the British capital—another victory.

"It's queer," Father said, "but those Londoners must feel the same way as Erna and Franz in Hamburg." At this point, Mother felt compassion only for her own relatives in danger and not for the worry-ridden people living in London.

In late summer Father's attention was diverted from the war news to home, to his pet subject, fishing. Evidently his silent prayers before eating lunch had strengthened Alex's confidence in him and both men enjoyed casual conversations. Avoiding the controversial subject of politics, Father had mentioned to Alex that he spent many summer nights fishing. Still in broken German, Alex had told him that as a civilian he had worked in the shipbuilding industry and loved to be near water. He had offered to build a large row boat for Father which he could use for fishing on a pond or river. Naturally, Father was delighted and he wondered how he could obtain permission for Alex to come home with him after work.

Only a few days later, Father's triumphant smile revealed to Mother that Meister Weiss, his trusted friend, had granted his request. The only stipulation was that Father had to guarantee Alex's return to the barracks before curfew.

"Alex is a good Christian; he will keep his promise," he assured Mother. From a lumber yard Father had bought the wood Alex had suggested and the following Saturday, he brought him home.

Our family got to know Alex well. He was a tall, blond man with broad shoulders and a quiet personality. Although he still spoke in a broken German, he and Father understood each other. While Alex displayed his expert skill in boat building, we watched with fascination as this big row boat took shape. How expertly he bent the wood, grafting each board neatly upon the other, explaining to Father that this technique would guarantee him a watertight boat. The project seemed to delight both men equally. Alex told Father that he enjoyed being away from the dreary barracks and now, having something creative to do, did not mind the strict 9:00 p.m. curfew.

Mother had invited Alex to join us at the table for supper, but he shyly and politely declined. Therefore, Father ate with him outside in the yard. Sitting on a pile of wood, eating their supper from the plates on their knees, both enjoyed a man-to-man conversation. Father was happy to learn boat building from Alex and told him that he was anxious to take the boat to the river Angerapp, a few kilometers west of Gumbinnen. In the small village of Mertinshagen, Father was on friendly terms with a farmer who had invited him to fish from his property adjoining the river. The boat would enable him to lay special lines to catch eel at night, a type of fish Mother considered a delicacy. We could read in Father's eyes how much he would have liked to take Alex along fishing.

"I don't dare press my luck too far," he told Mother, regretting the stringent rules at work regarding Polish prisoners.

The two men rarely discussed politics. Father considered it too controversial, too dangerous a subject. In late fall when their project was near completion, I watched Father explain his fishing equipment to Alex, showing him how to repair a ripped net.

During these weeks it had become Mother's routine to prepare an extra sandwich for Alex. She put it into Father's lunch box, from which he could easily hand it to Alex. It was a small way in which Father was able to show his appreciation to Alex for his generous help in building the boat. One evening, however, he came home from work angry and told Mother that his fanatic Nazi foreman had tapped him on the shoulder, implying a threat in his statement.

"Are you aware that you could run into trouble for feeding the Polack?" he had asked, revealing his displeasure. Mother reasoned that the foreman must have been watching and worried if he would file a complaint against Father. We knew this could have grave consequences as it was against the law to co-mingle with prisoners, to help or feed them. Even private conversation could be misinterpreted as passing on important secret data, which was an act of treason, granting either imprisonment or a death sentence. Yet Father was not too concerned, explaining that he knew the real reason for his foreman's remark.

"It must irk him to see me pray before eating my lunch. He used Alex's sandwich as an excuse to call me 'to order.' " Father's explanation made sense. The foreman was an atheist, believing along the Nazi trend that in the Third Reich, under the leadership of their almighty Hitler, no one needed to pray to an outdated God, and Father added:

"These brothers have a lot to learn; just wait and see." Yet from now on, Father was especially careful when handing the sandwich to Alex. It had to be done in a quiet corner or unobtrusively when passing each other. Nevertheless, Alex continued to get his sandwiches and Father continued to say his prayers.

It was too late now to put the boat into the water. Father was going to wait until spring after the floods had receded. He was happy and proud about the finished boat, a true masterpiece of craftsmanship. It was wide and roomy, with the two polished boards across the middle, allowing seating for four. As a final touch, the two heavy oars were hooked to the side, ready to be used by two strong arms in the spring. Father had offered to pay Alex for his work, but he had refused to accept the money.

"No money, you my friend," he had told Father, evidently appreciating the fact that Father treated him as a friend instead of a prisoner, sharing his food and honest conversation with him. One day shortly before the boat was finished, Alex had told us that he worried about his own family. He had not heard from anyone since September, 1939. The sad look on his face made me realize that we Germans were not the only people concerned about our families; prisoners were too.

When the boat was finished and stored away safely, Father again concentrated on the news. In the meantime, Stalin's troops had occupied the Balkan states and our geographical neighbors to the north: Lithuania, Latvia, and Estonia. Recalling a discussion he had had with his trusted friend, Meister Weiss, the two men were of the opinion that danger was brewing in the east. Neither could understand Hitler's pact with Stalin, reasoning that a strong feeling of distrust still existed between the two countries, stemming from the years of 1914 to 1918 of World War I. Mother did not want to be reminded of this dreadful period in which she as a youngster experienced the occupation of Gumbinnen by the Russian armies. Reasoning that we, as ordinary people, could not change our country's state of war and, as if trying to push her fearful memories out of her mind, she concentrated her efforts around the house.

In late November when Father read the headline to Mother about Molotov's visit to Hitler in Berlin, she asked what implications this could have. Father's answer was brief and to the point.

"I hope this does not mean war with Russia," he replied. He spelled out that men of the caliber of Hitler and Stalin did not honor pacts; that their foremost concern was to gain power. Mother, obviously not happy with Father's reasoning or too fearful about a possible war with Russia, accused him of being pessimistic again.

"I wish you would at least acknowledge the facts," she tried to persuade Father. Over the radio victory after victory was announced and the paper was proclaiming the same: Germany was going to win this war. Father, however, saw beyond these facts, he read the truth between the lines. One other fact contradicted these official proclamations—the fact of the many shortages, shortages apparent everywhere.

* * * * * *

It was close to Christmas again when Mrs. Geier, who lived farther down on the Beethovenstrasse, stopped Mother outside, offering beautiful fabrics for sale. To my astonishment, Mother politely refused to buy. After Mrs. Geier had walked away, a look of disbelief on her face, Mother explained that Mrs. Geier's husband had been stationed in Paris for some time and that these fabrics obviously were stolen.

"I refuse to wear a dress made of stolen French merchandise. I will not soil my hands with something obtained in dishonesty," Mother said to emphasize her point of conviction. That moment Mother stood ten feet tall in my mind. She spent endless hours altering clothes or going through the tedious job of tearing out an old dress and making a smaller one for one of us instead of doing something wrong. She never complained about the amount of work she had with sewing, baking, cleaning, gardening, or canning. As if to compensate for the many shortages, our garden this year had yielded an especially abundant harvest. Rows of glass jars, filled with a variety of vegetables and fruit, were lining the shelves in the cellar. Also, the bins, piled high with potatoes, assured us plenty of food for the coming winter.

As the war now dragged into the second winter, the government had installed *Winterhilfe*, a service in which housewives were urged to volunteer with collecting clothes or knitting socks, mittens, shawls, and ear muffs. These items were sorely needed for families who had either lost their home in a bombing raid or their breadwinner in the ravages of war. Mother, always willing to help, gave gladly what she could spare. By now Ursula, Herta, and I had learned to knit and we spent many evenings unravelling old sweaters and knitting new ones from the old wool.

The second Christmas approached and the war was not ended. One evening, however, Father surprised us with good news. The factory was giving a Christmas party. All the children of the working men were invited. Frederick jumped up from the bench, letting out a joyful "Hurrah! When? When?" Father announced that it was scheduled to be three days before Christmas Eve and Frederick stormed for the calendar, counting the days. He could hardly wait. When the day finally arrived, Father took Ursula, Herta, Frederick, Maria, and me to the party. Mother stayed home with Andreas. He was too small to make the long trip.

With our shawls covering our mouths, we were bundled up for our walk to the factory. Frederick had started to run ahead, and in his excitement, accidentally took the short-cut along our garden fence, passing the Thorne's house on the Franz-Schubert-Strasse. Turning left, our troupe headed north to the railroad crossing. Passing it, we made a turn east and walked down the "Black Road" along the tracks to the factory. Today the huge complex of buildings did not look quite as forbidding as usual. The two big Christmas trees gave the dark gate a cheerful and inviting touch. With a wave of his hand, Father checked us in with the porter and we trudged up to the huge dark, wooden hall located in the back of the factory complex. Many people, men, women, and children were heading in the same direction. There must have been hundreds.

Entering the enormous hall, I was surprised to see so many lights, giving the effect of summer brightness. Someone ushered us to a row of seats near the back and, after having settled comfortably, I noticed the wide, colorfully decorated stage in front of the hall. Two enormous Christmas trees, ablaze with light, flanked it on either side and lit the speaker's podium standing in the center. Although the noise and chatter in the crowded hall bothered me, it felt cozy to warm up after our long walk. Suddenly a bell rang and the crowd fell silent. A well-dressed man, taking his stand at the podium, greeted everybody present and then got lost in a long-winded and boring speech. My ears registered only fragments of it.

"Let us praise Dr. Ley and the Arbeitsfront standing firmly behind him! Thanks to our men at the factory for putting in extra hours of work and effort. Let us renew our pledge to back our beloved Fuehrer to make his ideals come true!" He talked on and on. Frederick got restless. Tugging at Father's sleeve, he asked when Santa Claus would be coming. Finally the speaker finished and, after endless applause, stepped aside. At the same time, through a wide side entrance, Santa Claus walked in. Wearing a red suit, he smiled broadly behind his huge, white beard and mustache. In expectation, Frederick and Maria had jumped up from their seats and, pointing her finger in Santa's direction, Maria called our attention.

"Look how hard he has to pull; the big sack must be very heavy." Frederick was anxious to find out what was inside of it. But Santa followed his scheduled program. A choir of girls dressed as angels in long white dresses with golden stars on their wings had caught my attention. Santa ordered them to sing "Silent Night, Holy Night" and encouraged all children to join them. It was fun singing along with the angels. Then he took out a long list and started to call out names of children, one by one, who went forward to receive a gift from him. Ursula, my bright sister, had figured out his system.

"All girls are receiving dolls in sizes according to their age, and the boys a variety of toys; either soldiers or football players, and he is giving out wooden building blocks for the toddlers." Herta had discovered that Santa was going down the alphabet and our name, starting with the letter "S," put us toward the end. Nevertheless, our turn finally came and when Father stepped forward with us, Santa handed me a box with a beautiful doll dressed in blue who could close her eyes and go to sleep. A brand new doll! And she was mine! I was so happy that I forgot to investigate the gifts the others had received. Then Father picked up the toy for Andreas and we returned to our seats. After singing a few more carols, the party was over.

It had turned dark outside and when we left the big hall, the factory looked forbidding again. Holding on to Father's hand, I was glad when we passed the gate and were on our way back home. The factory with its huge, fiery smelting furnaces looked like hell to me. I was afraid of the place.

Mother heard us as we arrived and she opened the door: "I have a hot soup ready to warm you up." Asking Father how the party had been, he replied with his dry sense of humor:

"They could have spared me listening to the high praises sung to Dr. Ley. Otherwise, it was all right."

* * * * * *

Another Christmas came around. This time our gifts were even smaller and all handmade but that fact did not dampen our spirits. Going to church, singing carols, and listening to Father read the Christmas story was so lovely to us that we almost forgot an ugly war was going on outside. The Christmas mail from our relatives, however, was a dreary reminder. The situation in

Hamburg had gotten worse, Aunt Erna wrote. Not only had the bombing been stepped up but the food shortage was becoming increasingly severe. Besides, Uncle Franz was registering the wear-and-tear in noticeably poor health. Aunt Tina from Koenigsberg wrote that Juergen, our cousin, had been drafted. So far, she did not know where he was stationed and was worried about him. On Christmas Monday, Mother and Father visited our relatives in town.

"We heard nothing but bad news," Mother sighed. Our cousin Willi had also been drafted, over which Aunt Frieda and Uncle Gustav were very upset. Mother and Father had not had time to visit Uncle Oskar and Aunt Ina. Therefore, I did not know whether Hans, my favorite cousin, had been drafted.

Determined to find out when school started after the holidays, I stopped by Uncle Oskar's store for a visit. Aunt Ina told me that Hans had started his apprenticeship as a radio technician and was attending school in Koenigsberg. For the next two years he would stay with Aunt Tina and come home only on weekends. That, at least, was good news.

On my long walk home from Aunt Ina's, the white snow crunched under my feet. The weather had turned very cold, and it occurred to me how much faster I could get home by bus. But the bus service to our Annahof area had operated for only a short while. It had been discontinued with the explanation that all cars, trucks, and buses were desperately needed at the front. All private cars, even Uncle Oskar's new beige Opel, had been confiscated by the government on a so-called loan basis, to be returned to their owners after the war was won.

Even this winter would pass, I consoled myself. Besides, I did not want to miss school. I had become friends with Helga, the girl sitting next to me. She had a sunny disposition and wore her hair in two thick brown braids. Since we favored different subjects in class, we had promised to help each other. Helga found mathematics easier than I, but in art and drawing she had problems, whereas I considered it a fun subject. I drew her and my own assignment in a very short time, but Miss Zahn, with her keen eye, recognized the drawing on Helga's desk to be mine.

"She'll get the grade but I don't need to ask who has drawn this," she said, giving me a knowing glance. Goodnaturedly, she did not embarrass me, but some lessons later she elaborated on the fact that in art, it was easy to recognize the artist in his work. Somehow she could always identify my drawings and, not wanting to rouse Miss Zahn to anger, we had to be very careful. I gave Helga's drawings only a few correcting strokes after Miss Zahn's explanation.

During intersession Helga had told me that her mother had been divorced but had remarried. Therefore, she had a real father, a step-father, and two younger step-brothers. To my question as to whether this was a confusing situation, she laughed.

"No, not to me. My father is in the army and I see him only occasionally when he is on furlough." To keep in touch with him, she wrote letters and everyone knew when she had received one. She would breeze into the classroom, waving the letter excitedly like a flag. After sharing some of the news with me, she fondly put it in one of her books where she collected her father's letters. Helga was also very fond of Miss Zahn, as were most of the girls in our class.

According to her profession, Miss Zahn was required to be a member of the National Socialist party. Contrary to general Nazi behavior, she was a very understanding and compassionate person and under her firm, teacher-like manners, she had a warm heart. Endowed with a roundish, mature figure, she was always neatly dressed and emanated motherly qualities, coupled with orderliness and cleanliness. Her gold-rimmed glasses added a touch of authority to her and only in the beginning had I noticed that she had two buck teeth. This slight facial flaw, however, did not prevent her from smiling or joining the class in laughter. To any girl in class who needed tutoring in special courses, even outside of her own subjects, she offered her generous help, free of charge. She was interested that every girl would get good grades and pass the course. I loved Miss Zahn; she held a warm spot in my heart. From the beginning, she must have recognized my shyness and when I answered a question correctly, she readily had a word of praise and encouragement. Sometimes the class strayed off the subject. On one of those occasions, Miss Zahn told us that she had spent her childhood days in the country and she had found it difficult to adjust to city life in Gumbinnen.

"On my first day I curtsied to every adult in the street," she recalled, "until my father explained to me that this was not necessary." She laughed with us as she recalled her childhood experience. In the small village where she had lived, she obviously knew everybody and curtsying to the people she met was part of good manners.

On another occasion, Miss Zahn admitted that her parents had always said grace at the table. This open acknowledgment of faith and prayer amazed me because, under the Hitler regime, this practice had almost vanished. She asked us to raise our hands if in our home grace was still said. I raised mine and so did a few others.

Did I detect a twinkle in her eyes when she looked at me, I asked myself. Ursel, the girl sitting in front of me, stated that her mother had taught her to pray at bedtime instead.

"Would you mind reciting your evening prayer to us in class?" Miss Zahn asked Ursel. Obediently, Ursel got up. Standing beside her desk, bowing her head, and folding her hands, she began to recite her prayer. In the middle of it, her sweet voice quivered and then she started to sob. Quietly, Miss Zahn walked over to her and put her arm around Ursel's shoulder.

"What is the trouble, dear?" she asked lovingly. Tearfully, Ursel replied that her mother had received a telegram the night before notifying her of the death of her brother. It had been her mother's only brother. The class became very quiet and many of us dabbed away a tear. Miss Zahn, handing Ursel her own handkerchief, whispered:

"I know how it feels to lose someone close. I lost my own brother last week." Tactfully, she changed the subject, taking our tender minds back to the course we had to study. Later, during recess, she talked to Ursel at length, consoling her privately. Miss Zahn was like a dear but stern mother to us.

During our lessons, she was firm. Her students had to know grammar and spelling, punctuation and sentence structure, in German as well as in English. Pronunciation of a difficult word was practiced over and over again until it sounded right. She taught us to write compositions in both languages, explaining that the sentence structure was different in English than in German. To study under her firm but patient tutelage was hard work, but at test time we remembered our subjects well and received high grades.

For the subject of mathematics, our class had a different teacher. His name was Mr. Stienke, yet all students in school referred to him as "Stinker," a title he truly deserved. I thoroughly disliked "Stinker," and did not know why he was exempt from the draft. I would have loved to have him sent anywhere, far enough to be away from me. He was loud and rough, and his habit of poking around his mouth with a toothpick while teaching betrayed his poor manners. Our feelings toward each other were mutual; he did not like me either. After some honest soul searching, I arrived at the conclusion that he could have only one reason to dislike me.

The incident had happened one day in math class. We had returned from recess and had taken a while to settle down to silence and attention. Meantime Stinker was anxious to review some formulae in algebra, writing them on the huge blackboard which covered the entire wall behind his desk. He wrote in a hurry. Finished with it, he posted himself before the podium and leaned backward to point out a specific formula. And then it happened. Evidently he had been to the men's room and, in a hurry, forgot to button his fly. While he leaned backward, a snap of his white shirt stuck out of his black trousers and sent our entire class of girls into a fit of giggles. Not knowing what was wrong, he turned his face to the class and caught me with a big grin on my face. It was a funny sight and I tried hard not to laugh out loud. In his fury he called me forward.

"You there, I'll wipe that grin off your face!" He fired the next problem at me, which I was to solve in a formula. Miraculously, the correct answer shot out of me and I hurriedly jotted the numbers and letters down in their proper sequence. I had shocked myself, math being my poorest subject. I had never gotten an answer so fast, so well. Stinker was disappointed because he would have loved to slap me across my face. Instead he growled:

"You're lucky this time," and snapped, "Sit down!" Not hesitating a second, I flew back to my desk, silently praying, "Thanks, Lord, for being with me."

After that, it was a situation of truce with Stinker always ready to dig up the battle axe, trying to get even with me. For many weeks thereafter, I did my math homework with diligence, careful not to provoke the beast in him again. Evidently he had complained about this incident to Miss Zahn but she, aware of his general unpopularity, made only a casual remark and then the matter was forgotten.

Homework had doubled since I had entered middle-school and it left me hardly any time for play. Almost unnoticeably the days were getting longer as the calendar registered the third week in February. Very unexpectedly one day we received the bad news that Aunt Frieda had had a serious accident. When Mother rushed to see Uncle Gustav, her brother, she found him in great distress. Aunt Frieda had broken her spine. He had returned from visiting her at the hospital where she had undergone emergency surgery. He kept accusing himself:

"Why did I permit her to help me stack hay in the loft above the horses' stables? Why?" he wailed over and over again. She had never done this work before but, because Willi was fighting at the front, she had insisted on helping. Underestimating her own weight and the strength of the flooring boards, she had broken through with a crash and fallen on a sharp cement edge in the stable. She was in critical condition and the doctors could not guarantee that she would ever walk again. Mother did not know whether a broken spine could be healed, but did not dare voice her fear to her brother.

"I do not understand what provoked Frieda to climb up to the hayloft; she was simply too heavy," Father said, shaking his head in disbelief. Yet faithfully for many weeks he and Mother went to visit Aunt Frieda at the hospital. She complained about a great deal of pain, but finally the doctor was hopeful that she would fully recover. Therefore, it came as a great shock when we received the news late in March that Aunt Frieda had died. Evidently she had died from internal injuries which had gone undetected. Uncle Gustav was inconsolable. Over and over again he asked why he had ever permitted her to climb up to the loft. He could not forgive himself.

Aunt Frieda's funeral was held on March 31, 1941. Ursula's confirmation was the same day. It was doubly sad. How could Ursula enjoy her special day when Aunt Frieda had been buried in the morning? Yet Mother's and Father's concern went beyond the day. How would Uncle Gustav manage his household and bring up his daughter Suzanne, who was not easy to handle? How would he keep the books? Aunt Frieda had taken care of these matters over the years. Someone had to help.

Mother had been looking forward to having Ursula spend her *Pflichtjahr*, a year of service in a household, at home. Her request had been granted by city authorities because we were so many children in the family. Hitler had installed this service so every German girl received adequate training to become a very efficient *Hausfrau*. Now Mother's hopes of gaining an extra pair of helping hands were dimmed because Father suggested that Ursula take care of Uncle Gustav's household until he located a reliable housekeeper. His business had to go on.

So instead of going to school, Ursula now headed to the Poststrasse every morning. A few days later she reported that, although she had the household and books well under control, to manage Suzanne created a problem. Our young cousin evidently had been thoroughly spoiled by Aunt Frieda and refused to cooperate with Ursula.

"Have patience. It will take time," Father encouraged her.

As Uncle Gustav owned a radio, Ursula often brought home the latest news. Hitler had ordered the occupation of Greece and Yugoslavia. King Peter II of Yugoslavia had been ousted from government, to which Father cynically remarked that it was most likely another of Hitler's victory strategies.

"How much I detest the propaganda minister! This liar, Dr. Joseph Goebbels, I cannot listen to his speeches!" Father shouted. Especially the three-fold *Sieg-Heil* at the end of each speech disgusted him and Father demanded to know where the *Sieg*, the victory, was, claiming that we had been waiting a long time now. And the word *Heil* had a double meaning. He could not understand how anyone could hail an unscrupulous character like Hitler who, in Father's opinion, was driving Germany into the abyss by provoking the whole world against us. Father had firmly decided not to buy a radio because he would not permit Goebbels' screaming voice in his own house. Father believed that Goebbels exaggerated and distorted the news to the point of untruth; therefore, he called him a liar.

Not that Father needed to have worried; radios and all other electrical appliances had become extremely rare and could be obtained only with special purchasing tickets. Father, not being a member of the party, would never have received one to buy a radio. Neither did he need one. The news was shouted from the rooftops. Yugoslavia surrendered in the middle of April and Greece only two weeks later. The paper carried a picture of the Acropolis with the Swastika flag mounted on top. With a hint of humor in his voice, Father said:

"I bet the Grecian gods are turning around in their graves at this sight."

Quite contrary to Father's opinion, in school and especially at Hitlerjugend quarters, Germany's victories were loudly proclaimed as great historical events. Our German armies, limited in number, were conquering one country after another. Great praise was attributed to General Erwin Rommel, proudly referred to as the "desert fox." He was gaining an enormous amount of territory in North Africa. And our Italian ally was bravely fighting on Hitler's side. Hitler's devotees and party members believed that no wrong could come from him. Seemingly, he was living up to his promise to make room for an ever-growing and expanding German population, his *Volk*.

I appreciated that in school we were not asked to voice our opinion regarding our government and at the Jungmaedel meetings I deliberately kept my mouth shut; it was safer that way.

When on May 10 the news spread through town that Rudolf Hess had flown to England, it sounded as if people had become daring enough to question Hitler's staff; after all Hess was considered the man closest to him. "Is his regime starting to shake? Are his trusted friends forsaking him?" Mrs. Barock, one of our more outspoken neighbors, had whispered this question to Mother. But the next day the incident was casually explained away, the paper stating plainly that Hess had gone insane and Hitler assigned Martin Bormann as his replacement. Life went on;

nothing had changed. Hitler sat firmly in the saddle.

Chapter V

War—Victorious

One evening only a few weeks later, Father arrived home with a troubled look on his face. He had gone to work especially early and, holding on to his bike, he had waited at the railroad crossing for a long train to pass. It was headed eastward and was loaded with heavy tanks and guns.

"I hate to think of its implication," he told Mother. But she reminded him that a war against Russia would be out of the question because Hitler had signed a non-aggression pact with Stalin a few months ago.

"Maybe it's in exchange for the many train loads of wheat we have received from the Ukraine," Mother reasoned, but this sounded completely illogical to Father.

"Hitler would not ship weapons to his rival, Stalin, pact or no pact," Father insisted.

Only too soon we learned the meaning of this shipment of war materials. It was 3:30 a.m. on June 22, 1941, when Father wakened us from our sleep. War had broken out against Russia. He urged us to get up and get dressed while he looked out the window to the east, intently listening to the distant rumble. Gumbinnen, our hometown, was only a short distance of fifteen kilometers from the Lithuanian border, a country occupied by Stalin's armies. Which way would the front move? Would Russian troops be in our town by morning? Desperately trying to waken, I could feel the rumble in the ground under my feet, transmitted by the cannonade directed toward Russia. Against the dark sky, a pink glow on the eastern horizon indicated that a big fire was raging in the distance. Mother and Father stood close together, fear and worry written over their faces, listening, praying. After two tense hours Father had to get ready for work.

"The rumble has faded into the distance," he assured Mother. The German armies were advancing into Russia. To be safe, he told Mother to keep us home from school. He would gather the latest news at the factory and report to us in the evening.

It was a tense day. Confined to the boundaries of our property made us feel fenced in and the lack of sleep kept our minds on edge. Soon our neighbors were up and Mrs. Gander and Mrs. Bergdoerfer rushed over to talk with Mother. Mrs. Gander, usually not interested in current events, was shocked about the latest development.

"Not a word of this was mentioned on the radio last night," she poured out to Mother. Mrs. Bergdoerfer reminded her of Hitler's speech given in May in which he had warned of a possible attack from Russia and Hitler's tactic to act first if need be.

"But so suddenly, in the middle of the night," Mrs. Gander stammered, still trying to recover from the shock. Mrs. Bergdoerfer worried about Russia's retaliation to Hitler's invasion, his breaking of the non-aggression pact. When will they strike back? Will it be today or tomorrow? Will they bomb the city? Will they throw back our front and over-run us? Mother, surprisingly, had calmed herself and resumed her household chores. Or was she afraid to think about the latest news, the war with Russia?

"None of these questions could be answered by standing around," she stated, and our two neighbors left, promising to keep Mother informed.

Later in the morning Mrs. Barock stopped by, seeing Mother in the garden. She cried very excitedly:

"My God, what is happening to our country? We have war all around us now. How is this going to end?" Mother tried to calm her, suggesting that we trust in God and keep praying. But it would also be a good idea to keep extra food in the house. Both women knew that more men would be drafted shortly and Mrs. Barock worried aloud, saying:

"I do not know what I'll do if my husband has to join the army. I cannot think about it." Wailing and worrying, she left, getting on her bike to hurry to the grocer.

During the early afternoon a courier came from the Hitlerjugend, advising us that all members would be picked up before nightfall. We would be taken to a schoolhouse in Adamshausen, a nearby western village. This prompt action was a precautionary measure to evacuate children. Authorities expected bombing raids on our city at night. Mother hurriedly packed some overnight clothes for Herta and me.

When Father returned from work and learned of our evacuation, he was reluctant to let us leave.

"I am fully aware of the danger. But where are you taking my girls?" he demanded to know. Only after the Jungmaedel leader assured him that we would be away for two nights only and had handed him a paper with the exact location of our whereabouts, did he consent to our leaving.

So Herta and I, equipped with a blanket and a gym suit, joined the noisy crowd. Having to stand up all the way in the old swaying truck as it stumbled along worn-out country roads was no fun and we were both glad to jump off at our destination. The school in Adamshausen, like most village schools, had only one enormous classroom. It was buzzing with girls and at least two hundred of us were ordered to spread our blankets on the floor and lie as close together as possible. Herta and I spread out one blanket and used the second one as a cover. Being dead tired, I had no trouble falling asleep, only to wake up suddenly as I felt something cold and wet against my cheek. Still groggy, I could not even scream when I saw a green frog look into my face. Jumping up, I realized that at least a hundred pairs of eyes were staring at me. The mischievous grins on their faces annoyed me. One girl sitting close to me explained defensively: "Your sister has been snoring loudly all night. She kept all of us awake. The frog was to waken her, not you." She picked it up by its leg and threw it outside. After that incident, the night passed quietly. Although the following day and night nothing disturbing occurred, Herta and I were glad to shuttle back home again.

Mother had news for us too. The rest of the family had spent two nights at the Bennert farm. Father had asked Mr. Bennert if he had room to keep our family over night and he had offered Father the hayloft. Frederick and Maria gave us their enthusiastic report.

"We had great fun sleeping in the warm hay." One of the cats had joined them and they were looking forward to going back tonight. It was a much more appealing idea than "camping out" with the Jungmaedel. At supper, Mother mentioned that the Ganders and the Barocks were going to join us. Ursula took a quick headcount. Our troop totalled twenty in number. Mr. Gander had received orders to spend the nights at the barracks because the military had issued a special alert.

Twilight was the best time for our departure, and Father

locked the door behind us. Frederick and Maria shouldered their *Tornisters*, into which Mother had quickly packed the most valuable papers and some warm night clothes. Father carried Andreas and Mother a shopping bag with emergency food. Father saw no need to hurry to Bennerts. Joined by our neighbors, the Ganders and the Barocks, we had covered half of the distance. As the sky slowly darkened, Mrs. Barock glanced backward and then shouted excitedly.

"Oh, the Russian planes are coming! Look at the 'Christmas trees' over the city!" Standing silently for a moment, we could hear a plane overhead flying at a very high altitude. Evidently it was a spy plane which had dropped the "Christmas trees," a lighting device used by the Russian pilots to light their bombing target at night. To us, it was a signal of acute danger. Father quietly ordered us to step up our pace while he kept an eye backward.

"If you hear bombs falling, everyone lie down flat on the ground," he instructed us. Yet we arrived at the Bennert farm without incident. The dog at the entrance gate announced our coming and I recognized Mrs. Bennert's dark silhouette in the kitchen frame. She greeted us with a wave of her hand and apologized that she did not have enough room in the house for so many. She motioned us to the hay barn, reminding Father of one condition.

"No matches lit, please." Father guaranteed her request, thanking her for letting us come.

Each family settled quietly in the hay, Frederick and Maria cuddling close to the red tiger cat. Only the women stayed awake, listening to Father as he frequently walked out to the yard, watching the sky, listening for Russian planes. But we were lucky. No bombs fell and before sunrise we arrived home again.

Two nights later, Father decided that we take the longer route to the Bennert farm via a country road, accessible from the bottom of the Beethovenstrasse in a wide half-circle.

"It's easier than crossing the meadows in the darkness," he reasoned. We were on our way for almost an hour and close to Bennert's neighbor, another farm, when suddenly, close behind us, a "Christmas tree" lit up. Mrs. Barock pointed upward, shouting:

"Oh, my God, they have spotted us! What shall we do? It is as bright as daylight!" Then a few more lights appeared closer to the city. Father ordered us to stay very close to the hedge surrounding the farm. Suddenly two men approached us, coming from the direction of the farmhouse.

"Hands up!" they ordered, "or we will shoot." Mother, closest to them, collected her wits.

"Just keep your guns down; we're from Gumbinnen," she called bravely. The two men, coming closer, yet still suspicious, explained they had mistakenly taken us for Russian paratroopers which they had thought were dropped by the plane that had just passed overhead. Only after they assured themselves that we were families with children did they relax and lower their guns. A short while later, Father interrupted the muffled conversation of the crowd.

"Do you hear the rumble? That could be bombs falling at a distance." One of the farmers thought it might be the noise of the front fighting in Russia. The next morning we learned that several bombs had fallen at the outskirts of town. Luckily, no one was hurt and no property damaged.

After the first week of battle, the pink hue in the eastern night sky diminished and then finally disappeared. As the war raged against Russia, drafting was stepped up and many more men left Gumbinnen to fight at the front. Father was still deferred for two reasons: because we were five children under fourteen and because his work at the factory was considered part of the vital war industry. As a result of stepped-up production to assure Germany the proclaimed victory, Father worked ten and twelve hours a day.

"Every so often we workers are showered with pep talk. We have to listen to fiery speeches, stressing the necessary increase of output. With every additional piece of farming machinery produced, Hitler can later harvest more grains in the Ukraine," Father told Mother with a tired look on his face. This was Hitler's goal—a goal to raise the additional food he needed to supply his armies at the many fronts. This provision included the Italian armies, the men fighting under the leadership of his ally, his bosom friend, the Duce.

* * * * * *

Only a few weeks after the outbreak of war against Russia, thousands of prisoners were taken and Gumbinnen received her share. Father talked about increasing problems at work because, hurriedly, many more barracks had to be built. The Polish obviously detested the new Russian prisoners. They had to be kept apart. Mother wanted to know why such hostility between the two nationalities existed. Father named two reasons. First, none of the prisoners were receiving adequate food and, second, the Poles were nationally and religiously fanatic, resenting the Russians and considering themselves superior to them. After their foreman had heard about a few serious fist fights, the Russian and Polish prisoners were separated by barbed wire.

"Even Alex keeps his distance from the new Russian prisoner who has been assigned to work with us," Father commented.

Some days later, Father brought up the subject again, telling Mother how rudely their Nazi foreman treated the Russians. Father said he had to turn away when the man hit one of them. It hurt Father; he could not help it. What troubled him was that he could not dare say a word, running the risk of getting arrested for siding with prisoners. It was a disturbing situation. Mother offered to pack an additional sandwich for the Russian working with Father, but he cautioned her to wait a while until hostilities had died down.

"Right now, I cannot risk getting caught feeding him." It gnawed on Father's heart to witness how inhumanly the Russians were treated, how often they were beaten or whipped. Being fed only once a day, they were forced to work ten or more hours.

"They are not permitted a moment's rest, many look faint and frightened," Father reported. Soon he would do something, I knew.

On my walks home from school, especially on warm days, I could literally smell a column of Russian prisoners marching to work. The odor was awful. Complaining about this to Mother, she amazed me. She excused them by saying that they consumed great quantities of onions and garlic, two spices which produced a distinct body odor. Mother remembered this fact from World War I when the Russians had occupied Gumbinnen, although she claimed that they had looked much cleaner then. The Russians of World War I had been a different breed, Mother recalled, because she had watched them attend outdoor Sunday services where they sang hymns or folk songs in the evenings sitting around campfires.

Yet these Russian prisoners in Gumbinnen still sang. Their spirit was not broken. It became a familiar sound to hear them sing as they marched to and from work. We assumed these to be army songs, quite different from our snappy German march music, yet melodious and usually sung in a minor key. Over the months, even we children hummed along with them. Maria even learned the text of one Russian song, although she never knew the meaning of the words.

One sunny July afternoon, Mrs. Gander talked to Mother across the garden fence, voicing her amazement about how far our German troops had penetrated into Russia.

"They will be in Odessa soon, the city in which I was born," she mentioned. We knew that she and her husband were *Volksdeutsche*, Germans who had lived in Russia under the Czarist regime, but who had returned to Germany in the early 1930's. Mother asked if she could understand the conversation among prisoners. Mrs. Gander replied that she possibly could if she listened closely. She pointed out, however, that it was forbidden for civilians to talk with prisoners. She was right. Life had become restricted. Not only did the authorities issue strict orders, many people stayed in the confines of their homes voluntarily. Father had ordered us to be home before dark as a safety measure. Without street lights in the city and the many prisoners in town, it gave us an uneasy feeling to be out in the dark. Besides, we never knew when to expect a surprise bombing attack. Mrs. Barock had stopped by and aired her worries.

"I do not like the idea that Elsa has to attend so many Jungmaedel activities at night; not that I mind her collecting clothes for the needy or picking herbs, but I object to her being out late. Most of all, I object to her seeing so many wounded soldiers in the military hospitals. Elsa is too young to see such sad sights, such maimed bodies." Her upset and worries clearly written on her face, Mrs. Barock rushed off on her bike.

* * * * * *

Summer vacation had kept me busy helping Mother in the kitchen or watching Andreas. When I returned to school in early fall, Miss Zahn made an announcement.

"Our school will move. The principal has received notice that our huge, new middle-school complex will be converted into a military hospital." She explained that very shortly we would transfer to the *Maschinenbauschule*, a technical school for machine construction which now was literally empty. The reason for this was that the majority of German students were fighting at the front. The move was great news to me. It would cut my walks to school to less than half the distance.

A few days later when the transfer was completed, I gingerly walked my new route to school, appreciating the extra time gained. Beyond the "Black Road," which had received its name from the added top layer of burnt out, crushed charcoal, I took the short cut across the service tracks to my left. Running up the steep end of a ditch, I passed some beautiful new homes on the Hermann-Loens-Strasse. Northward I breezed up the Walter-Flex-Strasse, crossing the wide, four-laned Hermann-Goering-Strasse from which I made a turn into the Luisenstrasse. In passing, I realized that Mrs.

Schoen, Aunt Marie's sister, lived in one of the apartment houses, and I intended to pay her a visit some day after school.

While absorbed in my thoughts, I had reached the end of the long row of three-story houses and, crossing the Adolf-Hitler-Strasse, I entered through the wide open, tall, wrought-iron gate, the north entrance to the *Maschinenbauschule*, the *Technikum*. The long, straight cemented driveway, flanked by neatly trimmed, lusciously green lawns, impressed me as a touch of luxury. The square, white, red-roofed building with rows of numerous, tall windows was now my school. It was our new middle school.

Once we had settled in our new surroundings, we buckled down to serious studies. Homework was heavy. One day Miss Zahn announced that new rules had been issued.

"Every student is required to attend the Jungmaedel meetings regularly; otherwise, his schooling will be in jeopardy." She read the notice to the class. I felt sick at heart. Life was getting rough. With homework increasing, it was a total waste of time to attend those idiotic meetings. I was distressed and as if Miss Zahn realized that she had touched a sore spot in many, added almost apologetically:

"Despite the order, I have to insist that homework be turned in promptly." During our lesson, I had difficulty concentrating. My mind was on this latest news. Having no choice in the matter made me dislike those meetings even more. These snips, as I had privately labelled our leaders, were determined to indoctrinate me according to the Dr. Goebbels or Himmler method, hammering national socialism into my disinterested mind. "Nerve," I thought. But I could not escape the ruling because I was determined to complete middle school.

Therefore, reluctant and resentful, I dragged myself to these weekly meetings. One day, one of Herta's classmates asked me if I was Herta's sister. To my question why she needed to know this, she replied in a snippy tone: "Just checking," and walked away. Telling the story to Herta, she reasoned that her leader must have been reporting her poor attendance, having brushed off Herta's excuse of having to help Mother in the garden as nonsense. We had to attend the Jungmaedel meetings we decided, at least for a while. Otherwise, we ran the risk of being transferred to Gisela Schwarte's group in which "problem" girls were specially drilled to align with national socialistic thought.

"No thanks," Herta joked cynically, "I do not care to receive this special attention." Obediently, we learned many Hitlerjugend songs, I listened quietly to the loud proclamations of victory, and watched the German borders extend over almost all of Europe. It amazed me how many volunteer hours our leaders would sacrifice in studying party material, with how much enthusiasm they delivered their subject. It left me cold. I had different interests. Glad when these sessions were over, I met Herta and we rushed home.

Contrary to the victory spirit of the Hitlerjugend, Father made gloomy predictions. It was September now. He was sure that a winter in Russia would immobilize our German armies, defeating them. He reminded Mother of Napoleon's attempts to conquer Russia and how he had been beaten in one of those Russian winters, returning to France a broken man. Evidently Mother did not want to envision Germany's defeat. It could be painful; it could endanger our lives. Therefore, she called the fact to Father's attention that our armies had occupied the Ukrainian city of Kiev recently, directing their new aim toward Moscow, Russia's capital.

"Hitler will never conquer Russia. God will not permit him to break the spirit of the Russian people as Hitler has predicted in his speech," Father emphasized with conviction. Occasionally he worried, asking himself what would become of us. Yet he had to leave this decision with God. Father was certain that if our family kept His commandments, God would not permit that anyone would pluck us out of His hand. As if to reassure himself and us, Father emphasized that we learn to trust God.

Recently it had become part of our German lesson that we be briefed on the latest war news. We learned that two major offensives were launched in Russia: one to the north, aiming for the city of Leningrad; the other to the south, aiming for the city of Stalingrad. With these two strongholds captured, Hitler's victory was assured, we were taught.

In late October, 1941, the unbelievable news broke through. Our famous German army was sixty kilometers from Moscow, the Russian capital. The tops of the Kremlin were in view on a clear day!

Visiting the Ganders in the afternoon, I listened to the end of Dr. Goebbels' enthusiastic victory speech: "...our heroically fighting armies, surrounding Moscow, will force Russia down on her knees! Glorious victory is now ours. Thanks and praise be to our beloved Fuehrer, Adolf Hitler. Sieg-Heil! Sieg-Heil! Sieg-Heil! Deutschland, Deutschland ueber alles, ueber alles in der Welt...." Our German national hymn was followed by the Nazi song: "Die Fahne hoch...raise the flag...." Then I heard seemingly endless applause.

Chapter VI

Trials and Tribulations

The next day Father read Dr. Goebbels' victory speech in the paper. He could not share Goebbels' fiery enthusiasm but instead pointed out that it was October, the beginning of winter, and the war was by far not won.

During our geography lesson in school, the front movements in Russia and other European countries had been indicated on a huge hanging map with red-headed straight pins. It was unbelievable how much territory our German armies had covered since September, 1939. Proudly, one of the girls in class volunteered to move the red pins ahead according to the daily newspaper report, marking Germany's newly captured areas.

One morning one of my classmates informed Miss Zahn that her father had accepted an offer to move to Poland where he was guaranteed to receive a large farm, which he considered a gift from the government and intended to turn into a productive and profitable enterprise. She expected her parents to move shortly and asked for separation papers from school. The day the girl left, Miss Zahn wished her "good luck" but, to my amazement, she did not smile. What were our teacher's thoughts, her feelings, I asked myself. Could she, a member of the party, silently agree with Father's conviction that this generous gift from the government was literally confiscated from Polish landowners and rightfully not German? I could only guess her thoughts, because questions like this could not be voiced in public.

At our Jungmaedel meetings, spirits soared high, set afire by one intoxicating victory after another. Our group leader, praising

Hitler's fantastic achievements, believed firmly that his prediction of the thousand-year Reich had come true. To her, it had already begun. Proud to be part of this new era, the young Hitler promoter was in a mood of celebration, as was the entire organization of the Hitlerjugend.

Father came home from work and told Mother that he had had a chance to engage in a political discussion with Meister Weiss, his trusted friend and confidant. They were debating Stalin's recent soul-searching speech in which Hitler's arch enemy had burnt the responsibility into the heart of every Russian soldier to defend his country, his beloved "Mother Russia." Meister Weiss had expressed the opinion that stabilizing the morale of Stalin's armies, coupled with a severe Russian winter, could tip the scale in their favor. He and Father intended to watch developments closely.

They did not have to wait long. Only a few weeks later, the first long trains, packed with wounded German soldiers, a great number suffering from severe frostbites, rolled into our station in Gumbinnen. Father was right about those bitter Russian winters. Many more men were drafted. Even Father's youngest brother, Uncle Karl, received his draft notice to fight in Russia.

"By now foreign prisoners are outnumbering German civilians at the factory," Father remarked. Mother's face showed that she worried. How much longer would Father be deferred? He was past forty now, ordinarily too old for the army, but the war was raging in its full fury and an enormous number of German men had been wounded or were lost in battle. Not that this fact ever flashed across the headlines, but the many families in mourning were a silent, sad reminder, telling the truth. Uncle Gustav also had received a letter from his son Willi. He was at the front in Russia; Ursula had brought the news home. The other news, our oldest sister reported, was that our cousin Suzanne was extremely difficult to handle.

"Has Uncle Gustav been searching for a housekeeper as he has promised?" Mother asked, and Ursula reported that the girl working as a waitress in the restaurant downstairs had been helping out. Mother firmly decided to discuss the situation with her brother, especially as she had great need for Ursula's help at home.

A month later Willi received a brief leave from the front. Announcing to his father the surprise that he would soon get married set off a heated argument between the men. Besides witnessing their ugly disagreement, Ursula had learned the cold truth about the Russian front. Willi had described how the

Russian tundra soaked by torrential rains before onset of winter had turned into a sea of mud, a condition which left our soldiers stranded and rendered most of their heavy machinery unoperable. But the worst situation, Willi complained bitterly, was to fight off the partisan groups, those fanatic Russian civilians falling into our soldiers' backs, killing many and greatly disturbing the so vitally needed supply lines. The onset of early frost left his unit with nothing but their dug-out trenches to sleep in, a hopeless predicament which turned the already low morale of the men and their generals into utter despair. Although Mother felt sorry that Willi had to return to such dreadful conditions, she criticized his disrespectful behavior toward his father.

"I don't like the mean streak in his character," she said perturbed. Mother attributed his tendency toward rudeness to the many years of active ice-hockey playing, which she considered a sport for ruffians. Mother sent word to her brother insisting that Ursula stay home by the end of November and Uncle Gustav reluctantly agreed to hire a full-time housekeeper.

* * * * * *

So Ursula assisted Mother at home, and the same day, November 30, 1941, Father read the news to us that Fieldmarshal von Rundstedt had resigned from the army at Stalingrad. This article confirmed Willi's report of increasing dissent among soldiers and their leaders. Father reasoned that Rundstedt was no coward, no traitor, but that Hitler was evidently pushing everyone of his men beyond endurance.

The urgent calls of the *Winterhilfe* for woolen shawls, socks, mittens, and ear muffs also confirmed that our soldiers in Russia were suffering during this bitter cold winter and were in urgent need of warm clothing. Mother, compassionate by nature, responded immediately.

"Instead of making Christmas gifts for ourselves, let's knit as many pairs of socks and mittens as we possibly can. It might save a few of our soldiers their hands and feet. Perhaps Willi, Juergen, or Uncle Karl would receive a pair we give," she said, hoping to ease the suffering.

The general mood of depression was intensified by the glaring headline on December 7th: The Japanese had bombed Pearl Harbor! Father was outraged. Pearl Harbor was an American port! Was this act of aggression a provocation to force America into war against us, he demanded to know. Only four days later came the answer.

Father had listened to Hitler's Reichstag speech at work, in which he had declared war against the United States.

"The man is insane!" Father exclaimed. "This will be the end of Germany; mark my word." Neither Mother nor any one of us tried to convince Father otherwise. We knew he was right.

As a result of the latest development, feverish drafting of younger men started. Many more men from our neighborhood left to join the army. Visiting Aunt Maria, Father's youngest aunt, living on the Mozartstrasse, I heard the sad news that her only son Erwin had also left. He had joined the navy a year earlier and, while in training, had confided to his mother that he was kept in reserve for a special secret mission. When Erwin bid Aunt Maria goodbye, he had asked her not to worry, even if she did not hear from him for a while. He promised to write as soon as he was permitted to. Aunt Maria told me in her warmhearted way that Erwin had embraced her, telling her not to cry any tears, yet gently reminding her of their faith.

"Just believe in God and me," he told her and encouraged her to be brave, to be strong. Nevertheless, recalling the day still brought tears to Aunt Maria's eyes. I realized that now she had only Waltraud, her daughter, at home. And only for a short while because Waltraud had announced her engagement and was going to marry a divorced sea captain living in Hamburg. Aunt Maria worried about the future.

"Will Uncle Richard and I be alone when we are old?" she asked, reflecting on her two adult children. As if to reassure herself, she told me that she prayed daily, asking that God be merciful and protect Erwin.

On my walk home, I decided to include in my evening prayers every relative and friend fighting at the front, including Erwin. Although Aunt Maria lived only a short walk away, I had met Erwin only on two occasions. He was much older than I and had spent most of his time away at school or in military training. Yet I admired him. He looked tall and trim in his neatly tailored navy uniform. I was not surprised that he had been singled out for a special mission. So many of the tall, blond, and blue-eyed young men were drafted into the S. S. to be Hitler's body guard, leaving them no choice in the matter. Aunt Maria mentioned that Erwin did not agree with the national socialist principles, but that he was an honest and gentle-hearted young man willing to lay down his life if this sacrifice guaranteed that his family at home would be safe in this cruel war. He could not tell his mother, however, to what secret mission he was assigned.

Uncle Richard, Erwin's father, worked as a foreman at the

Telegraphenbauamt, headquarters from which telegraphic installations were supervised. Too old to be in the army, he worked frequent night shifts at the plant as it was shorthanded in staff. Uncle Richard was the youngest brother to Father's mother and of the same strong, even-tempered, and generous stock, a man to whom the welfare and happiness of his family were most important. He and Aunt Maria were quiet people with a strong faith in God. Praying together as a family, Aunt Maria confirmed, had given her the strength to promise Erwin that she would be brave, that she would not cry. It was close to Christmas again and I knew how much she would miss her only son.

* * * * * *

That Christmas was a dreary one. All hospital beds in town were filled with wounded soldiers. Mother's thoughts went out to Willi, Juergen, and Uncle Karl. Where in the vastness of Russia were they? What would their Christmas be like? Freezing in a dug-out? The thought made me shiver. From nurses and volunteers working at the overcrowded military hospitals, reports leaked out that many of our young soldiers were badly frostbitten. Some had arrived without ears and noses, and others needed to have hands or feet amputated to prevent them from dying of gangrene. As this disheartening news spread, and in the face of so much suffering, our Christmas spirit was considerably dampened.

Father decided it was inappropriate to attend the Christmas party at the factory but suggested instead that we all go to church. It would be the first Christmas service for Andreas. Our favorite Pastor Preuss was scheduled to deliver a service at the Salzburger Kirche, a small church less than an hour away. Knowing Paster Preuss' popularity, Father urged that we be there an hour ahead of time to be assured of a seat. We got into our heavy winter coats and Mother bundled up Andreas. Motioning out the window, she commented about the weather.

"We might still have a white Christmas; look at the heavy overcast." Frederick had hoped for snow all week, anxious to get out his sled.

We had trudged past the railroad crossing and were half way down the "Black Road" when I noticed a few white snow crystals on my sleeve. As I watched them melt, a few more fell on my lips, leaving them moist. Then Frederick discovered them and, pointing upward, shouted:

"It's snowing; it's snowing!" Within a short while the wind whirled the white flurries around as if in a dance and deposited them on the side of the road against the dried grass. When we reached the church, almost an inch of snow was covering the ground. Shaking the white fluff off our coats and shoes, we entered the sanctuary and realized to our dismay that the church was already filled. Father blamed the blowing snow for holding us up, and pointed up to the stairs leading to the balcony.

"We can sit there," he said. It was still better than standing up through the service although we had to crane our necks a bit to see Pastor Preuss. For Andreas, now two years old, attending church was a new and exciting experience. The lights on the big Christmas tree next to the altar had caught his attention and his blue eyes sparkled with fascination. When soft organ music poured down from the choir loft, he was anxious to venture away, curious to find its source. Father had to hold on to his hand tightly. The congregation joined in with the music and Andreas watched us very attentively singing the first carol. He managed to stay quiet during the time of prayer but, toward the end of Paster Preuss' sermon, he got restless. Glad that the last carol was sung, he tugged at Father's sleeve, pulling him to walk up front to see the tree. We waited until most of the crowd had filed out and then took him to the side of the altar to look at the tree and the creche. Ignoring Father's explanation of the creche, Andreas pointed toward it, calling excitedly:

"Look, a donkey!" He laughed and Mother suggested that we hurry home. Also, Maria and Frederick were anxious to leave. The fluffy snow outside now lay three inches thick.

Stamping the snow off our shoes, we were glad to arrive home and Mother put some wood on the still glimmering coals in the huge cornerstove in the kitchen. Soon it was nice and cozy. After our brief meal, we gathered around the tree to sing more Christmas carols. We children sang in a high soprano, and Mother blended in harmoniously with her favorite alto voice. Although Father occasionally missed a key, to me, our family choir sounded almost professioal.

After Father's closing prayer, Mother surprised us with modest gifts, one for each in spite of the tight economy. Father had secretly baked some cookies and decorated a gingerbread man for each. Andreas' delight was infectious but, after having investigated everyone's gift, he leaned against Mother and started to yawn. It was the bedtime signal for all of us.

* * * * * *

"Another Christmas has come and gone, but the war is still

raging on," Father observed with resignation a few days later. He had been visiting Oma, his mother, who lived on the Fromeltstrasse. She had received a letter from Uncle Karl in Russia. In his note he stated that for many days the temperature had dropped to a bitter cold 30° below zero. He did not dare complain outright about lack of warm clothing but begged Oma to send him warm underwear, sweaters, socks, and mittens, reminding her not to forget his fur earmuffs. On the side of his letter he had scribbled a brief note.

"I wish I was home in your warm kitchen." Father, reading between the lines, was positive that Uncle Karl had not dared to write about the grim conditions at the front for fear of censorship and not to alarm Oma. But the situation in Russia must be extremely critical. He did not have to point out the stark proof. It was obvious. So many wounded soldiers in our town hobbled around on one leg, had one arm amputated, or their heads bandaged. One look around proved the bitter truth. The war was grim and, by far, not won. One thought now foremost in Mother's mind was how much longer Father would be deferred. She had visited Mrs. Schurat, a neighbor living up the street who had received a brief telegram advising that her husband had died at the front. The tone in which these notices were phrased angered Father. "He died the death of a hero for his Fatherland."

To Father, these words sounded like mockery. "Mr. Schurat died in Russia. He might have frozen to death in a blizzard; he could have died of exhaustion at Stalingrad, fighting day and night without getting sufficient rest or food," Father said perturbed. He was certain that Mrs. Schurat would rather have her quiet and gentle husband at home instead of having him honored as a dead hero. The telegram was an insult, Father felt. Mother prayed that Uncle Karl, Willi, and Juergen would not have to join the fierce battle at Stalingrad, a city over which our own armies and the Russians fought bitterly.

When I returned to school after the Christmas holidays, I was shocked to see that Helga, my classmate, wore a black dress. Her face looked pale and when I cautiously asked her how her holidays had been, she started to sob.

"My father died," she said. "I received notice the day before Christmas. Now I have no father, only a mother."

It was sad. I cried with her, sorry to have asked the question. Then we quietly started with our lesson.

During recess when Helga had regained her composure, she told me that her mother was still uncertain if her father was dead or if he was missing because none of the bodies were sent home for burial. She and her mother were torn by the question: could someone have made a mistake, a possible misidentification? All Helga had received was her father's identification number, no personal belongings. It was gloomy in class. No one dared to talk about Christmas and I noticed that over the holidays, the big hanging map of Europe had disappeared from the corner. Not a word had been mentioned about it. Obviously, no one would volunteer now to set the red pins backwards, indicating our front's gradual retreat. Many students wore a black armband around their sleeves. They were in mourning for the family member they had lost in Russia.

The war was taking its toll and Father did not need to remind Mother that our troops had long since lost sight of the Kremlin, of Moscow. Instead, they had retreated two hundred kilometers, moving rapidly, frighteningly close to home.

"It's just a matter of time," Father stated, but Mother had no comment. Did she hate to think ahead of the final outcome of the war? Father, as if reading her thoughts, reassured her. Each member of our family had kept his hands and conscience clean, having hurt no one, having stayed out of the dirty business of the national socialist party. Father was sure of God's promise that those who kept His commandments would not be plucked out of His hand.

"Each person will receive what he deserves," Father stated, believing in a just God. Yet only a few days later I doubted. Where was God in these days of war and horror? Father had returned from work and gave us an unbelievable report. The Russian prisoners had eaten one of their own men! As Father told Mother about the details, I felt sick to my stomach, hoping this gruesome story would not be true! But it was.

In the morning when Father had arrived at the factory, he noticed a commotion. Questioning Meister Weiss about it, Father learned that two Russian prisoners had just been hauled away on a truck to be shot. Because of hunger, they had killed one of their inmates who had been sick, boiled the flesh, and eaten it. Interrogation of the other prisoners revealed that all of them had eaten of the dead man's flesh. The bones had been found under the floorboards of the barrack after a furious and inch-by-inch search by the S. S. The report sounded unbelievable, inhuman. What savagery! Father was very upset, but much more disturbed about the reason, the cause for such bestiality. He and Meister Weiss were aware that the Russian prisoners had received only one meal a day, a watery soup of either cabbage or turnips, no meat. This hunger treatment was Hitler's retaliation order in which he claimed to have proof that our German prisoners in Russia were deliberately starved to death. Yet those Russian prisoners at the factory had to work a hard twelve-hour day, not to mention the rough treatment they got from their cruel Nazi foremen.

"I am ashamed that this bestiality has taken place right where I work, right in my hometown," Father confessed. He insisted that from now on, he would take another sandwich along to be sure that at least the Russian working with him would be fed adequately. He did not care about his foreman's watchful eye. Mother made him promise, however, that he would hand the food to the man unobtrusively. Father would make certain that from now on, no further prisoners would be missing at role call.

"How did Alex react to the gruesome news?" Mother asked and Father said his face had looked horrified. Alex claimed that such savagery could never have happened among the Poles. Yet Alex did not convince Father. He knew that hunger hurt and that the Polish prisoners were fed a better diet and more often than the Russian. To the Russian prisoner working with them, Alex talked only if necessary but, otherwise, kept his distance.

No one in the family felt like eating dinner. As we sat around the table, Father insisted on praying and encouraged us all to do the same. He believed that only diligent prayer to a just God could rescue our country from this state of peril.

Hitler had ordered another stiff retaliation measure. For every German prisoner starved to death in Russia, one Russian prisoner in Germany would be shot. Father considered this order an act of cruel murder and a violation of the laws of international warfare. Hitler evidently observed none of these laws. He established his own rules and regulations. The Fuehrer had assumed total charge of the military and, even at home, his tight grip could be felt everywhere. Civilians were closely watched. Herta and I were asked tricky questions at the Jungmaedel whenever we had dared to skip a meeting.

"Did your parents detain you from attending? What is their reason? Are your parents members of the party? Why not?" Our leaders asked. This treacherous method was to enlarge the party and to "purify" the German Volk of "misfits." Our life was not easy, realizing that our family was on the list of misfits. It was most difficult for me to keep my mouth shut or give a dumb but safe answer when, inside myself, I felt like screaming at our snippy leaders, defending myself, yelling my real thoughts into their cold faces. But I had to overcome those boiling emotions of rage and revenge. Besides, Father convinced us that all revenge was God's business.

* * * * * *

As our school had moved from the Moltkestrasse to the *Technikum*, my daily walks did not take me past the Wilhelmstrasse any more. Therefore, I saw Aunt Ina and Uncle Oskar only occasionally. Yet my love and admiration for them was the same. As a matter of fact, I missed them. Aunt Ina had taken my younger cousin, Trude, into her household and I was a bit jealous. Having visited her recently, Aunt Ina told me that Hans had completed his schooling and had been drafted. Momentarily he was stationed in the northwestern province of Holstein but, being in the army's communications division, he expected to move around a lot, to be transferred frequently. She would never know where Hans would be next; he could be in Greece, North Africa, France, or Russia. The thought of Russia made Aunt Ina uneasy and she worried.

"For Uncle's sake, I hope Hans comes back alive," she would say.

Uncle Oskar had placed all his hopes in his only son, wishing that he continue the business after he would be old enough to retire. I had never thought this far ahead, but I hoped and prayed that God might protect Hans, my favorite cousin. Life had become so uncertain. Yet a lot of homework kept my mind on tiptoes. Writing term papers and learning vocabulary left me no time for brooding.

I was eleven now and had the option to enroll in a course to study a second foreign language, French. But Miss Zahn suggested that, being the youngest in class and of fragile health, I should not burden myself with more demanding homework. Therefore, I joined the one half of the class in a music session with Mr. Baeker, my homeroom teacher from grammar school, while the other half studied French. Mr. Baeker was now on the staff of the middle school and I was happy to see him. To fill the classroom, the boys from our parallel class had joined us and Mr. Baeker taught us to read notes. I enjoyed music, especially the traditional folk songs with their prosaic lyrics. Mr. Baeker found it helpful to play a new melody for us on his violin, his favorite instrument, and he began to tune it. The screechy whining of the strings made me giggle, reminding me of Hans' violin practices. I tried hard to conceal my amusement while Mr. Baeker concentrated intently on the tuning. Satisfied with the sound, he played a new song and the entire class tried to sing it. First time around, the voices sounded rather whimpery but, after repeated practice, we finally learned the tune. At least, so I thought.

"Someone in class is still singing one note incorrectly," Mr.

Baeker insisted. The class tried again, over and over, but each time Mr. Baeker's anger was rising. One note did not sound right to him. The peculiar feeling crept over me that he stared at me while venting his fury. Yet I was certain that I sang the tune correctly. While he did not mention anyone's name, after half an hour of more practice, I was nervous. Why would he indicate that I sang the tune wrong? Trying not to provoke him any further, I dediced it to be safer to whisper the word, but not sing the critical note just to be sure. That did it! He screamed, waving his bow at me furiously, threateningly. Now I knew he had singled me out. Why? My mind screamed. I had sung the song correctly. He insisted this someone was singing the note wrong intentionally, which obviously was the reason for his fury. Far from it; I would never do something so mischievous. I? Never! But that very moment the school bell rang—thank God—and the whole class breathed a sigh of relief. Everyone stormed out of the class room, including me.

During recess two of my classmates pounded me with questions.

"Why did you so recklessly provoke Mr. Baeker to such a rage?" It was difficult to convince them that I had not done so and had sung the note correctly. Even months later I could not explain to myself what had actually happened. I never willfully nor accidentally disagreed with Mr. Baeker. Perhaps except for this one dumb note! He, however, did not seem to forget this ugly incident for years. I was certain he had crossed me off the list of his friends. As a result of this fateful day, I received a bad mark in music in my term paper. Momentarily, I was disappointed, but I promised myself to improve my grade during the fall term. Right now, summer vacation had begun and I enjoyed the prospects of several weeks of rest and play.

Planning to skip as many Jungmaedel meetings as possible, I was wondering what kind of an excuse could grant me a leave of absence. Mother had requested in a letter to the city authorities that I be sent to a farm for several weeks, hoping that I would gain a few pounds.

"This might transform your beanpole figure into something resembling a girl," she teased me. A few days later, returning with Lisa from Ganders, Mother happily announced that her request had been granted. She had received a written notice that I was to report at the *Rathaus* in town two days later. The good news filled me with excitement. I was going away to a farm or to some family on my first real vacation. This notice took care of the Jungmaedel meetings quite naturally; it was great!

* * * * * *

The day arrived quickly and, equipped with a small satchel of summer clothes, Herta and I arrived at the *Rathaus* on time. Herta had insisted she walk the stretch with me. To our amazement, we found a large crowd gathered and Herta joked. "Every girl in town seems to be going on vacation." Everything happened so fast. I had handed my notification to the woman registering all girls and, only a few minutes later, a blond, well-dressed lady stepped over to me.

"I'm Mrs. Stock! You will spend four weeks with me," she said with a faint smile. As if to explain further, she added that the trip would not be long. She lived about eight kilometers northeast of Gumbinnen. In the same breath, as if to cram a lot of information into me at once, she mentioned she was certain I would like her two small children.

"You will spend a lot of time with them," she rambled on. Herta gave me a consoling look. I was not going on vacation; I was handed a baby-sitting job! I felt betrayed. But since Mother was not in reach for a quick consultation, neither Herta nor I dared to object to this rude order. My heart sank; I had nothing but disappointments to register lately.

But Mrs. Stock was in a hurry. She was accompanied by a gentleman whose name I did not catch at the first introduction. He took my satchel and, following Mrs. Stock on her heels, headed for the parked car on the Magazinplatz, both completely ignoring Herta's presence. Turning around, before following the two hurrying strangers, I quickly waved Herta good-bye and caught a glimpse of disappointment on her face as she started to head homeward again. Trudging next to Mrs. Stock toward the car, I asked myself how this man had managed to keep his car while all other private cars had been confiscated by the government. When the man opened the car door, ordering me to take the back seat, it occurred to me for a split second to decline his offer, to run away and take refuge with Aunt Ina instead. Would my refusal to follow this order cause Mother a problem? I quickly asked myself and then obediently took my seat in the back. I felt disappointed, betrayed. I was angry.

When the two sat in the front, the man slammed the door shut and started the car with a rough jolt. He made a screeching turn and drove off the cobble-stoned Magazinplatz. I gave our MOOSE, the bronze statue, one last glance as the car turned into the Koenigstrasse. Mrs. Stock must have noticed my dead silence and I was positive that disappointment was written across my face. Turning to me with a thin smile, she explained the landmarks we passed: the Koenigsbruecke, the river Rominte, the "old" and "new" Regierung. Trying to conceal my ill mood, I politely answered that I had lived around here and knew the area very well. She did not seem to believe me, giving her male friend a knowing glance, a smirk but, when we had turned into the Wilhelmstrasse and passed Uncle Oskar's store, I pointed to his name plate, saying in an ill-concealed growl:

"He is my uncle." I mustered all my restraint not to throw the car door open and jump out. Realizing this would have killed me, I turned my head the other way to see if I could catch a glimpse of Mrs. Schwartz's candy store. To add to my disappointment, I saw a new name in the window. The store had a new owner. Now it was a fish store. How awful! It took only a few more minutes and then we passed into unfamiliar territory. The houses were spaced further apart, followed by another new settlement area. I never knew the Wilhelmstrasse was so long and led right out to the country. I never had ventured out this far. The villages we passed along the road were unfamiliar to me. Again, Mrs. Stock made an effort to break the silence.

"We have only two more kilometers left." My ears perked up at this news. Maybe I could walk the distance back one day. Then my situation was not entirely hopeless and my depressed mood lifted slightly.

We passed endless fields of wheat, rye, clover, and summer oats almost ready for harvest. Cows were munching peacefully on luscious green pastures.

"What a sight of contentment," I thought. To the left were white ducks swimming on a pond and a red-legged stork stalking the knee-high reeds for his favorite delicacy: a green frog. Mrs. Stock brought my wandering thoughts back with a comment. Her daughter Ingrid would arrive home within a few days from Treptow for a summer visit. This report was encouraging news and I asked Mrs. Stock toward which profession her daughter was studying. Mrs. Stock's reply was vague, mentioning that Ingrid had no specific future plans. She surprised me in saying that she felt her daughter attended school for one reason only: to get away from home. The man driving the car gave Mrs. Stock an understanding glance, as if he shared her opinion. What would be wrong with this woman that her daughter, still a teenager, preferred to live away from home?

The violent rattling of the car jerked me out of my thoughts. It was bouncing along a dirt road over dried-up wagon tracks, leaving behind a cloud of whirling dust. I had trouble keeping my balance in the back seat. A moment later, Mrs. Stock pointed to a red brick house, partly hidden behind a huge oak tree.

"This is our house; it also serves as the village school," she said, turning toward me. At the same time, the man slowed down the car, ending our shuttle. Two flaxen blond children came running across the big open yard and Mrs. Stock introduced both as her "two small ones." Turning to them, she loudly scolded them for running out on the road.

"What a rough greeting," I thought. The man coolly handed me my satchel, smiled gallantly at Mrs. Stock, and drove off, a cloud of dust trailing behind him.

With one glance, I sized up the village: five houses on the left side and seven on the right. That was all; I was stuck at the end of the world! How could I spend four weeks here without dying of boredom? What isolation! Yet Mrs. Stock's rushing did not allow my thoughts to wander. She urged me on, wanting to show me the room. She remarked in her cool and efficient manner of speech that I would be sharing it with her daughter. The big wooden front door led into a dark hallway, from which one door opened into the classroom. With authority in her voice, she explained in clipped phrases:

"This is our school. All grades are in one classroom because the village is small." Since her husband had been drafted, she was the substitute teacher for the children. What pride in her voice, I thought. But Mrs. Stock had no time to linger. She rushed to enter another door on the opposite side of the hall, urging me to follow her, and told me that this would be my room for the summer. Ingrid would share it with me. Her daughter was used to sleeping next to the window; therefore, the bed standing toward the door would be mine. Mrs. Stock left me no choice in the matter. She allowed me a few minutes to unpack my things and ordered me to come into the kitchen as soon as I finished. The other rooms she would show me later. With that remark she left, closing the door hard behind her. I took one deep breath, looked around the room, and glanced out the window. It faced the village dirt road, no pretty sight. Washing my hands and face in the sink, I stared at myself in the mirror. Not even a trace of a smile was on my face. Neither the airiness of the room nor its light decor could lift the heaviness from my heart. I did not like it here; as a matter of fact, I hated it. A hard knock at the door snapped me back to attention and Mrs. Stock asked impatiently:

"Aren't you ready yet?" So I rushed out and she hurriedly introduced me to the five-year-old boy and the little girl, not quite two.

"She is trained already; she will be easy to handle," she mentioned. Telling me to take them for a walk at once while the sun was still out, she instructed me to hold on to the little girl's hand. The boy would show me their daily route of a walk and, whisking us out into the yard, she dismissed us.

For having barely arrived, I had received a mouthful of instructions, to which I had not answered one word. But I was anxious to get away from this overpowering woman. She reminded me of a gendarme; worse yet, a snappy sergeant. Did she expect me to click my heels and stand at attention? Small wonder her daughter tried to stay away from home.

So I walked the two children across the road, up a grassy path dotted with wild flowers. The little girl happily picked a bunch, while her brother had run far ahead with a net, trying to catch butterflies. I sat down in the grass, trying to figure out why I had been sent to this disagreeable place. Had my God forsaken me? What was my crime to deserve such punishment? What was I expected to learn from this experience? To become a babysitter? Why did I deserve such rough treatment? My dream of a happy, carefree vacation on a farm had gone up in thin air. If the thought had only occurred to me to bring a stack of books from home; they would offer some consolation and help me to struggle through these four weeks of confinement.

As the sun was getting close to the western horizon, I felt a sudden chill in the air. It was time to go back to the house—the prison. Mrs. Stock demanded to know where we had lingered so long; supper was ready. A woman from the village, handling the cleaning and cooking in the household, had prepared the food. Although the supper on the large, round dining room table looked appetizing, I could swallow only a few small pieces. My stomach felt tied together. Mrs. Stock reminded me that it would be best to get up early in the morning because she was still teaching school. In the village summer vacation started later than in Gumbinnen. Finally, Mrs. Stock put the two children to bed and I could retire to my room. Feeling dead tired from traveling and exhausted from tension, it did not take me long to fall asleep.

When I heard a loud knock at the door the next morning, the night seemed to have vanished. My second day started. At the breakfast table, Mrs. Stock announced that her daughter would arrive in two days. Stressing that Ingrid would be interesting company for me, because of her outgoing personality, Mrs. Stock indicated that she had noticed my silence. I had no desire to engage in conversation with her.

The sun was out, the air felt warm, and I spent another day

with the two children. The following day passed in the same manner; then the day came when Ingrid arrived. Mrs. Stock had picked her up at the station in Gumbinnen. A girl of sixteen, Ingrid gave the appearance of an adult more than a teenager. She was tall, well developed, and resembled her mother in her figure and movements. What distinguished her though was a much softer voice and an easy smile, two qualities for which I immediately liked her.

At night we talked a while in our room. Ingrid had given her mother orders not to waken her early in the morning. She was tired and wanted to sleep. Ingrid should have permitted her mother to knock at our door because I would not have been jolted out of my sleep so abruptly. Mrs. Stock's shrill, shrieking voice was penetrating through the wall from the direction of the classroom:

"I will teach you, you duncehead!" And a loud smack followed. Horror-stricken, I bolted upright in bed. It was Ingrid's mother, her voice resembling that of a wild, vicious animal. The noise had wakened Ingrid also and she sleepily commented:

"She sounds bad; it must be one of her off days again." To Ingrid the noisy commotion confirmed that she was home again. Realizing my shock and bewilderment, she tried to calm me.

"My mother can be very good and she can be very bad. She has a violent temper," she affirmed. A confirmation of the latter was unnecessary. The whole building resounded with Mrs. Stock's screaming. After a while, the raw, loud voice died down and, matter-of-factly, Ingrid mentioned that her mother seemed to be through with her tantrum. It was time to get up.

At lunch time Ingrid casually told her mother that we had heard her screaming fit. Mrs. Stock's excuse was that the walls were not built strong enough. Evidently she ignored the fact that the school was built like a brick fortress, with a hallway between the two walls! Unbelievable!

Several days later Ingrid complained to me about boredom and suggested that we both visit one of her classmates who lived a few kilometers down the road toward Gumbinnen. It would be a long walk, but she wanted me to come along.

"Mother has used you long enough as a free babysitter," she said, but urged me not to mention her plan to her mother. We would leave immediately after lunch while the children were asleep. So we did.

We arrived at her friend's place, a farm close to Gumbinnen, after two long hours of walking. Ingrid got engrossed in a long conversation with the young man for whom she obviously cared a lot. Upon my prodding, we finally left and started our hike back.

Ingrid realized that she had grossly underestimated the distance. We would not arrive home before dark. As we turned into the yard in the early evening, we were greeted by Ingrid's furious mother. Demanding to know where we had been, she yelled at me for deserting the children, waving her arms threateningly in the air. Calmly, Ingrid followed her into the living room, while I fled to our room and undressed hurriedly to go to bed. As I pulled the covers over me, Mrs. Stock ripped the door open, stormed in, and yelled at me:

"Where have you been?" Telling her that we had taken a walk, exactly what Ingrid had instructed me to say, she raged and screamed, threatening to hit me, accusing me of lying. The torrent of shouts and threats did not seem to end. Then abruptly, she slammed the door so it shook the whole house and stormed out, still raging. In a state of horror and panic, I lay in bed as if paralyzed. Never in my life had I heard such a raging fit of a tyrant, a woman nonetheless.

When Ingrid entered the room, she shocked me with a smile on her face, saying that this experience would teach her mother a lesson that neither she nor I were her hired baby-sitters. Eventually her mother would stop fuming.

"Sorry she frightened you, the roaring lion. I should not have made you lie," she added apologetically. I was speechless. How could anyone take such coarse, rude treatment so calmly? I prayed that God would take me away from here, fast, please! And I promised that I would never again lie to anyone for any reason. I should have known better anyway.

Early Sunday afternoon, Ingrid called me back from my walk, telling me the news that Father had come to visit me. I ran to the yard, leaving the two children behind. God had heard my silent pleas! His answer had come quickly. Why had I not started to pray sooner? He might have spared me this awful experience. With one glance, Father must have realized that I was unhappy. In his calm but determined manner, he told Mrs. Stock that he would take me home at once.

"Her four weeks are not up yet," she angrily objected. Disregarding her grumbling, I hurriedly threw my clothes into my satchel and within minutes I was ready to leave. Father had looked Mrs. Stock squarely in the face.

"My daughter can't afford to lose any more weight," he remarked firmly.

Too glad to leave, I waved Ingrid a quick good-bye and got on the bike in front of Father. God had sent him to rescue me from a raging tyrant. The ride went quickly. Passing Uncle Oskar's store

89

on the Wilhelmstrasse, I was happy to see familiar sights again. At home Father described Mrs. Stock to Mother as a typical Nazi, a loud mouth, a cold-blooded woman without any feeling, very demanding and selfish. Mother was dismayed. With one glance, she estimated that I had lost ten pounds and promised herself that she would never again be tricked by the city authorities to send any one of her children on a so-called summer vacation.

My experience had proved that we were used as free labor by the worst kind of party members.

Chapter VII

War—On Bended Knee

It was still early in the summer and the rest of my vacation I was able to spend at home, carefree and happy.

Summer evenings were now long and balmy and I spent most of my time outdoors. As we lived too far away from town to attend regular Sunday school, Pastor Preuss had made special arrangements for us children living in Annahof. At the Waldschloesschen Restaurant in nearby Fichtenwalde, we met once a week on a weekday to be taught by Miss Graupner, our Sunday School teacher. She knew the Bible by heart and lovingly told us the many stories of Jesus healing the sick, forgiving sins, and teaching his disciples. In her tender way, she was able to make an invisible God real to me. He was alive; I could talk to Him. I enjoyed Sunday school, and our group usually numbered as many as thirty children from the neighborhood. We attended even during the cold winter months and sometimes, during late summer, the farmer Didt, located at the southeastern end of Annahof, volunteered his large garden for Sunday school. We loved to crowd together on the wooden bench surrounding the big old apple tree or sit in the soft grass, cross-legged, to listen to Miss Graupner's stories. From our song book, she taught us many songs. Her most favorite was "Fairest Lord Jesus." When we sang it, I could feel my heart grow warm; it was a beautiful song.

Miss Graupner told us that this song was very popular among missionaries and that many children in Africa were taught to sing it. They were black children and God loved them too; they were part of His immense creation. Miss Graupner had a special talent to expand our horizons, to help us think beyond our small selves, to train our young and impressionable minds to reach out far into the world, God's creation. We loved her and, after our lessons, we were often permitted to pick up ripe apples from the grass, a special treat granted by the generous farmer, Mr. Didt.

In Sunday school I gained the inner strength to deal with the Jungmaedel meetings effectively. I learned to understand that hate was a sin and Father had taught us early in life that the revenge was the Lord's. Father's faith was monumental. He amazed me by saying that Hitler's regime, ruthless and tyrannic, could not possibly continue to exist under God's rule of righteousness and love. It had to fall because it was not in accord with God's law. Yet Father did not seem to be afraid of the prospect of this fall. He was certain that God would protect us so that our family would not be harmed in the process. Those who kept God's commandments would not be plucked out of His Hand.

"What makes me sad, is knowing that so many lives are lost, sacrificed for no other reason than to satisfy Hitler's hunger for power," he said, expressing his true feelings. I could understand Father's logic and agreed with him that God would not let trees grow into heaven, as he referred to Hitler symbolically. But I was frightened to realize that the removal of Hitler could possibly involve the loss of our home, our nation. What would become of us, our family? I was not ready for a total defeat; I was not yet willing to die. As I became more aware of the uncertainty of life, I prayed more often and much more sincerely. If the situation in our country grew worse, God was the only one to whom we could turn.

During the summer the position of our armies at the Russian front took a turn for the better. By August our brave soldiers had reached the Volga north of Stalingrad and the paper carried a photograph of the Swastika flag flying on Mount Elbrus. Maybe we would capture the Russian oil fields; maybe our armies had superior war equipment to that of Russia; maybe Germany still had a chance to win the war.

Mrs. Barock had stopped by to exchange some news with Mother one day.

"Did you know that Italian troops are now fighting in Russia?" she asked. Mother did not, although she was aware that Italy was one of Germany's allies. Mrs. Barock said her husband was of the opinion that Italian soldiers would never have the stamina to fight in Russia during winter. When mother relayed this news to Father later, he agreed with Mr. Barock's opinion. It would be a better strategy to use Italian soldiers in Africa, a climate closer to their own but, for a Russian winter, they were physically unfit.

Only three months later, it was mid-winter again in Russia and bitter fighting was reported around Stalingrad. By November, General Paulus and his 6th army had been encircled and Hitler had ordered an airlift to fly in food, medical and war supplies, bringing home thousands of sick, frostbitten, and wounded soldiers. Here was Father's proof, a stark, sad proof. Not that he blamed the ill-suited Italian men for this loss, but he confirmed that if our own German soldiers could not withstand 30° below zero weather, how could the Italians? Many soldiers were reported to be deserting and running over to the Russians. Our German military had received orders to shoot deserters, the newspaper reported. Hitler considered desertion as an act of treason. Mother worried:

"I hope and pray that Karl, Juergen, and Willi are not in Stalingrad or else we might never see them again."

The fierce battle around Stalingrad raged on for weeks, right into the Christmas holidays. As many families on our street knew from the sparse correspondence they received that their members were fighting in Russia, it was a sad and gloomy Christmas. No one in the neighborhood dared to celebrate. It would have been an offense in the face of those families who had received notices of the dead and the missing. One question haunted every family: will our father, our son, our brother, our relative ever return? The focus of everyone in Gumbinnen was on Stalingrad. Our neighbors asked over and over again: will General Paulus and his 6th army be freed? I heard this haunting question at school, at the Jungmaedel meetings, in our street, and at home. Father was following the news reports closely. The first week in January of 1943, a bitter cold month, Father read that Russian soldiers had offered Paulus the white flag of surrender, but the brave General had not accepted it. Father asked himself if it could have possibly been Hitler's strict orders not to accept the white flag. This fact would never be printed in the paper. Throughout January, we all held our breath about Stalingrad. The Russian artillery was still firing into the city, a sea of rubble and smoke.

Then on February third came the deadly news: Stalingrad had been lost, including General Paulus and his entire 6th army. The paper stated that our soldiers had fought bitterly and heroically to the very last man. Father closed the paper in silence that evening.

"Where is Willi, Juergen, Uncle Karl?" we all asked the same silent question. Many years later, we learned the sadistic truth about Stalingrad. From the very few who had survived their long, defeating imprisonment in Siberia came the account. Father's youngest brother, Uncle Karl, had been one of the witnesses. Father had guessed right. Hitler had not permitted General Paulus and his men to surrender! They had to fight or die!

But at this time, in February, 1943, Oma had received the sad and unnerving news that Uncle Karl was missing in action. A few short weeks later came more bad news: the *Schuster*, Father's brother-in-law, was also registered as missing. We did not know whether the two men were dead or alive.

As long as the incredible disaster of Stalingrad had hung like a huge, black cloud of suspense and depression over our city, no one had paid attention to the developments at other fronts. In November of 1942, Anglo-American forces had landed in Morocco and Algiers. Under Montgomery's direction, they had forced General Rommel and his men back hundreds of kilometers. El Alamein was lost. Father wondered if all of Africa was lost. I worried about Hans. Not having visited Aunt Ina for a while, I had lost track of his whereabouts.

By now Mother was reluctant to open mail. She feared it might contain bad news. Aunt Tina had sent a letter from Koenigsberg telling us that our cousin Juergen had died in Russia. But that was not all. Trudel, Aunt Tina's youngest daughter, had been engaged. A few days ago she had received a telegram stating the cold fact that her fiance was missing in action—and Trudel was pregnant. Aunt Tina wrote sadly to Mother that she found it easier to deal with the problem of an unwed mother than to lose her only son.

"What heartache," Mother sighed. I felt sorry for Aunt Tina; she was so kind, so even-tempered, so noble.

On my way home from school a few days later, I stopped to visit Aunt Schoen, as we called her. She was a sister to Uncle Wilhelm's wife and lived on the Luisenstrasse. Mr. Schoen worked for the post office. He was an older looking man with a big but fragile frame. A bushel of tousled salt and pepper curls topped his square face. Because of his severe nearsightedness, he wore thick, dark-rimmed glasses. He was a very quiet man and spoke only rarely. It seemed to take all of Aunt Schoen's gentle persuasion to draw him into a conversation. Their three children were older than I and the oldest son, Peter, was in the army. Dietrich, the second son, had been drafted into the S. S. This fact worried Aunt Schoen because she was certain that Dieter, as she called him, would never have volunteered to join. Yet, dutifully reporting at the S. S., he had been told that he had the physical qualifications for it. Over six feet tall and slender, with light brown hair, and keen, blue eyes, the S. S. expected him to consider his draft a privilege. He was also expected to follow orders. Aunt Schoen looked troubled and told me that Dieter was still in Gumbinnen for training. The strict orders he was given to carry out worried her.

"Dieter is troubled by his new duties. He confided to me one day that he has been assigned to take stenographic notes of Pastor Preuss's sermon on Sunday morning," she told me. This assignment disturbed Dieter because he knew that the S. S. was searching for anti-party evidence in our pastor's speech which would be sufficient reason to arrest him.

"What treachery!" I gasped. Everybody in town loved Paster Preuss, and Aunt Schoen assured me that she and Dieter did too. He did not dare refuse to carry out the order. As a result, he might be sent to the front lines in Russia, to be used as cannon-fodder, Hitler's way of getting rid of misfits, undesirables.

Therefore, Dieter obeyed the order and, to be absolutely certain not to incriminate the Pastor, had skipped writing down parts of the sermon, those parts that had contained even the slightest possibility for misinterpretation. One day Dieter had been questioned about the missing pieces. Aunt Schoen told me that Dieter had answered that the minister had been speaking too fast, that he had to skip a few words on his note pad.

"I worry about Dieter," she sighed.

It did not take long until he was shipped to the front anyway. Aunt Schoen never knew where he was stationed because he was permitted to write only under a coded address. Now she had only Luise, her youngest daughter, at home. Luise was a leader at the Jungmaedel and obviously enjoyed her function. She was a few years older than I, but I never liked her. I considered her flighty and spoiled. How could a girl over fourteen permit her mother to polish her shoes? Only Ursula, my oldest sister, was able to get along with Luise. I thought the reason for it could possibly be that Ursula had an eye on Peter, Luise's oldest brother.

Meantime, Ursula's *Pflichtjahr* had long since passed and she had started to work in April, 1942. To become a secretary, she had to serve her two years as an apprentice, during which she attended classes in accounting, typing, and stenography, on certain days of the week, and the practical application she got at work. During the years of her apprenticeship Ursula received a limited salary but, once she passed the examination, she would be a full-fledged secretary-bookkeeper and, with the substantial increase in salary, be able to support herself. Ursula, conscientious and ambitious, was proud to be working and reported that she enjoyed the congenial surroundings at Woelbing and Co., the lumber firm where she was employed. As the first of us children was now on her way to financial independence, Herta was expecting to receive approval from the city authorities to spend her *Pflichtjahr* at home, assisting Mother with the many household chores. But, instead, a few weeks later, Mother received a disturbing and embarrassing notice which declared our household unfit as a training ground. Instead of working with Mother at home, Herta had to report to a family in the center of town. The name, address, and date were listed at the end of the form.

Mother was stunned. Who in city authority could declare our home unfit, suggesting sloppiness? Nobody had visited her. But then Mother recalled the day when Mrs. Thorne had knocked at our door at 8:00 a.m. unannounced and without invitation. She had brushed past Mother into the kitchen, commenting in a snippy tone that it looked disorderly. The breakfast dishes were still in the sink. Mrs. Thorne disregarded the fact that only minutes ago we children had left for school. That day Mother had been very much annoyed about such an early intrusion, not allowing her time to straighten up the house. Even people with the slightest knowledge about etiquette would not dare visit anyone before 11:00. It was downright impolite. Now Mother realized that this early and unannounced visit was her adversary's vicious intention to produce evidence that our house looked disorderly so that Herta would have to spend her *Pflichtjahr* away from home. Mother was outraged.

"What viciousness! This treacherous woman!" she cried. Discussing the problem with Father in the evening, he suggested that it was wiser not to fight this official notice. Instead, he reminded Mother of the scripture, quoting: "The revenge is mine, sayeth the Lord."

It took Mother and Herta several days to swallow their anger, but finally both agreed with Father that it was wiser not to make an issue of this betrayal. We were on the "Black List"; we were not members of the party; we were watched. Father reasoned that Mrs. Thorne must have expected Mother to lash back at her which would have given her the opportunity she had longed for—to send Mother to prison, or God knows where. But, thank God, Mother had restrained herself and we were positive that Herta would manage to struggle through her year.

As Mother had guessed, the family to which Herta was assigned for her *Pflichtjahr* were Nazis, both husband and wife active members of the party. While both attended every function, it was Herta's duty to wash the dirty diapers daily for the young baby. It was not the hard and dirty work that offended Herta because she had carried a heavy share at home, but it was the woman's bossy manner and the multitude of fleas in the family's bedroom which Herta had discovered to her greatest horror.

"The woman is outright sloppy; she leaves her dirty personal items either in or under the bed. Balls of dust are in every corner," Herta reported in disgust, explaining that our house with six children had never looked as messy as this. She insisted on changing her clothes entirely when she arrived home in the evening, fearing that she might bring home fleas. The woman did nothing, no cooking, no cleaning, no laundry. Neither did she care for her small baby but left every chore to Herta, her *Pflichtjahrmaedel*. Father considered this treatment tyranny at its worst where *Nazi-Bonzen*, as he called them, took ruthless advantage of non-members, knowing no one would dare to complain.

The ruthlessness of the Nazis did not change even when the situation on the many fronts grew critical. They ignored the fact that the remnants of German-Italian troops were thrown out of Tunisia, a definite indication that the war had taken a turn against Hitler. Our troops were retreating on every front, the Anglo-American forces keeping right on their heels. Although Hitler must have recognized the steady loss of territory in Russia, he never openly admitted the fact and, instead, promised his bosom friend, the Duce, that he would send reinforcements to him in Italy. Where will he take the men from? Father asked. He considered Benito Mussolini another fanatic, possibly a trifle less dangerous than Hitler.

During the summer of 1943 came the surprise news: the Duce was arrested! In a revolt, he was forced out of the political picture! Father was glad. He also raised hopes that this successful move in Italy might encourage the small, underground opposition in our country to remove Hitler, Germany's war-hero. After these many years of a hopeless war, Father had no qualms wishing Hitler dead, because he felt an assassination might even be too mild a punishment considering how many millions of people the man had on his conscience. Hitler was sinister, the Devil's accomplice. Yet Hitler continued to live. The situation at the front grew steadily worse and the clamps around civilians at home closed tighter and tighter.

Before our summer holidays started, a notice was passed around in school advising that every able hand and body had to join in the effort to assure victory. The order notified each student to report at the Jungmaedel quarters for our assignments. I resented the fact of being cheated out of my well-deserved rest after a term of hard school work, especially since the Hitlerjugend was in charge of the summer assignments. Realizing that we had to meet at the *Rathaus*, the same place where Mrs. Stock had picked me up the previous summer for my fateful baby-sitting "vacation," I was on guard.

"How can I possibly get out of this restriction?" I strained my mind. The letter "S" of my name put me at the end of the list, giving me a chance to talk to those girls who had already received their assignment slips. Checking with a few, I discovered the old trick—non-members of the party were ordered to do hard farm and field work, whereas members were either dismissed or given clerical office work, an easy task. I decided to fight this order.

When my name was called, I told the girl that I had a medical certificate from my doctor exempting me from strenuous sports, mentioning that this fact should exempt me from this summer work assignment. Shattering my hopes, the girl snapped at me, adding in a sly tone:

"We have a way of finding out whether or not you are able to work." Calling over a classmate of Herta's, she told her, with a grin on her face:

"Take this slip of paper over to Dr. Hex; she will decide if this one can work or not." Momentarily, I felt the compulsion to jump at her throat and strangle her. I was boiling; my knees were shaking in rage. Yet my guard did not hestitate a moment. She started to move and I had to follow her to the doctor. This beast had ordered me to be examined! For a moment, I thought I would burst, that my mind, my body could not contain the rage within. Then one phrase hit me: "The revenge is mine—the revenge is mine—the revenge is mine." My mind screamed this assurance over and over again until we reached the doctor's door.

I had walked as if in a trance, not even noticing that Dr. Hex's practice was located on the Wilhelmstrasse, several houses beyond Uncle Oskar's store on the opposite side of the street. The girl, assigned as my guard, had not said one word on our way, while I kept my mouth nailed shut. She rang the bell and the doctor herself opened the door. From the note the girl handed her, the doctor sized up the situation at once. Looking straight at me, a faint but honest smile on her face, she seemed to be trying to spare me further embarrassment, and asked me a simple question:

"Don't you think it would be easier just to say 'yes?'" Barely opening my mouth, I agreed and we were dismissed instantly. I had to work during the summer whether I liked it or not. Flying down the Wilhelmstrasse, ignoring my guard, I stormed into Uncle Oskar's store. There I vented my rage. Pounding my fists on the counter, I screamed and I cried. Aunt Ina listened patiently until my tirade subsided, after which she calmly read the details of my assignment. In my fury, I had not even unfolded the paper. Mentioning that the office to which I was assigned for work was a few houses away, almost next door to Dr. Hex, Aunt Ina picked up the phone. Briefly she explained my situation to someone, then hung up.

"Mr. Holz knows your mother; just go over and see him," she said, and added, "Stop by before you go home," dismissing me with a smile and a pat on my shoulder.

When I hesitantly entered the dingy office, a tall, white-haired man greeted me, extending his hand. I accepted it shyly, and followed his encouraging motion with which he ushered me to his desk, while, in passing, he casually introduced me to three other girls in the office. While I sat on a chair next to his desk, he explained to me that I would work under the supervision of the senior girl, his head bookkeeper, and I would be adding up columns of figures or running brief errands. A bank deposit had to be made daily. Closing his introduction, he smiled.

"I know your mother. We were in the same class. Give her my regards when you get home."

The blond, slender senior girl then took me in her charge, mentioning that she had been Ursula's classmate. My hostilities were melting and I shyly answered her questions regarding my sister, after which she handed me several long sheets of paper. The columns of figures were endless. Above all, she expected me to add them in my head because the apprentice, training to become a bookkeeper, was using the only adding machine in the office. I tried it. What drudgery! My mind still had not digested the recent affront. For lack of concentration, I had to start those columns over and over again, arriving at a different result each time. This was maddening, yet I was determined to add up these numbers correctly. My new supervisor, sensing my despair, consoled me that adding figures in one's head was no easy task, a task requiring time and practice.

At the end of the day, I was totally exhausted from the emotional strain and concentration. My report to Aunt Ina before walking home sounded more like a complaint than an achievement. I tried to tackle the job two more days. The head bookkeeper had been re-adding every column I had totalled and had again arrived at different results, correct results. She was a genius; her mind worked as fast as the adding machine, producing the correct total. Realizing that my struggle with these long columns was a waste of time and effort, the girl let me run the errands. The rest of the day I wasted with sharpening pencils and handling the minute amount of filing. I was bored. Complaining again to Aunt Ina about my plight, she made another phone call.

"Now honestly, Mr. Holz, do you need her at the office?" I heard her say half jokingly and half in earnest, to which he replied negatively. Cautioning him, however, that the Hitlerjugend might check with him about my attendance, he assured Aunt Ina that he would give them an appropriate answer. I was free, free for the rest of the summer! Thanks to my Lord and Aunt Ina, He had freed me from this boring assignment without my direct prayers for it. It was miraculous. On my way home, stepping gingerly, I reasoned that possibly because I had forced myself to control my anger a few days earlier, this self-restraint had paid off in giving me this freedom, this reward.

Now I could spend the summer at home helping Mother while at work Herta suffered under the pressures of the Nazi woman who was her boss.

"This woman does not allow me a moment of rest. She pushes me around and criticizes everything I do. And I try so hard to please her," Herta complained bitterly. Therefore, Father decided to find a different place for her. He was aware that Herta would not be permitted to stay home for the balance of the year, but he was determined to stop the abuse she suffered.

It did not take him long to solve the problem. He returned home late one Sunday afternoon from fishing at the Angerapp where he now enjoyed the use of his boat. Having told the farmer, who stored the boat for him over winter, about Herta's predicament, Mr. Matzat suggested that she complete her *Pflichtjahr* with them, helping on the farm. His own daughter, close to Herta's age, stayed at home serving her year.

"I know my daughter would like the company of another girl," he emphasized. Mother was reluctant about the suggested change at first because Herta was fragile and not very strong, but Herta's immediate enthusiasm changed her attitude. Herta, arriving home late and tired that night, breathed a sigh of relief.

"Working on a farm cannot possibly be harder than serving this harsh Nazi woman hand and foot," she reasoned. Then Mother worried about something else. She feared that the woman might not accept Herta's resignation. So Father decided to settle the matter personally. After meeting her, he regretted not having freed Herta sooner from this tyrant. Herta was happy. The chicanery was over.

Taking a few days to pack her clothes, Herta showed Mother her shoes. They were in terrible condition. The long daily walks to and from town had worn out the wooden soles.

"Do you think I could get a new pair within these few days?" she asked. Father promised that Mother would hunt up a purchasing ticket for a pair and he would bring them along on his next fishing trip.

The following Saturday, Father packed Herta and her suitcase on his bike and off they went to the Matzat farm in Mertinshagen. Mother expected his return anxiously on Sunday, curious to know how Herta had reacted to her new surroundings. Father, with an assuring wave of his hand, reported that she was happy because Hilde Matzat had rushed her off for a horse and buggy tour around the village after breezing her through the house and the farm. The girls had become friends instantaneously.

Hearing this good news eased Mother's mind. Now she could concentrate on preparing the house to accommodate Aunt Erna and Uncle Franz for several weeks. Since the recent arrival of their son, Gerd, both were suffering from nervous exhaustion. The many nights they had spent in the bunker in Hamburg were taking their toll. Uncle Franz suffered from ulcers and Aunt Erna's nerves desperately needed a rest. Mother had invited them for a visit. The clean air, the food, although meager, and sufficient rest would restore both quickly, Mother reasoned.

The three arrived in July. It was a warm and sunny day and Andreas appreciated a playmate close to his age. What disappointed him, however, was that Gerd, his young cousin, could not yet walk. He was less than a year old. But Andreas was determined to teach him and Gerd was obviously anxious to learn. Although Aunt Erna was on edge and in a snappy mood at first, she relaxed after a few nights of sleep. The ample food supply in our kitchen amazed her after experiencing many years of severe shortages in Hamburg. Chickens and eggs from the stable and the plentiful choice of vegetables from our garden soon registered as additional pounds around Aunt Erna's middle and filled out Uncle Franz's drawn face. Gerd, shortly before his first birthday, followed Andreas' cheerful encouragement and made his first hesitant steps. Andreas was overjoyed.

"Look, Gerd can walk!" he cried to Mother, pulling excitedly at her sleeve. Every day their radius of adventure widened and soon the two women found them sitting at the edge of the pond, much to Aunt Erna's concern. Yet Andreas proved to be a reliable baby-sitter. Gerd never fell in.

Meantime, Father had taken Uncle Franz on several overnight fishing trips to his favorite spot, the Angerapp. The enthusiasm with which they returned conveyed that both enjoyed the sport. Discussing politics, however, was an entirely different matter. Here their opinions widely separated. Usually Father avoided the subject, knowing Uncle Franz's leftist, radical attitude, but often Uncle Franz deliberately steered their conversation in this direction.

"Do you have to broadcast your opinion while you are a guest here?" Aunt Erna retorted, criticizing her husband for his views. Therefore often a major disagreement between the two and a lot of noise were the result. This problem distressed Father. He loved a peaceful and tranquil atmosphere in his house. Whenever he or Mother saw need for a discussion, both usually took a long walk together. They never voiced their disagreements or fought before us children. Yet despite our overcrowded house, Uncle Franz's vacation passed quickly and he soon had to return to Hamburg, to his work at the wharf. Aunt Erna and Gerd stayed on for a few additional weeks. Gerd had gained almost ten pounds and was obviously very happy. He and Andreas had become bosom friends, a fact Aunt Erna observed with delight.

What delighted Aunt Erna further was that Mother taught her to sew. From Father's old pants they made two new pairs of shorts—one for Gerd and one for Andreas. Uncle Franz soon wrote for Aunt Erna and Gerd. He missed them, their company, Aunt Erna's care. Obediently, she packed her suitcases, leaving Gerd's baby carriage with us. Her son had learned to walk; she did not need it any more. Tearfully, she wished us goodbye.

"How I dread to go back, back to the long nights in the bunker and the continuous search for food," she cried. Mother promised to send her regular food packages with items we could spare, which eased Aunt Erna's mind. Andreas regretted losing his buddy, especially since he had been teaching Gerd many new words which enabled the two to carry on a nearly perfect conversation.

* * * * * *

After his controversial visitor had left, Father again concentrated on the news. Several months had slipped by in a turbulent summer. Now it was the end of September, 1943, and, to Father's amazement, the newspaper again reported on Russian cities, cities which had made headlines at the outbreak of war against Russia. Our troops had won and lost the Donets and the cities of Orel and Smolensk; they were retreating, coming frighteningly close.

"How long will it take until we have the Russians at our

doors?" Father worried. "How many more of our soldiers have to bleed to death until Hitler acknowledges defeat and capitulates?"

Hitler evidently had no intention to capitulate and his mouthpiece, Dr. Goebbels, screamingly continued to proclaim victory, totally disregarding the heavy losses. As bitter fighting continued, leading into another severe cold winter in Russia, Uncle Gustav received a telegram: Willi had died for his Fatherland, the death of a hero. Uncle Gustav was inconsolable. Willi had recently been home on a brief furlough. He had made a special effort to reconcile with his father with whom he had had a major disagreement over his surprise marriage. Now, only weeks later, Willi was dead. Mother's heart went out for her brother.

"Life is dealing him one hard blow after another," she wailed. "He has not yet recovered from Aunt Frieda's sudden death, and now Willi is dead." The only fact that she appreciated, despite the sadness, was that Willi had reconciled with his father before he died. At least, the grudges had been removed between the two. Mother strongly believed it to be a bad omen for anyone to die leaving an unresolved quarrel behind.

When Mother visited her brother the next day, Uncle Gustav told her why he was so upset. On his last furlough, Willi had met with one of his hockey friends for a few beers at a neighborhood bar. A minor disagreement between the two had flared up Willi's hot temper and resulted in a fist fight in which Willi injured his equally rough friend. Instead of arresting Willi for the crime, the police had noted the details, shipping him back to the front immediately. With a crime on his record, Uncle Gustav speculated that Willi had not returned to his previous unit but, instead, was put into action right at the firing lines. Here, most likely, he had died the death of a hero!

"Cannon-fodder," Father remarked sadly. Hitler did not waste lives of able-bodied men keeping them behind bars; they had to be put to use to fight for their Fatherland and, if necessary, die. Willi had paid dearly for his crime. Mother felt sorry for her bereaved brother.

But having a multitude of household chores on her hands did not leave her time for mourning or brooding. As the food situation was rapidly growing worse, Father decided to bake bread for us. Mr. Matzat, the farmer with whom Herta was serving the balance of her *Pflichtjahr*, had offered Father wheat and rye grain. Although Mother at first could not see the use for this commodity.

"If we soak them a night, the wheat berries can easily be chopped in a meat grinder," Father explained. Mixing it with our meager flour rations, he could stretch our bread supply, if not triple it. As soon as Father had located a baker in town who was willing to bake the loaves in a sufficiently big oven for us, he set out to work.

It was fascinating to watch him. After Mother had taken turns with us to work the soaked grains through the meat grinder, Father mixed it with the prepared sourdough and the flour. Pouring in small amounts of water to give it the perfect texture, he added salt and caraway seeds for flavor, working the mass of dough with his two strong hands. Preparing four eight-pound loaves at a time, it took all his strength to mix the dough thoroughly. Allowing it a night to rise, he had to repeat the hard kneading process the next day. Forming four equal-sized loaves in huge baking pans, they were ready to be taken to the baker.

"Who is going to volunteer?" Father asked. But seeing no hands go up, Mother voted that Frederick would be the one most suitable for the job; first, because he ate the most bread and, second, because he could take them to town on his way to school. Father placed the tins securely on our hand-wagon, covering the precious load neatly with a linen cloth. To keep him company, Maria walked with Frederick to the bakery. Although Frederick had only grudgingly consented to his new chore, he could hardly wait to get home with the freshly baked bread after school.

"It smells so good," he said, drawing the aroma in with his nostrils. Naturally, he was entitled to receive the first crunchy end. The bread tasted delicious, even without butter. As we used to argue over the ends, Mother had to rotate them. But often Frederick brought the breshly baked bread home and Mother discovered that one or two ends were already missing. The fact did not need an explanation; Frederick deserved to have first choice on the crust. About once a month, Father baked bread. Watching him, we realized it was very hard work; yet he never complained. Instead, he was grateful to be able to feed us while the food shortage reached critical proportions in major cities, especially in the densely populated Ruhr area.

* * * * * *

Father was of the opinion that not even the invention of the newest weapons could assure our country victory. Nevertheless, the Japanese dead-sure method in applying the one-man torpedo flashed across the headlines. Father considered this act a last frantic effort and suicidal in its operation. Those Japanese marines who volunteered to man these torpedoes, riding on it and aiming it at dead-center of an enemy ship, were expected to die in the explosion. The sacrifice of their lives, voluntary as we were led to believe, was to assure victory to their country and ours. This was the newspaper's interpretation of the matter, praising each marine lost in such action as a hero.

Many years after the end of this furious war, we learned the sadistic truth about the one-man torpedoes. This was the secret mission to which my much admired cousin, Erwin, had been assigned. He barely escaped his deadly call for duty; it was a draft to action and not a voluntary service as we had been led to believe. Meantime, the newspaper was filled with distortions about our country's situation, still proclaiming victory in every article. In Annahof every day a new rumor flared up.

One rumor kept the women in our street mystified and excited for several days. A few neighbors had seen strange, disc-like objects in the night sky. As the newspaper had given this strange occurrence only minute coverage, somewhere on the back page, Mrs. Barock suspected a cover-up.

"What are these mysterious lights zipping through the sky at night? Could they be new Russian spying devices?" she questioned Mother. "Could the Russian scientists in a joint effort with the American technicians have developed a new weapon? Could it wipe our country out in one single blow?" "Why does our paper ridiculously refer to these highly maneuverable and noiseless light devices as 'flying saucers?' Are we ever told the truth? Do you think there is a link between these objects and the much whispered about V-2, a remotely-controlled missile which was designed to wipe out England in one massive blow?" she continued her questions, serious questions. Yet neither Mrs. Barock nor Mother had a reasonable answer to this mysterious phenomenon. Dr. Goebbels apparently ignored such subjects. He continued to scream about victory. Germany was going to win this war!

The frequent drills during class, however, and the increased piles of sandbags against the basement windows of our schools testified differently; yet we were told these were precautionary measures only. So far, no bombs had fallen in Gumbinnen. Therefore, our attention in class was undisturbed. Soon we were absorbed in a new subject—geometry. Although Stinker taught it, I enjoyed it thoroughly. For several weeks I had turned in my homework correctly, which resulted in improved marks. Stinker had forgotten about the fateful incident that happened several years ago.

One day, after five long and tiring sessions, we had one more subject to sit through, geometry. Stinker entered the classroom briskly, slamming the door behind him. The entire class sensed it. He was in a bad mood. Mentioning that he was going through a quick review, he held up a wooden triangle and asked the girl in the front row which type this was.

"I do not know. We have not yet discussed this specific triangle," she answered shyly, looking fearful. Annoyed, he ordered her to come foreward, showing the triangle to the class. The second girl gave the same answer: we had not discussed it.

"What? You don't know? I'll wake you up!" he screamed furiously and slapped the girl. Snapping at the first girl to give the triangle to me, he hissed the same question in my face. I did not know. Yet hardly waiting for my answer, he reached out to slap me. Realizing his intention, I quickly held the triangle before my face in protection. With one hard strike, he knocked it out of my hand and pushed me hard and rudely against the desk behind me, almost breaking my back. As I held it in pain, sitting down crying, he raged on and slapped half of the students in class until someone insistently knocked at the door. This reminder brought Stinker to his senses and he decided to check his textbook.

We had not yet discussed this triangle! Although realizing his error, he did not apologize to anyone for his raging fit. After racing through the next lesson, he stormed out of class, leaving the door behind him wide open. Our class, petrified, disturbed, and crying, poured out after him to see Miss Zahn. Without knocking at the door, we stormed in and disrupted her lesson. From the sobbing and talking jumble of the girls, she finally realized what had happened. She did not request proof; she had heard Stinker's raging voice resound along the hallway.

"He is impossible," she admitted. Miss Zahn devoted her next entire English lesson explaining to us the infamous uneven-sided triangle and in a moment's time every student mastered the subject.

Although many parents complained to Director Dr. Bruch about Stinker's bad temper and signed statements requesting his removal from the faculty, he did not leave. He never turned into a lamb either. Although he curbed his slapping, he maintained a state of truce with our class. What I resented more than his rudeness was the fact that my enemy had finally and unexpectedly gotten even with me, mistreating me without reason.

Aware of my shyness, Miss Zahn had offered to tutor me in math in her spare time as we had walked home together for a stretch. Although I declined her offer, shortly thereafter she visited us by bike in Annahof during summer, asking Mother to sell her a few pounds of potatoes and some eggs. The food situation was growing worse, even in Gumbinnen, located in the heart of Germany's farm country. Mother knew that Miss Zahn lived alone and had no food resources other than her food stamps, which allotted her to buy painfully small rations. Meat and butter were measured by the gram; therefore, staples like potatoes and vegetables had to satisfy the hungry stomachs.

"How will our country get through another winter?" asked Father. The Russian grain bin, the Ukraine and the city of Kiev were lost and, judging from the experience during the two previous winters, it was most likely that the Russians would again gain the upper hand.

"How long will it take them to over-run East Prussia?" he worried. But Dr. Goebbels still sounded his victory trumpets. It made Father angry. Several of our neighbors who had never dared to voice a different opinion than the one proclaimed through the press looked discouraged and now talked more freely. Having lost so many of their men and relatives, they were depressed.

"What did they die for?" they asked Mother with bitterness. Many Nazi women who had Polish maids at their disposal complained about their recent rebelliousness, their refusal to work endless hours either for minimal pay or free of charge.

Shopping at Mrs. Schneider's grocery store one day, I witnessed one of these encounters. Mrs. Schneider had kept her pretty Polish maid restricted to private quarters. Therefore, it surprised me to see the girl breeze into the store, totally disregarding Mrs. Schneider's orders.

"I will meet my Polish friends. I no care what you say!" She yelled and stormed out, leaving a speechless and embarrassed Mrs. Schneider behind. Trying to conceal her anger, Mrs. Schneider waited on me and complained bitterly about her difficulty in managing the Polish girl. On my way home, I wondered why Mrs. Thorne, Mother's adversary, had never rated a Polish maid. It had been the thing to do, a status symbol, so to speak, in Nazi circles. Perhaps they were granted to outstandingly active members only. I realized that Aunt Ina never had one either.

With winter on its way again, our visits to relatives became rare. Cold weather, deep snow, and our worn shoes did not permit us to take unnecessary walks. For two years our class had taken on extra girls from the Ruhr area, Hamburg, and Berlin—cities which had experienced heavy bombing and were reduced to little more than rubble. These students had fled to their East Prussian relatives to be safe. Now, as the Russian armies advanced steadily, they moved back home, preferring to spend many nights in a bunker in a major city in Western Germany than to be captured by the Russian hordes. These Russian and Mongolian hordes were taking bitter revenge because Hitler had broken the non-aggression pact and attacked their country.

Nevertheless, Hitler made every effort to halt the retreat of our armies. Boys sixteen years old were drafted and men past forty, and only after a minimum of training, were thrown into the fighting lines.

"How long will Father stay home?" I worried and noticed that Mother smiled less these days. Those few men returning home wounded considered their injury a God-given chance to stay alive. They reported tragic scenes from Russia. While the Russian soldiers attacked, fired on by their commanders with loud shouts of encouragement, our young men jumped out of their trenches, ready to defend themselves. But ill-equipped and untrained, they were mowed down by Russian machine gun fire. Those young soldiers surviving such an attack cried during the long dark nights like children crying for their mothers.

"It is a pity. It breaks my heart," reported one of our neighbors, hobbling around on one leg and crutches. The old-timers, soldiers with experience, were unable to handle the situation; it was hopeless. Knowing their predicament, their doom, we watched the boys from our street leave for the front. Heavy-hearted, we asked ourselves a silent question:

"Would we ever see them again? Would we ever be able to sing along with Herbert Ross while he played his harmonica?" Walter Schurat, Herta's close friend had to leave on such short notice that she was not allowed enough time to rush home from Mertinshagen to wish him goodbye. His mother wept uncontrollably, seeing her only son leave after having lost her husband in Russia not too long ago. Her three younger daughters could not console her. Yet Walter left bravely. He considered it his duty to defend our country, to guarantee his mother and his sisters safety at home. Several months later, Mrs. Schurat told Mother that Walter was stationed in the west, south of Hamburg, for training. This news was at least a consolation; he was not fighting in Russia.

* * * * * *

After a depressing, dreary, and seemingly endless winter, another spring started. One look around the neighborhood revealed that only children and older men were left in our street, all able-bodied men were fighting at the front. The year 1944 had crept in quietly, unobtrusively. As my confirmation approached in early spring, Mother and I hunted for a suitable dress. The traditional white dress had long since vanished. It was neither available nor did anyone dare wear it while half the nation was wearing clothes of mourning. In almost every family, someone was dead or missing. It took a long search to locate a dress that fit my beanpole figure. Mother settled for one in navy blue.

"In a black dress you resemble a corpse," she commented dryly, as I stood in the dressing room. Although I was not enthusiastic about the style of my new dress, it fit me and served its purpose.

On Palm Sunday, Pastor Preuss held our communion service, during which I knelt the first time in my life. It was a very long and somber affair and I whispered a question to Father:

"How long will this session last?" But he did not answer me and I had to remain on my knees, my mind able to focus only on their soreness instead of our dear pastor's guidance for my life. Finally, our turn came to walk to the altar where we received the wine and bread, the communion. Returning to our pew, we were permitted to sit down. Only then did I comprehend the holiness of its symbols. Jesus had also died for me, letting me share His life, His body, His blood. Would I be required to share in His suffering, His death? I was too young to suffer, too young to die, my mind reasoned in defense. These thoughts disturbed me and I firmly pushed them out of my mind. Yet God knew what was best, Father had taught me; therefore I readily placed my hopes and trust in Him.

Preparations for a small celebration marking my confirmation demanded a lot of attention and ingenuity because hardly any baking ingredients were available. Coffee grounds had to substitute for cocoa and the limited sugar ration dictated that Mother could bake no more than three cakes. This meant that we could not invite visitors either. The food was sufficient only to serve us and a few neighbors who might come to congratulate me. Not even Aunt Ina could attend my confirmation party; it was depressing.

The cool and overcast weather on Easter Day blended in with the generally dreary mood. Although I was disappointed in having no celebration, receiving several neighbors as congratulants made the day stand out slightly from any other. It was my day, the day I promised to live a Christian life, no matter how many trials I had to withstand. God had offered His guidance, His care, and I had accepted it, saying "Yes" at the altar. Realizing that my entire life lay still before me, I was curious what it might have in store for me.

With summer approaching rapidly, these thoughts of the future retreated to the background of my mind. Working toward another year of finals in school, studies occupied every spare minute. Two more years and I would graduate from middle school. My term paper showed signs of encouragement; my grades were improving. But instead of the usual joyous dismissal for vacation, all classes were ordered to join in the big auditorium to listen to a speech. The Director, Dr. Bruch, delivered it and immediately we recognized its importance. Only sketchily did he size up our country's situation, voiced his optimism that we would win this war, but stressed the fact that any student who had attended four full years was considered a graduate from middle school.

"Anyone who wants to receive a certificate to this effect, please see me after dismissal," he said, barely emphasizing this point. Only very few students did, however, and, as usual, we wished each other a good summer. This was the last day I saw any of my teachers and classmates until many years later, after the total collapse of our country. Very, very few survived.

During the summer, Father followed the news very closely. In early June, the Anglo-American forces had occupied Rome, at the same time launching a major offensive on the shores of Normandy. Only two weeks later, as if by joint force, the Russians pushed forward in their first, forceful summer offensive. Watching these developments worriedly, Father decided that Herta should return home.

"Our family should be together at such a critical time," he insisted.

Father's main focus was on the Russian front. Mother wondered if it would have been wiser to follow Aunt Erna's invitation to join them in Hamburg.

"I do not believe that the Allied troops will permit Russia to capture German territory. I am sure that they will advance quickly from the West," Father reasoned.

In the midst of this confusion came the blaring news that Hitler's headquarters in Rastenburg, East Prussia, had been bombed. It was another assassination attempt. Yet Hitler was still alive. Father commented dryly:

"This man must have a pact with the devil. It looks as if he will protect him until our country is totally wiped out."

Only four days later, our family was struck with horrible news: Father received his draft notice. He had to report to the recruiting center on July 25, 1944. Mother was in a state of shock, of panic.

"He has to fight at the front, just before the doors close," she wailed, a stream of tears soaking her face.

And so, Father left our house quietly the next day after placing his big, warm hand on my head, uttering a prayer and a blessing for each one of us.

Chapter VII

Flight From the Beast—Step One

Even now, as our city was in a state of confusion, the organization of the Hitlerjugend did not allow its members a moment's rest. Only two days after Father had left, the girl who had been given the embarrassing order to accompany me to the Nazi doctor the summer before told me a gruesome story. One night her family was wakened by the screams and moans coming from the direction of the railroad station near where they lived. Her father, driven by these heartrending groans, hurriedly threw on his clothes and went to investigate. Employed at the railroad, he took a shortcut to the station by crossing numerous tracks. What he found was a sight of horror and Karin repeated his story to me. In the station stood a battered passenger train from which many windows were missing. Her father peered into the first car. Once his eyes adjusted to the darkness he discovered it was packed with hundreds of wounded German soldiers. Many were covered with fresh blood; some were obviously unconscious. But no doctor or nurse was in sight to assist these battered souls to stop the bleeding or hand them water to cool their bodies burning with fever. Their moans and screams gripped at her father's heart, causing him to race back home. With tears streaming down his face, he tore out every piece of bandage in the house, ripped clean sheets to strips, grabbed all the medication he could find, filled a bucket with cold water, and dashed back to the train to lend as much help as he possibly could. He would not permit his wife to go with him.

The train had evidently been quietly pulled in at night, not to scare civilians, and was left standing in the station after the locomotive evidently had been removed to dash off and bring in another load. This newly arrived trainload of wounded must have been the reason why the BDM drummed together all Jungmaedel, ordering us to visit one of the military hospitals. We were urged to cheer the wounded with singing and to bring along some food ready to eat. For this purpose Mother had quickly cooked a big bowl of pudding and chilled it the night before to be ready for me the next day.

According to orders, I met the group of girls at the assigned hospital. Upon arrival, I was directed to take the food to the kitchen. This done, we waited only a moment until the last one of our group of girls arrived, including our leader. A head nurse ushered us one flight up into a large hall.

"These are severely injured soldiers," she explained in a low whisper and then hurriedly disappeared. I counted approximately thirty beds along the walls. Some of the soldiers sat up in bed as our entering had stirred general curiosity.

Our leader gave us the key note to one of the scheduled songs and we blasted off, determined to cheer these desperate souls. After finishing the second song, both peppy Hitlerjugend melodies, one of the soldiers sitting up motioned me with a determined gesture of his hand to come over. Talking from his bed as I drew closer, he hissed through his teeth in disgust:

"Where do you get the nerve to scream such offensive nonsense? Over in the corner one of my comrades is desperately fighting for his life. Can't you see? Are you blind?" I was dumbstruck and, thank God, the singing stopped as each girl was visiting with a soldier sitting up in bed.

This soldier, no older than his early twenties, ordered me to sit down at the corner of his bed. While I followed his instructions obediently, he fired his frantic questions at me.

"Have you ever paid attention to the nonsense you are singing?" he demanded. At times I had, but not very seriously. This urgent question, however, refreshed my memory: Today Germany belongs to us and tomorrow the world. We had sung this one, the song that had made me ponder its words in 1939. The brown-haired soldier continued hurling questions at me.

"Do you realize that the Russians have crossed our East Prussian border and are less than fifteen kilometers away? Are you aware that Goebbels is leading all Germans by their noses, army and civilians alike?" Then he demanded to know how many sisters I had. Whimsically, I told him I had two older ones and Maria, a younger sister.

"Now listen! I have seen horror with my own eyes. This was the gruesome fate of civilians who believed Goebbels' lies, civilians who stayed at home until the Russians invaded their territory." Furiously, urgently, he pounded his experience into me. One day when his unit recaptured an East Prussian village, he found a whole family dead, their tongues nailed to the kitchen table. Another family he found on a farm crucified against their barn wall, man, woman, maid, and children. Asking me directly and insistently if I wanted to be raped, butchered, or deported to Siberia, I started to tremble so violently that I had trouble concealing it.

"If you don't want these atrocities to happen to you and your family, then leave! Leave!! Leave before the Soviet tanks are at your door!" I knew he was telling the truth. The Russian soldiers, he explained with bitterness, were handed a ration of straight Vodka with their meals. As a result, they were totally drunk when they received orders to attack and treated German civilians in the barbaric manner he had just described.

The young soldier urged me, begged me to leave Gumbinnen, to run home and start packing. As soon as I was able to control my violent trembling, I got up from the corner of his bed. He thanked me for the pair of knitted new socks I had brought him. With resignation, he mentioned that he had a shell splinter removed from his leg. He would live, but his friend in the corner might die for nothing, not to mention those countless thousands who had died before him and the countless other soldiers who had returned home crippled, without arms, legs, noses, and ears.

I did not wait for the rest of the girls to leave. As I turned around at the door, the soldier tiredly lifted his hand to motion me a goodbye. Storming home the long way, I decided to leave Gumbinnen. We had to leave! No matter how Mother would react to my decision, I was going to evacuate as soon as I saw a chance, even if this action meant disobeying her orders. Only after I had reached this decision did my mind recover from this frenzied state of panic. I had not noticed the road, the time, or anything else when I arrived home.

Bursting into the kitchen, I announced to Mother that I was going to leave home and would start packing immediately.

"Why! What happened? You look white!" she asked anxiously. When I gave her the reason, telling her of the soldier's blunt and urgent report at the hospital, she sank on a kitchen chair and cried bitterly. Sobbing, she told me that Father had given her strict orders not to leave Gumbinnen. He had reasoned that our house belonged to us and no Russian had the right to take it from us.

"Where do you intend to go?" Mother asked through her tears.

"Westward, the direction everybody else is going," I assured her, amazing myself at my own firmness and determination. During the last few weeks many Nazi families had left Gumbinnen quietly under the cover of darkness. Herta and Maria had crowded around us and Maria, holding on to my arm, cried:

"I want to go with you." Herta immediately decided to join me as she did not want to take the risk of being murdered by the Russians. Mother, slowly gained her composure.

"If you all leave, I will not stay home alone; I will go with you," she reasoned and let out a deep sigh. Ursula, returning from work, agreed with our decision. Against Father's will, we would evacuate as soon as the means were provided by city authorities, who had begun to organize evacuations.

Meantime, Herta and I started to pack the most practical clothes, including woolen sweaters and our coats to be prepared for the oncoming winter. Hastily we sewed together bags of coarse linen, securely fastening two straps on the top. Frederick and Maria, the two smaller ones, could carry them in knapsack fashion on their backs. Andreas was too small to carry anything. So Herta and I prepared a bundle for each of us older girls to carry.

"Some day Father might thank God for our decision," Ursula stated matter-of-factly. This eased Mother's mind about acting against his will. Yet the fear of the unknown, the chaos among the people in the city frightened her. She had never been confronted with such an emergency situation. As Father had left only a few days ago, she had to handle the problem alone.

"What will happen to us? Where will he ever find us?" she worried and sobbed intermittently. After a helter-skelter meal, Ursula joined us with the packing. Mother was useless and we were afraid she might suffer a nervous breakdown. We three girls worked feverishly into the night, even managing to sew a big duffle bag, into which we intended to squeeze two of Mother's light summer feather beds. This task accomplished, we fell into bed, totally exhausted. Grateful that our family would soon be out of this immediate danger, I slept well.

The next day Herta and I set up a plan and made substantial progress with our packing. It had been Herta's brainstorm to pack our cousin Gerd's baby carriage with linens and towels and securely wrap the huge smoked ham Father had bought from the Matzat farm and tuck it in on the bottom.

Mother came downstairs and, to our relief, looked better. While we were tying the duffle bag, she told us that she had had a dream before she woke up. She vividly described the details to us.

"I recall that I was with all of you in a dark place. It resembled a bunker. Then I heard enemy planes approach in waves and drop their bombs. With each new wave, they moved closer and closer, as I was anxiously estimating by the detonation of bombs. I knew the next wave that came would hit us. Panic stricken, I listened for the roar of the advancing planes. But they never came; we were safe!" After Mother had wakened, still breathless from panic, she had pondered the meaning of the dream. Certain that it indicated we would survive this turmoil, she felt relieved about acting against Father's will. Herta and I exchanged glances. Understanding of the message in her dream would stop her crying as she must have been torn between our decision to leave and Father's instructions to stay at home.

Ursula, the cool-headed one in the family, suggested that Mother pack all legal papers and documents relating to our property and withdraw as much cash from the bank as she could get. Both left together, Ursula to go to work, and Mother to do her important errand, while Herta and I completed the packing.

"I will tuck in extra socks and underwear for each of us, even two sets for Father, in addition to packing his dark suit," Herta told me. Her organized mind seemed to function at its best. I decided to wear another of Father's sport suits over my own clothes and his winter coat over mine. It would weigh me down heavily, but it was easier than carrying such heavy clothes. Besides, Father would need his civilian clothes when the war was over and he returned from the Army.

When the bare necessities were packed, Herta and I relaxed for a moment. Glancing around the house, I realized that everything else had to stay. I remembered having watched over his shoulder as he painted the low basket of blooming cacti when we still lived at the Kasernenstrasse. I was also very fond of another painting, the old barn at sunset. But at the moment, these were luxuries and perhaps some day Father might paint again. This was not a time to bemoan the loss of things. Lives were much more precious than belongings.

Our neighborhood was buzzing, each person consulting the other about what to do. Everybody was worried. We had notified Mrs. Gander of our decision to evacuate. But we would wait until we received the official notice. She and Lisa started to pack hurriedly. Mrs. Barock and Mrs. Adomeit, two other neighbors quickly tied some bundles together. We could not check activities farther up the street because Mother had given us strict orders not to leave our property until she was back.

Returning before lunch, Mother mentioned that Ursula had suggested giving every one of our relatives in town Aunt Erna's address in Hamburg. Obviously, each family had to find their own means of evacuation because we lived too far apart. But via correspondence directed to Aunt Erna, we could locate each other later. This suggestion was an excellent idea and Ursula offered to notify Aunt Ina and Uncle Gustav by telephone from her office. They could then convey the information to Oma at the Fromeltstrasse.

Now all we could do was to sit, to pray, and to wait. But we did not have to wait long. Late in the afternoon, a courier breezed by on his bike, announcing that whoever had decided to leave Gumbinnen should have their bags packed, securely labelled, and outside tomorrow morning—August 12, 1944.

"No more than one bag per person is permitted. And each family has to handle their own baggage. Horse-drawn wagons will pick you up," he announced and hurried off, leaving people standing dumbfounded, leaving them to answer their own questions.

After this brief notice, our street buzzed like a hive of disturbed bees. Women were screaming and complaining about the short one-day notice. If they were determined to leave the city, however, before the Russians arrived, they had to pack in a hurry. As I walked over to our neighbor to check with Mrs. Gander on her progress in packing, I noticed that the radio was on. Mrs. Gander kept abreast with the latest developments. I did not believe my ears. Dr. Goebbels was still screaming victory while the Russians had already passed our East Prussian border. Father was right; Goebbels was a liar. Mrs. Gander would have been wiser not to listen to the news. It was totally distorted; it was untrue.

Thank God, we had finished our packing. Our problem was to decide what to do with our animals. Before leaving, Father had sold the larger ones—the sheep and the pigs. We still had over a dozen chickens and one big, white goose. Mother would have liked to cook the goose to provide some food for us on our way, but Father was not home.

"But whom can I ask? Who of our neighbors would volunteer to kill the goose in this chaos?" she fretted.

Quietly I battled with myself. I loved the goose; it was such a pure white, beautiful animal. When it came home at a day's end from a swim in the pond, it usually tilted its head, looking up at the kitchen window as if to say: "I'm fine; how are you?" How could I kill this sweet thing? But someone had to do it. With shaking knees, I told Mother I would volunteer to do the job, begging her to keep her fingers crossed so that I would do it right. Some time ago I had watched Father kill a duck.

"The animal has to be knocked unconscious with one strong blow," he had explained. This blow would prevent the animal from feeling the pain. Then the main artery had to be cut quickly with a sharp knife so the animal would bleed fast and die before regaining consciousness.

So, heavy-hearted, I set out to catch the goose. Knowing me, she tamely sat down, tilting her wings upward so I could grab her. Equipped with a heavy piece of wood and a sharp kitchen knife, I had gone behind the animal stable. Chasing Frederick away, I demanded to be left alone in order to concentrate and not cause the goose unnecessary suffering. Taking a deep breath, I knocked the animal in the head. It swayed, so I had done the job right. Quickly I cut the main artery at the side of her head. As I held her tightly between my knees, it was not easy to get her in a new position to grab her two feet and then hold her up, head down, to let the blood run out quickly. The poor thing jerked a few times and I had trouble holding her tight. But within a few minutes, the goose was still. My stomach started to turn, but I swallowed hard and wiped away a tear with my sleeve. After covering the blood on the compost heap, I silently handed the knife and the goose to Mother. While she was busy plucking and cleaning it, I went off to the pond and sat on a stump. I prayed that I would never again have to kill an animal.

In the evening Ursula had arrived at a solution to the problem about the chickens.

"I will run over to Aunt Maria and ask if she would agree to feed them; then, one by one, she could use them until they are all killed," she said and Mother liked the idea. Aunt Maria gladly agreed to do Mother this favor. So everything was settled as well as we could. Ursula was expected to stay on the job until the last minute. The industry had strict orders to keep operating as long as possible. This fact made Mother nervous and, to ease her mind, Ursula agreed to evacuate with us. Some days later she could return to Gumbinnen if her boss insisted on it.

Although the sirens had sounded several alerts during the day, no bombs fell. In the evening we quietly sat down for supper and had some of the cooked goose. No one really enjoyed the meal. The remainder could be wrapped quickly and taken along.

Morning came fast and we got up early to be ready in time for the pick-up. The sun was out, promising a beautiful day, but nobody noticed. One by one we carried our bundles out of the house, piling them up at the entrance gate. Frederick had posted himself in the middle of the street to keep watch so we would not miss the wagon. The rest of the linens, the furniture, the lamps, and all other household items had to stay behind.

"They have already started the pick-up at the lower end of the street," Frederick announced, judging by the commotion he could see. Peering down the street, I saw several farm wagons which evidently had been drafted from farms close by for the purpose of evacuation. One family after another passed our house on their way to the train. Word spread that we would not be taken to the station in the city but instead would board a train parked on a track close to Annahof, a track that was used to ship industrial loads. We were given the explanation later that here, at the western part of town, we ran less risk of being bombed or attacked by the guns of low-flying Russian fighter planes.

"I am glad that you decided to pack the baby carriage," Mother mentioned to Herta. We were permitted to take it because, with four wheels, it was mobile. Also, Andreas was only four years old and would tire easily. With the duffle bag tied on top, it looked like a gypsy load, but the carriage was a practical device and this was all that counted. Very soon we realized how quickly our arms tired from carrying our bundles.

Ursula had given Aunt Maria a spare key to our house, but Mother decided it would be more practicable to leave the stable unlocked. "What difference does it make if someone helped himself to what is left behind," she commented, "because the Russians will arrive sooner or later and confiscate everything."

After locking the front door, Mother counted the heads of her children. Assured that no one was missing, we waited for our turn of the pick-up. Mrs. Gander and her six children were already on the wagon moving toward us and we were ordered to squeeze on behind them. The soldier who was in charge of our evacuation helped Mother on the wagon, handing her the baby carriage and Andreas. Then the rest of us, one by one, climbed on. We had to lean hard against the sides to gain a secure foothold because the harvest wagon on wooden wheels would rattle and sway considerably once it started to move. Our family was on and we were moving, though painfully slow. But now I was certain we would get out of this dilemma, out of Gumbinnen before the Russians over-ran our town.

Between Annahof and Fichtenwalde, we boarded a long passenger train on an open track. It had been pulled out of the station in the city to make our evacuation inconspicuous. Soldiers helped us handing us our bundles, the baby carriage, and to climb on, speeding up the operation. Each large family was assigned one open compartment. On one side of us was the Gander family and on the other the Barocks.

Ursula, Herta, and I arranged our baggage. Having seated Mother and Andreas as comfortably as possible, I glanced out the window. In the distance I saw our street, the last one in town, and I recognized our house by the red front door, matching the red roof. A thought entered my mind: "Would I ever see our house again?"

But the huge locomotive puffing past me diverted my attention. Looking out to the side, I was amazed at the length of the train. It seemed endless. By now, the last car was filled and soon a short jerk indicated that the locomotive had been attached. Anxious to move on, I wondered how long it would take. In this commotion, no one had noticed how fast the time had gone. Mother checked the small alarm clock she had taken along and it was almost noon. Suddenly we felt another jerk and, almost unnoticeably, the train was rolling. As Mrs. Barock realized this, she started to cry hysterically.

"Our street, our house; we may never see them again," she sobbed, leaning against her husband's shoulder. Mother, watching his helpless attempts to console her, dabbed her eyes with a handkerchief. It was a sad scene. I assured Mother it was better to be alive and safe then to stay home and run the risk of deportation to Siberia. Herta was glad Mother did not lose her composure and Ursula very attentively kept Mother's mind occupied.

"I hope Father will remember Aunt Erna's address in Hamburg. I hope he will write to her and inquire as to our whereabouts," Mother said. She had sped a letter off to him, notifying him of our decision to evacuate. "Will he receive the letter?" she worried.

Although the train rolled very slowly, within a few minutes our hometown, Gumbinnen, had shrunk in the east and then disappeared behind ripe wheat fields. Even searching, I did not detect sadness in my heart. Instead, I thanked God for having taken us away safely and before the Russians occupied our city.

* * * * * *

Once Gumbinnen was out of sight and Mrs. Barock had dried her tears, she inquired about our destination. No one knew. We did not even know whether the army or civilian members of the party were in charge of our evacuation. Later in the day, however, we heard that the commander of the train had received orders to discharge his load in the southern part of East Prussia. After having spent close to five hours on the slow moving train, we pulled into a small station and were ordered to disembark. Rothfliess—no one had ever heard of this place. As we had not remembered to bring a map, we did not know how far we had travelled.

Farmers from the area who had received orders to shelter one family each crowded around the station. We were assigned to the Behrend farm in Lautern and Mr. Behrend, a stocky man with dark hair and a thick mustache, introduced himself to Mother. Although his square face looked forbidding, in his awkward manner, he tried to be helpful. While assisting Mother to climb on the harvest wagon, he explained that he did not have room for all of us but that Ursula and Herta were welcome to stay with his neighbor. Having securely loaded everything on his wagon, including the bulky baby carriage, we climbed on.

"What a shame this trouble had to happen to our country," he said, trying to make conversation with Mother and, with a firm "hue-hott," ordered his horses to go. Obediently they pulled away from the cobble-stoned area before the station.

According to my estimation, we were by far not out of danger. In this rural part of East Prussia, the Russians could still over-run us. For the moment, however, we were safe. It was getting dark and, as we slowly rattled along dirt roads, we passed shrines of the madonna or saints. We were entering Catholic territory, an area totally unfamiliar to us. Finally our rumbly ride ended as Mr. Behrend halted his horses before a big house on a very large farm. Jumping off quickly, we helped Mother to get down. While Mr. Behrend unloaded our baggage, a tall lady dressed in black appeared in the doorway. He introduced her as Mrs. Behrend, his wife, and I realized that her thin "hello" neither sounded warm nor friendly.

They had been ordered to shelter us; therefore, we literally imposed on their privacy. We had never had such an experience before, but Mother amazed me by stepping forward, warmly extending her hand to the woman.

Mrs. Behrend took it, apologizing that she had prepared only one big room, the only one she could spare, but we were welcome to live in it. Following Mrs. Behrend up the creaky, wooden stairs, I was glad to have a roof over my head. Like the farm house, the room looked old with its hand-hewn beams against the ceiling and had only a minimum of furniture. It consisted of two big beds and a small cot, a portable old-fashioned clothes closet, a wood-burning stove, a table, and an assortment of old chairs. As if reading

Mother's mind, Mrs. Behrend confirmed what her husband had told us before.

"The two older girls are welcome to sleep at our neighbors, the Seefelds," she said and turned around to introduce the three girls who peeked into the room. Emma and Theresa, the two younger girls were her own daughters, but Gertrud Seefeld, the neighbor's daughter, had come over to help Herta and Ursula carry their baggage. Gertrud appeared to be Herta's age and her honest smile assured Mother that her two older girls would be in good hands.

When the three had departed and Mrs. Behrend had excused herself, Mother sat down and took a deep breath. She looked tired. Realizing we had not eaten all day, I unwrapped the cold goose. I found some dishes in the closet and went downstairs to pump water. It felt good to shed my triple layer of outer clothing and wash my hands and face. For the first time during the day I was hungry. So were Frederick, Maria, and Andreas. We ate heartily and then went to bed, dead tired. The straw mattresses felt like sleeping in heaven. Mother slept with Andreas, Maria with me, and Frederick on the cot. God had provided for us even now.

The next morning Ursula and Herta came over early. They had enthusiastic reports for Mother.

"The Seefelds are a friendly and understanding couple, glad to have us," Herta said. Besides Gertrud, they had a younger daughter, very frail but a lively girl. Ursula told us that the Seefeld farm was much larger than Behrend's.

"They also own two important conveniences—a radio and a telephone," she added, happy about this surprise. Mrs. Seefeld had offered to let Ursula call her boss in Gumbinnen. Evidently the Russians had been beaten back over night and her boss told her that business in town went on as usual. Conscientious as she was, Ursula assured him that she would report back to work shortly. Mother worried, but Ursula promised to join us in Lautern once the situation at home grew critical. Reluctantly, Mother allowed Ursula to return to Gumbinnen. Gertrud Seefeld gave her a ride to the station by horse and buggy and Herta happily accompanied the two.

Mother had scraped together a meager breakfast of bread and butter and, as soon as Frederick's hungry stomach was filled, he set out on an investigation of the farm. From the window he had seen several horses and a young boy. He was going to take a closer look. Mother knew it was also time to replenish our dwindling food supply. The clatter of dishes from downstairs told us that Mrs. Behrend was up. She gave us directions to the village, reminding

Mother to register with the village authorities so we would receive our food stamps. Having promised our three neighbors to keep in close contact, Mother was curious where the Ganders and the Barocks were located. Andreas went with her. Maria and I promised to wait until she returned, after which we planned to visit Herta at the Seefeld farm. From the window Maria had watched the two Behrend girls disappear into a stable with pails.

"I bet they are going to milk the cows," she said. "I would like to look around a bit." As if Mrs. Behrend had heard her wish, she knocked at the door and invited us to roam around the farm. Maria smiled happily and joined Frederick who introduced her to Ewald, the Behrend's young son. It had taken Frederick only a short while to realize that Ewald was an expert rider and he had asked Ewald if he would teach him to ride a horse. It looked so easy, so natural. Ewald led his shining, brown stallion to the stable wall and from a ledge swung himself on to the animal, without saddle, without reins, holding only to the stallion's long mane. Frederick was fascinated; he was determined to learn to ride. Meantime, Emma and Theresa had come out of the stable, carrying two pails of fresh milk. Maria's curious eyes persuaded Theresa, the younger one, to show her the cows.

"I counted more than twenty," she enthusiastically reported later, "and three small calves are in the stable." When Mother and Andreas returned from the village, it was past noontime. They brought back good news. At the registration office, Mother had met Mrs. Bohn who informed her at which farm the Ganders and the Barocks were located. Mother's bulging shopping bag confirmed Frederick's hope; she had bought food. He was hungry and begged Mother to prepare a fast lunch.

Upstairs, Mother whisperingly reported that the village was totally Catholic and had only one church. From Mrs. Bohn she learned that Protestants were officially forbidden to enter. This news meant that here in Lautern our family could not attend Sunday Service.

"I'm glad Father does not know this. He would be very unhappy," Mother stated. She had counted many private shrines on her way, assuming that Catholics were devout people; at least, this was her impression. We had to live there and try to understand them.

"The registrar called us "Fluechtlinge," refugees," Mother announced, and I squirmed at this label. Nevertheless, it was true. We had fled from Gumbinnen, fled from the approaching Russians. Although true, I did not like the word. It had a degrading connotation to it, implying that we were second or third grade citizens.

Frederick, bursting into the kitchen to check the lunch situation, focused my mind on immediate matters. At least we had a chair for everybody. When Mother took over Father's function to say grace, I realized we had many reasons to be grateful: we were alive and we were safe.

Maria and I hurriedly washed the dishes and then walked over to the Seefeld farm. Their yard alone we estimated to be over two acres in size. Maria pointed to the big, white dog tearing at his chain, announcing us. "He is huge!" she said.

"It is a Saint Bernard," I explained to her as we got closer. It was a beautiful animal, the size of a calf. Herta and Gertrud had heard the dog and came out to greet us. They had seen Ursula off earlier. Taking us into the house, Gertrud introduced her mother, Mrs. Seefeld, a quiet lady. She smiled easily and her manners and movements put an air of dignity about her. A lanky young girl, about eight, walked into the kitchen.

"This is my little sister. The men are out working in the fields," Gertrud explained. Showing us the room she shared with Herta, I understood why Herta was happy here. The room was large and sunny and, although old, decorated in cheerful colors and polished, expensive furniture. While Gertrud was giving us a quick tour of the house, I guessed it to be double the size of the Behrends. One corner of the living room was arranged as a private altar, as a costly statue of the Madonna indicated, and I was glad Maria did not make remarks or ask curious questions. She contained herself until we were on our way back.

"Did you see the statue of the Lady? Who is she?" she wanted to know. All my religious ingenuity was required to make the Holy Mother concept plausible to her. Maria tried hard to understand.

Meeting Mother and Andreas who were out for a stroll around the Behrend farm, we exchanged notes about our impressions. Mrs. Behrend had offered to sell Mother milk daily and eggs as we needed them. This was important news because we now realized how much food our garden and animal stable at home had rendered. Mother also appreciated the fact that the Seefelds had a radio and Herta could keep us informed about the latest developments at the eastern front. The heart of the village where we could buy a newspaper was more than two kilometers away.

Returning to the farm, we saw Ewald and Frederick on horses. Mother worried about Frederick but he, although still sitting stiffly in the saddle, waved at her. Mother could not share his enthusiasm in learning to ride. "It looks too dangerous," she said.

"I'm going to ride without a saddle later," Frederick proudly announced as he dismounted, "then we can gallop like Indians across the prairie." He brushed aside Mother's well meant advice to be careful by changing the subject and making his famous announcement that he was hungry.

As I helped Mother prepare vegetables for a soup, she wondered how long it would be until we could return to Gumbinnen. The potatoes in our garden would soon need to be forked out and the rest of the vegetables would go to waste. We missed Father's homemade bread. Would we have to go hungry living on a farm?

* * * * * *

A few days later, Mother received a letter from Ursula. She had arrived in Gumbinnen without difficulty and found our house in order. In the mailbox was a letter from Father informing us that he was stationed in Italy. Behind the fighting front, he worked as a baker in the food division. Ursula had rushed off a reply telling him of our evacuation to Lautern and giving him the address of our new location. The city looked eerie, she added, after more than half the population had left. She slept at Aunt Maria's house, checking our own after work.

"I'm so glad that Father is not in Russia," Mother breathed a sigh of relief and, for the first time, she ate heartily. Herta visited us after dinner, mentioning that the next weeks would bring hard work as the Seefelds were beginning with the harvest. Behrends had a long standing agreement with the Seefelds to join efforts and share the machinery and manpower. To fill in for the farmhands now fighting at the front, prisoners were working at the farm. Behrends had two Russians and the Seefelds had several Russians and Poles, including a Polish maid.

Theresa had told Maria about the background of their two prisoners. The older one, a quiet and fair-haired man, was from White Russia, a very devout man whom they very often found praying. Anton, the younger one, however, came from the Caucasus.

"He is a Cossack and has a violent temper," Theresa said, pointing him out with a glance of her eyes as he crossed the yard. His coarse, unruly black hair and thick mustache added to his forbidding appearance. We decided to stay away from Anton because Theresa stated that even her quiet, strong-minded father had difficulty handling him. Even the two Russians didn't seem to get along.

"Especially when harvest time comes around, Anton gets balky. He resents the hard work," Theresa added. Hearing this news, Mother cautioned Frederick about Anton, suggesting that he avoid him and never provoke him to anger.

Within a few days the threshing was under way and the machines howled from morning until dark, spitting out clean, dust-free grains into sacks on one side and bales of yellow straw on the other. Herta and Gertrud helped at Behrends and then the machinery and manpower moved to Seefelds to do their threshing. The two girls were glad when the hot and dusty job was done. Herta looked sunburnt and well. Country life, although hard, seemed to agree with her.

Maria, however, had been complaining about a pain in her upper leg, which Mother had brushed aside for a while.

"Most likely it is a muscle strain. We are not used to walking up and down such sloping terrain," she said. Nevertheless, Maria continued to complain until one day Mother took time to investigate her leg. To her horror, she detected a large, red swelling on Maria's inner leg and, touching her, she realized that she was running a fever. Alarmed about it, Mother asked Theresa where she could locate a doctor but learned in disbelief that the village of Lautern did not have one.

"Here, the nuns from the convent are rendering medical services," Theresa explained and volunteered to summon one to Maria's bedside. By now she was unable to walk.

Only an hour later, Theresa arrived with Sister Benedictine. Maria, visibly frightened by the long, black habit, started to cry. But the nun casually sat down on the corner of her bed, talking softly to her. Within minutes, she persuaded Maria to show her the troublesome leg. Diagnosing it as a severe glandular infection, she gave her medication to bring down the fever. She would be back in two days and if by then the pus-filled head had not broken, she would have to cut it. After instructing Mother how to change the black ointment twice daily, she left.

"I don't want to be cut," Maria cried after the nun had left, and we understood her fear. Theresa came to see her after dinner and, hearing of her young friend's predicament, made a suggestion.

"It might sound ancient or superstitious," she said, "but I know that cabbage leaves draw out infections. It's an old home remedy." Maria was anxious to try it and Theresa soon returned with a big, freshly washed leaf and put it over the black ointment application. Mother had to tape it down with many sizeable bandaids because Maria, suffering great pain, threw herself around in bed, restless, unable to sleep. To keep the room as quiet as possible, I took Andreas for a walk to the Seefeld farm. Frederick was roaming around on horseback with Ewald somewhere in the fields. Mother stayed at Maria's bedside, cooling her feverish head with a damp cloth.

Toward evening as we entered the room, Mother motioned us to be quiet. Maria had finally fallen asleep. We prepared dinner and, to avoid making any noise, talked in a whisper. Suddenly, Frederick clamored up the stairs, throwing the door open, asking if dinner was ready. He wakened Maria. Mother was ready to slap Frederick, but Maria told her that her leg felt wet.

"I think the boil broke," she said to Mother, anxious to have it confirmed. It had and Mother called down for Theresa to tell her the good news.

"The good old household remedy—it works," announced Theresa triumphantly, glad to know that Maria's suffering was over. When Sister Benedictine returned the next day, the ugly redness and swelling had receded and she assuringly patted Maria's head.

"Brave little soldier," she said, but Maria did not tell her about her secret, the cabbage leaf, only giving her a wistful smile. The fever was gone; she felt better.

* * * * * *

Late in the evening, Herta dropped in to tell us that Ursula had called. She reported that the city had been quiet and that the front had come to a standstill. She had forked out all the potatoes in our garden. The leased patch behind the pond, however, she could not handle. It was too much work. While I was getting bored, having no school to attend, no work to do, I suggested to Mother that I take a train to Gumbinnen and bring in the last crops and would fork out the potatoes behind the pond. Not used to the idea of letting anything go to waste, Mother accepted my offer.

When Mrs. Bohn visited us the next day and heard of my plan, she promised to walk with me to the station of Rothfliess. I did not have much to pack, but Mother prepared a long list of items she needed. We did not have enough pots; she needed more cutlery; but, most of all, she needed the food we had stored in the cellar, especially the chickens and meat Mother had lined up in glass jars.

Early the next morning, with dew still on the ground, Mrs. Bohn arrived and we walked the long stretch to the station.

Equipped with Mother's long list and her suggestion to be cautious, I left, enjoying Mrs. Bohn's cheerful company.

"Stop running. I have difficulty keeping up with your pace," she kiddingly told me. She felt tired lately and I recalled that only a year ago she had lost her oldest son, Martin, in whom she had placed all her hopes.

"If Martin could be here, it would not be so difficult," she said as if reading my mind. Her husband, a notorious drinker, had been drafted recently. Now she was in Lautern with her two younger boys. Trying to steer her mind toward a lighter subject, I asked in jest if she had brought enough money and a big bag to do some fancy shopping in Rothfliess. We both laughed, knowing that it was only a large village with a few empty stores.

We arrived at the station and, luckily, I had to wait only a few minutes. As the train moved out, Mrs. Bohn waved goodbye, sending along her regards to our street, the Beethovenstrasse, and I promised to extend them. Glancing out the window as the countryside zipped by, I wondered whether the farmers outside were bringing in the crops for their own use, or for the Russians. Viewing the peaceful scenery, it was difficult to believe that our country was at war. But Father was in Italy. This was stark proof of the fact. The thought never occurred to me that Father might never return home. We needed him; Mother relied on him. He had to come home.

After several hours of travelling, having changed trains in Insterburg, my thoughts took a jump as I recognized the outskirts of Fichtenwalde. Seeing the so familiar barrier drawn at the railroad crossing, I felt as if I were returning from a long dream. Lautern, did it exist? Within minutes, the train stopped at our station in Gumbinnen and I jumped off. The city had not changed; it had not been bombed. Carrying my light, almost empty bag, I walked to Ursula's office where she had instructed me to meet her. After introducing me to her colleagues, she excused herself for leaving a few minutes early, and we took off. On our way home, she told me sad news.

"Uncle Richard died. He was hit by a splinter of a bomb dropped by a single Russian plane one night when he worked his shift. It happened just before he was ready to go home," she said and added that since then Aunt Maria has grown very quiet.

"Lately I have avoided walking along the tracks and do not take the 'Black Road' home," Ursula explained.

Railroad tracks had lately been targets for Russian planes and she did not want to risk being near them in case of a surprise bombing attack. The war was still on, I realized, and the Russians not too far away. Passing the machine factory, we crossed the railroad at that point and walked the long way through Annahof to get home. Stopping at Aunt Maria's house, we found her dressed in black. She was glad to have company and we promised to be back after supper.

It seemed strange to enter our house. Everything was standing in the same place, yet it seemed empty. Our family was missing. As Ursula had pointed out earlier, very few families had stayed at home. Annahof looked deserted. While we prepared dinner, Ursula cautioned me not to venture far from the house during the day. Not that I would have had the time for it, but I assured her I was not afraid to be here alone. To be afraid in our own house was a ridiculous thought anyway. Ursula was the conscientious one in our family; she never took chances. After dinner we walked to Aunt Maria's house. She mentioned that it was a good feeling to have life in the house again.

"Waltraud urges me to move to Hamburg and stay with her," she added, but she was waiting for Erwin's ideas before making a decision. Since Uncle Richard's death, she relied heavily on Erwin, her son.

Aunt Maria and Ursula had developed the habit of going to bed early because once or twice a night the howling sirens would waken them. I had just made myself comfortable in the bed next to Ursula's when the sirens sounded. Throwing a coat over our night clothes, the three of us scrambled down the cellar stairs. Half an hour later, the alert was over. The rest of the night passed quickly and undisturbed.

As Ursula left for work in the morning, I walked home. Pulling our handwagon and a fork out from the shed, I set out for our leased patch behind the pond. It was approximately half an acre, but I was determined to fork out all potatoes. Father would be proud of me; nothing would be wasted. During the afternoon the sun grew hot and, having brought home five wagonloads of potatoes, my back ached. One more basketful had to be carried down to the cellar, then my day's job would be done. Straightening my back, I recognized a boy walking toward our house. It was Manfred Schukat. He was glad to see me.

"I noticed somebody at your house, so I came over to check," he explained. As most people had left, it was not safe in our neighborhood any more. He had seen prowlers. Watching me with the basketful of potatoes, he asked if I had returned home to do this job. I agreed. Although he thought it to be wasted effort, believing that Russians would eat our potatoes, he promised to round up another volunteer and help me with the job.

129

For the next week, Manfred and his younger brother joined me in my project. I did the digging and the two boys carted the potatoes home, carrying the heavy baskets down to the cellar. To show my appreciation, I offered them vegetables and meat in glass jars. It saved Mrs. Schukat the cooking. Ursula had also taken many jars to Aunt Maria.

When my job was done and the last basket of potatoes was in the cellar, filling the bin to the brim, I looked forward to spending a few days around the house, nursing my aching back and relaxing. As the boys knew I was the only resident on the upper end of the Beethovenstrasse, they paid me a daily visit to check that I was all right.

"So far, Gumbinnen has not had a severe bombing," Manfred mentioned one late afternoon. "We have been lucky." I agreed with him and enjoyed the warm sun as I sat on my favorite stone, our property marker. In the midst of our conversation, a fast approaching roar cut through the stillness. In a second it shot over our heads, over the pond. We were speechless—it was a Russian fighter plane zipping past as low as tree-top level. The two boys, recognizing the red hammer-and-sickle emblem, threw themselves on the ground. I was dumbfounded, watching the plane cut a fast curve behind the pond and, as quickly as it had approached, disappear, crossing the southern end of the street, toward the direction of the city.

"Did you see the pilot and the machine gun pointing downward from the cockpit?" Manfred shouted, brushing the dirt off his shorts. I had, and drew a deep breath to recover from the shock. Fifteen minutes later, the siren sounded an alert; by then it was all over.

Ursula came home earlier than usual and insisted that I pack and leave the next morning. She had heard the lowflying plane, evidently a spy, and realized that the situation was growing dangerous. Quickly we filled Mother's list, testing the weight of my heavy bags, but still adding one item after another—pots, silverware, chicken in glass jars. The bag with a sizable piece of smoked ham alone seemed to weigh a ton.

"I will carry it, even if I have to drag it behind me," I joked while we were on our way to Aunt Maria.

After another interrupted night, we got up early and Ursula accompanied me to the station, carrying the extra bag. I urged her to persuade Aunt Maria to leave. Waving Ursula goodbye, I made her promise to join us in time in Lautern. She agreed.

It was October 16, 1944, when I returned to Lautern after spending more than two weeks in Gumbinnen. Ursula had telephoned Herta announcing my arrival at the Rothfliess station. When I got off the train, lugging my heavy baggage, I saw Herta and Gertrud. They had come to pick me up. Telling them about my adventure, Gertrud asked why Ursula still had to stay in Gumbinnen and work. Herta criticized the city authorities for keeping civilians on the job until the very last minute, endangering their lives. Mother was glad to see me, but worried about Ursula. "Why didn't she come along?" she asked, and then investigated the contents of the bags.

"Oh, the chicken! The ham! Wonderful! Now I have the stock for our soups," she exclaimed with delight. Frederick was anxious to cut and taste a piece of ham.

When I sat down to relax, Mother told me that Mrs. Bohn had died. I was shocked. Only a few weeks ago she had walked to the station with me. Asking about the cause of her death, Mother told me that, no matter what the doctor's opinion was, she was convinced that Mrs. Bohn had died of a broken heart. Losing Martin, her son, her only hope, had broken her spirit. It was sad and Mother continued, saying that after the funeral, the two boys had been taken to a distant relative.

It was getting late as we had talked for a long while. Mother and I walked downstairs with Herta, Gertrud having driven home ahead of her. Taking a deep breath of the balmy summer air, I noticed a pink hue on the horizon in a northeasterly direction and mentioned it to Herta. We looked at each other knowingly, then listened intently, holding our breath.

"Can you hear the distant rumble?" Herta asked with foreboding in her voice. Yes, I did and we hated to explain to Mother what this meant. Gumbinnen was either being severely bombed or under heavy artillery fire! Ursula was still there! Mother panicked.

"Why didn't she come with you?" she wailed. But nothing was gained in worrying. Herta dashed off to the Seefeld farm.

"I will listen to the latest news over the radio, maybe it is not Gumbinnen," her voice trailed off as she ran toward Seefelds. But it was! She came over very late to confirm the stark fact. Then she ran back to stay glued to the radio. The uncertainty had kept us up. Only Frederick, Maria, and Andreas had gone to bed. Mother and I sat on a bench in the yard, listening to the rumble. While I was staring, I was praying. God could not, must not let Ursula die in this fire, I pleaded.

Herta had promised to return. Where was she? More than an hour later, we heard someone running toward the farm again. It was Herta. We recognized her as she came closer. Calling her, she shouted back to us: "Ursula is safe!"

"She called from Insterburg. She will take the next night train to Rothfliess," she puffed, totally out of breath. Quickly we threw on a sweater to be protected against the night chill and the three of us walked the long, dark road to Rothfliess. It was in the early morning hours when Ursula climbed off the train. Her face smudged, her hair unkempt, she was still in a state of panic, having trouble collecting her thoughts to reconstruct what had happened. In fragments she told us the story.

On October 16, a few minutes before 6:00 p.m. while she was clearing her desk at the office, she heard planes overhead and, immediately thereafter, bombs started falling, some very close. The office staff dashed for the bunker, located in the yard. The lumber yard was heavily packed with wood supplies. While one by one they filed into the bunker, the sirens howled a late alert. They held their breath sitting along the walls of the dangerously swaying bunker while bombs were falling closely around them. This bombing attack lasted until 7:30 p.m.

As one of the men cautiously opened the door, he shouted that the wood in the yard was on fire, blocking them in from every side. They had to act immediately if they did not want to burn to death. Fortunately, blankets and water were part of the bunker equipment. Her colleague ordered each one to soak a blanket, throw it around himself, covering his head, and run through the flames. Heading for the office building was their only way out.

"The smoke choking us was worse than the searing flames," Ursula cried, recalling her horrible experience. Miraculously, everyone had made it through alive. Assembling and recounting his terrified staff, her boss ordered each one to dash home as fast as possible. It was getting dark and the streets were cluttered with rubble from collapsed houses with smoldering debris. At least the bombing had stopped and Ursula thanked God for having shipped me off to Lautern in the morning. She realized that Mother, hearing about the bombing attack, would be sick with worry. Not having to be concerned about me, Ursula hitchhiked her way out of the city to Insterburg. No trains were running out of Gumbinnen. Carrying only her handbag, she had called Herta at Seefelds from the station. She had transferred to the first train heading in a southerly direction to get to us.

"Thank God!" said Mother, and we knew it came from the depth of her heart. Washing the smoke and dust smudges from her face and combing her singed hair, Ursula finally calmed down. Herta took her to the Seefeld farm as the sun was about to rise. Falling into bed, I thanked God for His help and protection. One phrase from the Bible crossed my mind: . . . and no one shall pluck them out of My hands.

The next day Ursula evaluated her situation. She knew that Mother would not permit her to return to Gumbinnen, although she had telephoned her boss and learned that the work force had so far not received official permission to evacuate. She had brought no clothes other than what she wore. Our hometown had been destroyed; at least the center was a heap of rubble. During the latest newscast, it was officially admitted that the Russian armies had launched another major offensive. By October 20, they had reached the eastern suburbs of Gumbinnen and were only eight kilometers away from the center of the city. The remainder of the population evacuated the same day as the rumble of the front moved frighteningly close. Many people, not relying on promised transportation, had walked westward, carrying only the barest necessities. The roads, choked with slow moving horse and wagon traffic, proved useless. A great number of our Gumbinnen people were over-run by the Russians at Nemmersdorf the same day. This village, a southern suburb of Gumbinnen, had seemed to be a possible escape route. To their horror, they encountered Russian tanks which had spearheaded south of the city and many of our friends lost their lives in a bloody massacre.

Many years later, Uncle Gustav, who had been on this trek, gave us his eyewitness account of the barbarous murders that had taken place at Nemmersdorf.

Having never been able to escape the claws of Bolshevism, despite his numerous attempts, Uncle Gustav had spent his life in East Germany. When he had reached retirement age, the prerequisite to obtain a visitor's visa to West Germany, he had visited our family and gave us his report about Nemmersdorf.

The trek, moving at a crawling pace southwestward, was of people leaving Gumbinnen. Uncle Gustav, having hurriedly loaded one of his coal delivery trucks with belongings, was one of them. Keeping an eye backward, he had spotted several Russian tanks advance across a field from the rear. In his panic, he abandoned his horses and the truck and rushed for the woods ahead across a field. He climbed into a tree and from his hiding place he saw to his horror that the tanks passed slowly along the trek and fired into it with their guns, mowing down everything that moved. Then they jumped out of the tanks and, with bayonets mounted on their guns, plundered the wagons. The daughter of the farmer, Didt, was on the trek and being pregnant had been hiding in their wagon. When Uncle Gustav saw her crawl out, evidently still unhurt, one Russian soldier, using the handle of his rifle as a club, slew down on her protruding stomach until she collapsed and died. Then the Russian pulled the fur coat off her body and stormed forward to grab more things from among the dead. Uncle Gustav was frozen in terror at the sight of such cruel murder. Not one civilian of the entire trek walked away—every one had been killed.

Under the cover of darkness, Uncle Gustav had fled back on foot to Gumbinnen, where several months later he was taken prisoner by the Russians. Immediately he was put on a work force and his ability to maneuver a truck gave him a certain advantage. For several months he was shuttling Germans, the few civilians who had faithfully stayed at home, believing the Russians would not harm them, to and from work camp. The Russian military had occupied the former German barracks in Fichtenwalde and usually did not venture out.

On one of these trips, Uncle Gustav took the liberty and walked up to our house on the Beethovenstrasse. As he opened the front door he was confronted by a Russian woman, a woman with typical Mongolian features, who was very much affronted by Uncle Gustav's intrusion. Yet he, bold in his nature, told the woman that this house belonged to his sister and, to prove his point, he urged the Russian woman to follow him outside and read the name plate at the door; it still read: SCHMELING in simple black letters on an oval white plate.

Having taken one glance around the kitchen, he noticed that the woman was using the kitchen furniture as firing wood; one broken chair lay in the middle of the room. The house was in disarray. But seeing the Russian woman get angry and nervous, Uncle Gustav left.

Although he had decided to live the rest of his life in Gumbinnen, even under Russian occupation, Uncle Gustav, with the remainder of the German populace, was transported to East Germany. The Russians considered the northern portion of East Prussia their own territory and as a result every German civilian was deported, every trace of the German language, street and store signs, removed and substituted with Russian names.

Uncle Gustav continued his story that he had tried to escape from East to West Germany several times, but each time he was caught. The Russians, accusing him of spying, locked him in a basement filled to his waist with water. They calculated on his hope to escape this punishment, and wanted Uncle Gustav to sign certain false statements. When this method did not work, he was put into a tiny cell, in which he could only stand upright, and every few seconds a drop of cold water would fall on his head. "It can drive a man insane!" he recalled.

But Uncle Gustav was stubborn, having nothing but his life to lose, he would not sign any untrue statement, and again he was released.

After his final attempt to escape, he was sentenced to ten years of hard labor in a uranium mine in Sachsen. He told us how he, together with other German prisoners, had to mine the dangerous ore with his bare hands, often lying flat on his stomach or in a kneeling position under ground. When he developed big ugly sores over both of his arms that would not heal from the exposure to raw uranium, he was transferred and assigned the job as a bricklayer. After many years of laboring "in darkness and hell," to use his own words, Uncle Gustav appreciated seeing daylight.

Although his sentence was shortened and Uncle Gustav lived and worked as a "free man" and later remarried in East Germany, he could not forgive the Russians for the cruelties they had made him suffer. Anyone who knocked at his door to solicit for funds to promote friendship between Russians and Germans was turned away with Uncle Gustav's detailed explanation for his reason.

"Anyone who forces me to stand in ice cold water, anyone who convicts me to dig uranium with my bare hands is not my friend," he recalled telling them bluntly.

What disturbed Mother most after her brother and his new wife had returned to East Germany was the fact that Uncle Gustav had shrunk in size at least five inches. Knowing him as her adult brother, Mother recalled that he had always been taller than she, but now he was several inches shorter than she.

"Could the overexposure to raw uranium have shrunk his entire bone structure?" she asked, shuddering at this incredible fact.

From Uncle Gustav's sad experiences we had learned even in retrospect after more than twenty years that we had thousands of reasons to be grateful. We had evacuated from Gumbinnen in time. We had been taken to Lautern as our first step. And we were safe.

But in late October of 1944 we neither knew whether Uncle Gustav was alive nor where he could possibly be, but, so far, we were safe and indeed grateful that Ursula had joined us in Lautern, unharmed.

Miraculously, the remaining handful of our army was able to halt the Russian advance by October 21 and throw the enemy back to the East Prussian border. This position remained almost stationary until January 10, 1945.

While everyone's attention was focused eastward, suddenly in November came the news that heavy Soviet troop movements were assembled south of East Prussia. It was assumed that the Russians had intended to cut off the entire province of East Prussia in another offensive from the south. It was time to pack. It was time for us to move on.

Chapter IX.

Flight From the Beast—Step Two

The news of Russian troops advancing from the south put my mind on the alert. Again, I started packing the little bit we had.

Although Ursula, being part of the work force, had been unable to return to Gumbinnen, she was assigned a different office job in the city of Roessel located a few kilometers north of the village Lautern. Mother kept in close contact with the Barocks, the Ganders, and Mrs. Adomeit. They had passed on the rumor circulating in the village that we might be evacuated within days. During the last two weeks even Mrs. Behrend's cool and reserved attitude had changed. Her usual aloofness vanished and, instead, she looked worried, standing in the doorway.

"If we leave here, where could we go?" she questioned Mother who mentioned that we were ready to move on. Mrs. Behrend, like so many others, including Father, believed that the farm was their property by right; therefore, no one could take it from them. She could not comprehend that these civil laws changed once a country was in a state of war. The Russians, we were certain, would not only confiscate their property and possessions but would take their lives or deport them to Siberia.

"Mother, I will leave even if you insist on staying here," declared Theresa, Mrs. Behrend's youngest daughter, determinedly because Herta and I had told her the wounded soldier's story I had heard in the military hospital in Gumbinnen. Emma, her older sister, had decided to leave with her. Herta had also persuaded Gertrud Seefeld to evacuate with her once the official notice released the work force.

The strict order that those girls who were old enough and able to work had to stay until the last minute upset Mother. She wished that Herta and Ursula could leave with us. The two, however, assured her they would keep in close telephone contact and evacuate together once the situation grew dangerous.

We would not have to wait much longer because I could feel the rising tension in the air. Anton, the Russian prisoner at the farm, was almost impossible to handle. He belligerently threatened Mr. Behrend that he would leave and join his Russian comrades not too far away at the fast approaching front. On Sunday afternoon the Polish prisoners and farm workers of the neighborhood, men and women, assembled for a feast in the patch of woods between the Behrend and Seefeld farms. They had asked for the meat of the pig which the Seefelds had killed in an emergency. Not caring about the possible contamination of it, the prisoners had planned a cookout in the woods. Soon the wafts of odor and voices streaming from that direction indicated that the party was in full swing.

"I'm afraid that Anton might instigate his fellow prisoners to start a riot," Mrs. Behrend said fearfully. Her worries, however, were unnecessary because the two Russians returned calm, Dimitri, the White Russian, arriving much earlier than Anton.

My greatest concern was to evacuate from Lautern in time. For several nights we had observed "Christmas trees" hovering over the village, the disturbing fact that the Russian front was close; they were mapping out the territory for attack. We remembered these "Christmas trees" too well; they were a signal of acute danger. Remembering also how Father doubted the news, we were not sure how close the Russian front was, how fast it was advancing. This uncertainty made me nervous. I started praying hard again. God had to find a way to take us out of here, in time, fast, please!

God always heard me, I knew, especially my pleas in desperation. Within a few days, in November, Mr. Behrend received official notice to drive us to the station in Rothfliess the next day. Mother was glad that our bundles were already packed. To leave Herta and Ursula behind, however, worried her immensely. Nevertheless, the two promised over and over again to stay in touch, to leave in time.

Arriving at the station we recognized many familiar faces and kept closely together with the Ganders, the Barocks, and the Adomeits. Mrs. Barock shared Mother's worry.

"Elsa also has to stay behind. She works in Osterode. Why do our girls have to be separated from us at such a critical time?" she asked Mother, complaining about the strict rules of the work force.

"Will they receive the official notice in time?" both women asked anxiously. But the train slowly moved into the station and Mr. Behrend helped us board, making certain that Mother took the baby carriage along with her few possessions.

As the long train started to roll slowly, we waved Mr. Behrend goodbye. Within a few days, he and his family might share our lot and be refugees. I realized the strange fact that people were unable to comprehend the situation of others until they experienced the very same. Was there no other way of learning?, I asked myself.

The train picked up speed. Seeing Mother settled between her long-time neighbors, I silently thanked God for our timely evacuation from Lautern. With each kilometer gained, we were getting farther away from the enemy, the approaching Russians. Mrs. Barock must have read my mind.

"I hope this evacuation is our last one," she sighed, "and that we will be taken far enough west to escape the Russians." Mother agreed with Mrs. Barock's hopes, wondering what our destination would be. Praying we would be transported beyond Berlin to the western part of the country, to be captured by the Western allies, I checked the passing stations closely. At the moment, our greatest concern was to pass the city of Danzig, the Free Port at the Baltic Sea, because we were aware that the Russian armies were aiming for this strategic point in order to cut off the entire province of East Prussia.

By noontime we had finally passed this critical check point and were travelling through the original "Polish Corridor," territory which Hitler had declared as part of Germany. Did he realize that his Great German Reich which he had predicted to last a thousand years was crumbling? Did he know that the Russians were on East Prussian soil, aiming for Berlin, our country's capital, I asked myself.

"I wonder if Hitler will capitulate before it is too late, before our country is totally destroyed?" Mrs. Barock asked Mother. But no one knew. Mrs. Gander had been very quiet, watching the countryside slip by.

"I never believed this could happen to Germany," she sighed as if lost in deep thought. She had believed Dr. Goebbels and his victory speeches. Perhaps she still did. But she had left her radio behind in Gumbinnen and for the last few months nobody had been able to listen to the news.

Frederick had posted himself at a window and called out the

stations as we passed. As the train stopped at a small town, he happily announced that the staff of the Red Cross was handing out food. This news, a drastic change of subject, perked up everybody. Tasting the hot soup and sandwich, I realized that my stomach had been empty. Once everyone was fed, our spirits lifted and Mother surprised me with a jocular remark.

"I feel like a gypsy with all these bundles," she said, assessing our belongings. The baby carriage with the duffle bag tied on top was a funny sight, Mrs. Barock admitted and, gypsylike, we did not know our destination.

Frederick, standing at the window, asked Mother what the abbreviation "Pom." meant. We then realized that we had passed the "Polish Corridor" and we were travelling through the province of Pommern. How far would we go, I wondered, and sat down in a corner. The monotonous shuttle of the train made me drowsy and I fell asleep. An abrupt halt awakened me and, trying to overcome my grogginess, I heard voices outside. Mother stepped over to the window and pulled it down. We had reached the outskirts of the city of Koeslin in Pommern. Again members of the Red Cross dished out food and filled baby bottles with milk. A man, rushing alongside the train, announced that our destination was the city of Cammin in Pommern. Immediately Walter Barock set out on a scouting trip through the train and found someone in the next car who had remembered to bring a map.

"Where is Cammin?" everyone asked at once and, in a joint search, we located it. Immediately my hopes sank. Cammin was still east of Berlin, close to the Baltic Sea, situated northeast of the Stettiner Haff. It was a considerable distance west from East Prussia, but was it far enough west? As refugees, we had no choice in the matter; this decision was made by government authorities.

"How long will it take us to get there?" Mrs. Barock questioned the man as he ran back to the head of the train. His answer was: "Before evening, if we are not delayed by air raids." Mother was glad to hear the news; it meant we would not have to sleep on the train because Andreas and Maria were complaining of getting tired. Not wanting to upset Mother with my worry, I prayed silently: "Let this be the last time we need to escape, dear Lord. Make sure we get through this chaos of losing a war safely and unharmed. Please!" Then a feeling of peace settled over me and the train continued to roll westward.

* * * * * *

Having left the cities of Kolberg and Treptow behind, several hours passed before church towers of another city were visible in the distance.

"This is Cammin," someone announced during a brief halt, "and we should arrive shortly." With a sigh of relief, I got up, stretched, then hastily straightened our compartment to make certain we would leave nothing behind. After crawling endlessly, the train finally pulled into the station. Red Cross personnel and *Volkssturm* men in green uniforms milled around the platform. Mother helped Maria and Andreas overcome their sleepiness, patting their cheeks. I handed our bundles, one by one, to a Red Cross man standing at the door who also helped me unload our baby carriage. On the platform at the station, Mother huddled together with our three neighbors.

To our surprise, the courier of our train announced that our load would not stay in Cammin but would be moved on to Dievenow by boat.

"You'll like the place. It's located directly at the sea shore," he encouraged us as he rushed on. Dog tired, none of us appreciated the news. But the *Volkssturm* men in green uniforms shuttled us quickly to the pier where a sight-seeing boat was docked to ship us to Dievenow. Our family and our three neighbors were the first to board, baby carriage and all, ready for a cruise. The crisp breeze blowing from the Haff helped us to overcome our tiredness and exhaustion.

As we approached the small harbor in the bay, I realized that Dievenow was a summer resort and our boat a cruiser for summer guests. Too bad that it was November; otherwise, we could enjoy the shore, I thought. But we were refugees; we were not summer guests.

In the hustle and bustle of unloading, I had hardly noticed the curious bystanders at the pier. Their cold glances, their sarcastic remarks about "refugees" now made me aware of the stark truth: we were not welcome. My heart cringed. Mother tried hard to follow the quick orders given by a *Volkssturm* man. She was holding on to Andreas who was sleepily stumbling along, pushing the baby carriage and keeping close behind the man who had told her and Mrs. Barock to follow him. I grabbed my bundle and rushed after them, glad that it was getting dark, making our bedraggled arrival less conspicuous.

As our gypsylike troupe was struggling behind the man along the main street, we were surprised to see him stop in front of an enormous, brown wooden house. Ordering Mother and Mrs. Barock to follow him, he whisked us through the back entrance and took us up a flight of stairs. Mother, having the four of us, was given two rooms and Mrs. Barock, having only two boys, was shown into one room, adjoining our quarters. It would be beautiful here in the summer, I realized, but noticing only one stove placed in the smaller of the two rooms, I knew we would freeze later in the winter. Even now, in November, the airy rooms with their high ceilings felt clammy and cold.

"Tomorrow you will receive more wood and coal from the owner; this will settle you," said the man, pointing to the meager wood supply at the door. Reminding the two women to register with the town authorities for their food stamps in the morning, he hurried off.

"You have to draw your water from the hand pump in the yard," he added, already half-way down the stairs. With stiff fingers, I unpacked the bedding, preparing the big corner room for the night. The three huge, drafty windows made it as cold as the outside.

"How could Maria and I sleep here" I asked myself, shivering severely. Mother now appreciated our having packed the two light featherbeds.

Having shed Father's extra clothes, but keeping my own coat on, I checked on the progress Mother had made. With a few splinters she had started a fire in the stove and the room was warming up quickly. A thin brew of grain coffee was steaming and Frederick devoured his sandwich while Marie and Andreas ate theirs with closing eyes. Mother and I cleaned up, numb from exhaustion, and moments later Maria and I crawled into one bed in the big, cold corner room, shivering ourselves warm under the one thin featherbed.

* * * * * *

Waking the next morning, it felt as if the night had passed in an inkling. Throwing on my coat, I stepped over to the window. It was a foggy, dreary looking morning. But something else captured my attention. Motioning Maria to be quiet, I listened intently and was positive that I heard the rushing of water.

"The sea must be very close," I told Maria who was anxious to get up and find out. After dressing hurriedly, we checked the "kitchen" in which Mother and the two boys had slept. The three were up and Mother was busy trying to scrape a breakfast together. Luckily, she had brought along some bread and margarine, a yellow mixture that turned green after a few days. By now, we had reduced the size of our smoked ham considerably but, using it sparingly, Mother cut away a few thin slices for sandwiches. So far we had not suffered hunger. The bitter coffee, made from dry roasted grains, was better than no coffee at all. Mother faithfully said grace before each meal. We were indeed grateful for our food, grateful for what God had provided for us.

"I have to go shopping and see what I can round up for dinner," Mother said, seeing her food supply dwindle. Consulting Mrs. Barock after breakfast, the two women reasoned that in Dievenow, on the Baltic Sea, fish should be available. Mrs. Barock suggested that Frederick and her son Walter venture out on a scouting trip to check the harbor where, upon arrival, we had seen a number of fishing cutters at the docks. The two complied readily because nothing could be more fascinating than to roam around the harbor.

Maria and I volunteered to wash the dishes and straighten the rooms. Therefore, Mother and Mrs. Barock got ready, Mother taking Andreas and Mrs. Barock her youngest son Martin along, they left to register for food stamps. Equipped with an empty shopping bag, they hoped to buy food somewhere.

Later in the morning, we heard heavy footsteps clamoring up the stairs. Curious, Maria peeked out the door to the corridor and whispered to me that a man was bringing us an armful of wood for the stove. Piling an even number of pieces against the wall of Mrs. Barock's room and ours, he mumbled something.

"Mrs. send this. For heat." Speaking a broken German and dressed in drab, wrinkled work clothes, we realized that he was either a Polish or Russian prisoner working downstairs for the owner of the house.

When Mother and Mrs. Barock returned before noontime, I was delighted to learn they had been able to buy some food. Although Maria and I were anxious to venture out to the beach, we prepared the soup for our noontime meal to free Mother for writing to Ursula and Herta. It was important that they knew where we were now located. These two letters had to be mailed immediately. One to Aunt Erna in Hamburg and one to Father in Italy, she would write after lunch.

"I rounded up a local newspaper. We have to keep abreast on the latest developments at the front," she said, glancing at the headline. It was sad news for our country. The Western allies had recaptured a considerable portion of France and Belgium. The article alarming Mother most, however, was that the Soviet armies were quickly advancing through Poland, aiming in a northerly direction, obviously determined to cut off East Prussia at Danzig. In this direction they seemed to throw their full force, because their westward move toward Gumbinnen had been halted. Mother could not find any news about the southern front in Italy. Knowing that Father was involved in that area made her nervous and she worried. Although Father had written to her that he was stationed with the mobile field bakery behind the front, he was still in danger. Not knowing whether our relatives had evacuated from Gumbinnen in time added to Mother's uneasiness.

"Where might they be? Did Oma, Uncle Oskar, Aunt Ina, Uncle Gustav, and Suzanne leave? Did Aunt Marie get out safely after the big bombing attack on the city? Who helped her pack and leave?" These were Mother's haunting questions.

"How will we ever find them in this churning chaos? How will Father ever find us?" Yet the answers were with God. All we could do was pray and trust in Him.

After I dropped Mother's letters into the mailbox across the street, she told us that she felt better. It was extremely important to keep in close touch with the two girls. Frederick and Walter had also returned from their scouting trip and brought back good news. The fishermen at the docks had told them to return in the evening and, depending on the size of the catch, would sell them a fish each if they could. Mother and Mrs. Barock were delighted.

"We may have fresh fish for dinner," Mrs. Barock smiled, reminding Mother that this news would mean additional food for which we did not have to use food stamps. It sounded almost too good to be true. Yet Mother thoughtfully commented that the Dear Lord knew how fast Frederick was growing, making him demand great amounts of food, and now He was providing the extra he needed. Our family liked fish and Frederick looked forward to a big piece at night.

"You have to see the sea," Walter Barock told his mother excitedly. Both boys had taken an excursion over to the shore, once their mission for the day was accomplished. Neither one had ever seen the Baltic Sea and the sight of the vastness of water behind the high dunes of the house had fascinated them. Hearing their enthusiastic report, Maria and I could hardly wait to run up the short walk to the dunes and see the water. We left Mother to finish the chores and disappeared.

Although the heavy fog had lifted, the sun was not strong enough to break through. Climbing up the narrow path to the dunes, the clammy breeze, laden with moisture, hit our faces. A strong north wind heaved the sea, creating waves more than five feet high which, thrown forward onto the sloping shore, lapped their tongues as if reaching for something. We ran down to the water, scooping up sand in our shoes with each step. Maria pointed to the horizon.

"Do you see the black smoke? What could it be?" she was anxious to know. It was a new experience for both of us and we guessed that it could be smoke from the fishing cutters. Amazed that the boats would venture out as far as the horizon, we let our eyes travel. The seemingly endless shoreline and the water touching the distant horizon filled me with awe. How small I was in comparison to this vastness, the Baltic Sea. I could easily visualize the beach with its pure white sand in the middle of summer. The sand would be dry and warm from the sun, and the water, a deep azure blue, inviting for a dip to cool off. In such a setting one could forget his problems, forget even that a brutal war was being waged. But now, in November, the gray sky merged with the gray of the water.

Walking along the shore absorbed in thought, I realized we had gone farther than anticipated. We quickly turned around and, stepping up our pace, walked back to the spot from which we had started.

"I could never get lost here," Maria assured me, pointing out that the peninsula on which Dievenow was located was very short and narrow. It had one main street leading through the town in an east-west direction. Several short side roads connecting the bay with the shore were all that made up the town of Dievenow. It was a very small summer resort. Reaching the cement boardwalk on top of the dune, we stopped to shake the sand out of our shoes. Maria suggested that we venture out to the other side of the beach tomorrow.

"Andreas will love the sight of the water," she added and we decided to take him along. Having recognized the large brown house from the dunes, Maria ran ahead. In the yard, however, she waited for me and pointed to an enormous stack of wood against the far side of the fence. "Look at all the fire wood," she said. Judging also by the black smudges in front of two low, wooden doors leading to a cellar, we were certain that the owner was a distributor of heating materials. This gave me a comfortable feeling. With supplies so close at hand, we might not have to freeze during winter.

Mentioning my optimism to Mother when we had climbed upstairs, she, however, put a damper on my hopes. Having gone to see the landlady downstairs to pay for the armful of wood delivered in the morning, Mother inquired about the possibility of buying a small supply of coal for the stove. The lady told Mother flatly that for this purpose she had to obtain a ration slip from the town registrar. "Without this paper, I cannot sell you any," she had said. Mother was disappointed because she knew applying for our ration would mean standing in line for hours. We could expect no favors from our new landlord. She explained that she ran the small business with the help of a Russian prisoner while her husband was stationed at the front. The lady had given Mother a tip, however, on how to get around in this area. The boat that had brought us the day before went to the city of Cammin on a regular schedule twice a day. This was good news.

"Perhaps I might be able to buy a few kitchen utensils in Cammin. I need them badly," she said hopefully.

As none of us had been able to enroll in school so far, we considered our stay in Dievenow an extended summer vacation, a fact that troubled Mother. We had missed out on a half year of schooling. How could we ever catch up on the lost education? But the small public school in Dievenow could not accommodate the many refugees. Besides, the lessons in school were frequently interrupted by air raids and even the native children spent many hours of the day in a bunker.

Having heard the news about frequent air raids from Mrs. Adomeit, who was located at the eastern end of Dievenow, Mother did not permit us to leave the house after dark. She insisted that our family be together in case of an alert. Our landlady had also told Mother which bunker we and the Barocks were supposed to use in case of an air raid. It was located close to the dunes, a safe distance away from the big wooden house and the huge pile of fire wood stacked in the yard.

Mr. Barock had joined his family recently. So far, he had been deferred from the army, but was on the work force and was assigned a job close by. Knowing Mrs. Barock's reluctance to discuss the reason, Mother did not ask questions but one day Mrs. Adomeit, a very talkative, tiny woman, spoke to Mother about it.

"Mr. Barock suffers from a lung disease," she confided to her. His haggard face with dark, deep-set eyes and his frail body confirmed that he was not well. Yet, a man of a quiet nature, we never heard him complain about his ailment. He had to report to the village administration in Lautern, however, and here in Dievenow, he was registered for the *Volkssturm*. This was a reserve made up of civilian men held ready for action in case of emergency. Mrs. Gander's oldest son, Karl, fell into the same category. As members of the work force, they were ordered to fill any job necessary to be handled. Both men had to report for work on the neighboring island of Wollin.

"Did you know that we have a very important military installation across the bay?" Mrs. Barock asked Mother excitedly the next day. She explained what her husband had told her, that the *Fliegerhorst* stationed on Wollin, a stone's throw across the Stettiner Haff, was packed with military planes. Then she lowered her voice to a whisper.

"My husband also told me that the V-2, our newest secret weapon, is launched from the western part of Wollin, close to the island of Usedom." This confidential statement from Mrs. Barock worried Mother, as she shared our neighbor's feelings.

"Why did we land so close to such a dangerous place, a place that must be a very important target for the enemy?" Mrs. Barock wailed. Trying to encourage each other, they reasoned that Mr. Barock, working on the *Fliegerhorst*, would inform them of the latest developments. If we were lucky, we might survive any possible bombing attacks and we would know in time whether or not we had to evacuate again. It was a small consolation but, in these times of chaos, a very valuable one.

* * * * * *

During our fourth day in Dievenow the weather was clear and sunny, a welcome change from the gray overcast. It had been a day full of adventure, a stroll along the beach and through the harbor, and we had gone to bed early. Only some short hours later, the monotonous sound of the siren wakened us. Scrambling into our clothes in the dark, we dressed hurriedly and waited. Only a few minutes later, the siren gave the danger signal. The on-and-off swelling of the alarm sounded like a herd of howling wolves close by. Torn out of my sleep, I could not talk. It took me a while to overcome my grogginess.

Joining the Barocks in the corridor, we hurried down the stairs and rushed across the yard to the bunker. Thank God, Mother had remembered to bring matches and a candle because, closing the heavily padded door behind us, we were enveloped by impenetrable blackness. Fumbling for the candle, Mother struck the match. The small flame of the candle giving off a glimmer of light enabled us to investigate our surroundings.

The bunker was damp and had three wooden benches made of rough, heavy boards around the three walls, leaving the wall with the door empty. A pail of stale water stood in the corner, that was all. As we huddled closely together on the bench, Mother motioned us to be silent.

"I hear something; it could be planes approaching," she whispered and, keeping still for a moment, all of us confirmed her suspicion. Russian planes were coming. Suddenly, Maria, sitting next to me, started to shake violently. The poor girl! Wakened abruptly and now freezing in the dark, clammy bunker, her young nerves, strained by fear, were registering the effects. I held her close but it took a long time before her trembling finally subsided. Almost holding our breath, we listened intently to the sound of the planes. Then we heard a rumble in the distance. Bombs were falling.

"How close could it be?" Mrs. Barock asked her husband anxiously. A short while later, the planes returned; they had dropped their deadly load. Over the years we had learned to differentiate between the sound of German and Russian planes. The engines of our own German planes had a lighter, higher sound than the low droning of the Russian which let up in strength and, seconds later, picked up again. Lately, Mr. Barock had noticed even a third sound—a sound which he attributed to either a British or American plane. It sounded slightly higher in tone than our German engines and the high, even pitch indicated it to be a much faster moving plane.

When the monotonous siren sounded again, indicating that the emergency had passed, we stumbled out of the bunker. From our path back to the house, we could see a pink, faint glow over the southern horizon.

"Could Stettin be on fire?" Mrs. Barock wondered. It was difficult to judge the distance across the water of the bay. Mother's distressed face expressed worry, yet she remained silent. Was she praying? I was because I realized how close we were to the *Fliegerhorst*, a dangerous target.

Rubbing our tired eyes, one by one we climbed up the stairs to the first floor, glad to resume our harshly interrupted sleep.

The next morning the paper confirmed that we had guessed right. The city of Stettin, located south of the Stettiner Haff at the mouth of the river Oder, had been severely bombed. Many civilians had died in the attack and much property damage was reported, especially in the harbor area. It also confirmed Mr. Barock's theory that the water of the Haff, acting as a very effective transmitter, had made it sound as if the bombing had been much closer. With trepidation, I realized the Russians were following us.

"How long will it take this time for the front to catch up with us?" Mother wondered, as if reading my thoughts. We had spent three months in Lautern. How long would we stay in Dievenow until the Russians were on our heels again? Glancing up to the stars, I prayed: Dear God, stay with us and protect us. Bring Herta and Ursula safely to us, please!

After the fourth day in Dievenow, our family had fallen into a daily routine. When the weather was sunny and clear, we could hear the putter of the fishing boats early in the morning. They would pass along the narrow channel between Dievenow and the island of Wollin and head toward the Baltic Sea around the tip of the peninsula. On such a day Mother counted on fresh flounder for dinner and she rarely was disappointed.

When Frederick heard the familiar putter of the boats returning to the harbor toward evening, he set out for the docks with Walter to pick up a fish for dinner. With beaming faces, the two boys returned shortly and, when they were able to buy an unusually large catch, Frederick looked as proud as a fisherman himself. He liked the crisp, fried flounder and Mother was grateful to be able to feed him. In addition, he could devour enormous amounts of potato salad, for which I had developed a recipe and prepared it on a daily basis. These were our staple foods, guaranteeing us a simple but nutritious meal every day.

Much as we enjoyed the fish on a clear day, we had learned to count on the other fact it guaranteed—an air raid at night. So far, the *Fliegerhorst* had not been bombed, but we could not be sure the situation would stay this way. One crystal clear night Maria and I watched a peculiar light going up into the dark sky, then halting for a second or two, after which it moved westward.

"Did you see how fast it moved? It was out of sight in seconds," Maria said, watching the light. Although we had heard from Mr. Barock earlier that the V-2 was launched from the city of Swinemuende on the island of Usedom, we had never seen it. This was Hitler's newest weapon, a remote controlled bomb in rocket form, steered from its launching site toward London, its destination. It was eerie to watch it move up and, at a calculated level, remain stationary as if undecided which way to go, and then speed westward. Although the V-2 was a subject not discussed in public, I reasoned that if we were able to see its take-off from Swinemuende, so could any enemy flying overhead coming from the east or west.

"How long will it take them to discover the launching site?" I worried, knowing that, once the exact location was pinpointed, the entire installation would be destroyed in an all-out bombing attack, which could happen any day now.

Mother's troubled thoughts, however, were going in a different direction. She had not heard from Father. Was he still stationed in Italy? Was he alive? Or had he been taken prisoner? These questions were haunting her, especially as the newspaper lately reported fierce fighting in Italy. Our German-Italian front was steadily retreating northward. Many soldiers were reported as missing. Where was Father? The uncertainty made Mother nervous.

While she anxiously waited for mail from Father, she had heard from Ursula and Herta. Both were glad that we had arrived in Dievenow without too much discomfort. Again both assured Mother that if the situation grew critical, they would leave together and join us here. Ursula reminded Mother that she was part of the work force and had to wait for the official evacuation notice from the city. Although Mother was familiar with this rule, it added to her fears.

"What will happen if the notice is released too late," she worried. Trying to keep her mind occupied with less morbid thoughts, I suggested that we take the boat to Cammin for a day. Knowing many of our neighbors from Gumbinnen were now located in Cammin, she agreed, hoping we would meet some people we knew. The boat ride had acted as a tonic and, returning home, Mother's spirit seemed revivified.

"I even bought some spoons and cups," she told Mrs. Barock, who met us in the corridor.

In order to ease my own worries, I started to read. The only book I had brought with me from Gumbinnen was my heavy German-English dictionary. Mother could not understand why I considered this book such a treasure. To me, it was the most important of all the school books I had owned. The need to keep my mind active made me search for a library. Although Dievenow was too small to have its own public library, I discovered that the bookstore across the street had a lending library as an extension. If I was missing at the apartment, Mother knew where to find me. I was scanning the rows of books for another intriguing title as a trade-in for the one I had just finished. My reading had become an obsession. Over a few weeks' time I was reading one book a day. Before getting up, I was reading; while doing the chores around the apartment, I was reading; taking the boat to Cammin, I was reading. Mother was concerned that I would ruin my eyesight from reading so much. But I was determined to read every book in the library across the street.

"What is it this time that you are reading?" she queried and I would give her a quick briefing on the story. She could never understand why I liked space stories. As far as Mother was concerned, only our own planet, the Earth, was inhabited with life. Her mind could not comprehend or imagine that the other bodies in our solar system and those in neighboring galaxies had some form of life. Not necessarily as we knew it, I reasoned with her, but different, because I firmly believed that God, being the Creator from Eternity to Eternity, would not waste His energy, but had created life from the beginning and was still creating life. Ruling this vastness we call space, and keeping it in precise order and timing, watching it evolve steadily, this was what I imagined to be God's role. Mother, after such a discussion, would shake her head in disbelief.

"How can a young girl's mind be captivated by such lofty subjects? I don't understand it," she often wondered. She was interested, however, in travel adventures. Someone daring to climb the Himalayan Mountains, venturing to the North Pole, or penetrating the Amazon jungle fascinated her and I gladly shared my stories with her. Nevertheless, once I finished a book, Mother hoped it would be the last one for a while. She did not share my enthusiasm, especially as I could have helped her more. Once I started a book, I was unable to tear myself away until I finished it.

Because of my mental haze, into which I had enveloped myself through reading, I only vaguely noticed the developments at the front. Now and then, Mother bought a paper. The news usually focused on heavy losses of men and war materials of the enemy. Mother had learned something from Father. To establish the approximate truth of the news, was to equal the given numbers in order to get a fair picture of what our own armies were losing at the same time. The picture was grim. One fact confirmed this. The latest draft notices included boys fifteen to eighteen years of age and men as old as fifty to sixty. It included everybody. Was this order Hitler's last frantic effort to win this brutal war? It had already taken so many lives of German men, young and old. Our country's human reserves were exhausted.

In the meantime, General Eisenhower's armies had passed the city of Aachen and were steadily advancing northward. Thank God, the advance at the eastern front seemed to have come to a halt. Ursula and Herta confirmed this fact by writing a long letter to Mother before Christmas.

As our family was not together for the holidays and the times were too chaotic, we did not feel like celebrating. It seemed as if even the elements reacted to the fury of the raging war. Late Christmas Eve the wind was whipping furiously, increasing as the time went on, pounding the waves against the dunes as if in a rage. Mother was panic-stricken.

"If the dam breaks, we will be lost; we will be swept into the bay," she said, fear and anxiety written on her face. Mrs. Barock did not help matters, mentioning that she had seen an enormous anchor on display at the fishers' museum, an anchor that had been washed ashore years ago when the dam had broken at the end of the peninsula in a severe storm.

"Marianne and I will walk up to the dunes and see how high the sea is," Maria suggested, hoping to bring back news that would calm Mother. The storm was tearing at the house, making its beams creak and groan. It felt as if it shuddered at times. Assuring Mother that we would walk only up the path behind the house, she reluctantly let us go.

Although we had put on our heavy coats, it felt as if the wind was determined to rip them off. Tying our knitted hats down with our shawls and covering our mouths, we carefully inched forward keeping close to the fence, literally grabbing it for support. The storm howled, tearing at bare trees, bending their crowns to the ground, whipping sand along the path and up our nostrils.

"Keep your eyes slanted as much as you can," I told Maria. The tiny grains felt like needles darting into our eyes. Having scrambled beyond the fence, we bent forward as far as possible, trying to stay on our feet and keeping the stinging sand out of our eyes. We were both determined to reach the top of the dune. Knowing we would not be able to stand up against the violent force of the storm, we crouched on our hands and knees, holding on to each other, shielding our eyes from the cutting sand. Finally, I was able to raise my head high enough to see the water. I was horror-stricken. The sea was one black, churning, roaring mass with mountainous waves at least fifteen feet high, tearing, ripping at the dunes, reaching as close as a foot from the top, lapping foamingly over the cement boardwalk.

"Oh, my God!" I stammered and choked. Maria, seeing my panic stricken face, insisted on seeing for herself.

"The water is higher than the street!" she shouted, retreating quickly. "Will the dam hold?" I did not know. Turning backwards in fright, I prayed feverishly: "Dear God, order Thine angels to hold this dam! Please order this raging storm to subside! Please protect us!"

Slowly we fought our way back, holding on to the fence for support, Maria tightly gripping my hand. She was petrified. So was I, except that I could not let her know. Debris was strewn all over the street and trees were uprooted. We had to fight the door open to get into the house. A gust of wind slammed it shut behind us. Maria and I were covered with sand from our hair to our shoes. Although I had intended not to frighten Mother, she could tell by the look on our faces that our situation was dangerous, if not critical.

"How high is the water?" she asked anxiously and Maria

blurted out, "Up to the top, higher than the street!" Frederick and Walter prodded their mothers to let them go and take a look, but Mother and Mrs. Barock did not permit it. While Maria and I were frantically trying to free ourselves from our cover of sand, I strained my ears listening to the furiously pounding sea, to the painful creaking of the house. Silently I continued my prayers. When I finally finished with the tedious clean-up two hours later, the storm had gradually subsided and we dared to go to bed. Thanking God for subduing the storm, for protecting us, I fell asleep.

Frederick and Walter were up early the next day, Christmas Day, and ventured out to the beach. Dievenow looked like a battlefield. Wooden planks, trees, branches, fences, and doors were cluttering the main street. The sea, as if she had exhausted herself the night before, lay in a calm gray. The shore was covered with bushels of seaweed, with planks and driftwood. Frederick and Walter were positive that a ship had gone down because they found beer cans and a lot of other debris in the sand. The newspaper, however, did not confirm the boys' assumption. Instead it listed another beach area where a dam had broken and property had been damaged extensively.

"Thank God that we got through this storm alive," said Mother, breathing a sigh of relief. Mrs. Barock agreed with her.

"We land-lubbers are not designed to live at the seashore; we feel uneasy at the sight of so much water," she said jokingly. I was glad she had not seen the black, churning mass and, with her funny comment, had snapped Mother out of her depression.

As Mr. Barock had mentioned to Mother that our front in the west was retreating steadily, despite Hitler's efforts to halt this tide with a major offensive, Mother again bought a paper. Fierce battles were reported from the Ardennes and a place called the Bulge. Heavy losses had been inflicted on both sides. Only a week later, by the middle of January, 1945, the Russians were attacking fiercely from the east. Another winter had started. Immediately Mother sped off a letter to Herta, telling her to be on the alert and evacuate in time. Ten days later, she still had received no answer. Mother became very much alarmed.

"Why don't they write? What is wrong? Were are the girls?" she kept asking, worried, anxious. To make matters worse, Elsa Barock had arrived in Dievenow two weeks ago. She had been working in Osterode, a city located in the southern part of East Prussia. Elsa told Mother that her firm had received a timely notice to evacuate. Lautern and Roessel were located even farther east than Osterode. Herta and Ursula should have arrived by now.

"Please, dear God, bring them here safely," I prayed, having the frightening feeling that something had gone wrong for Herta and Ursula. But I could not discuss my fears with Mother. She was already in a state of panic.

"Where are the two?" she kept asking over and over again, not knowing what to do. To appease Mother, every night Maria and I walked to the bus stop, hoping to pick up the two girls. But two more weeks had gone by and they had not arrived.

Then came the most frightening news. On January 27, 1945, the Soviet armies had encircled East Prussia at Danzig. This meant that those who had not gotten out that day would be taken captive. The thought sent shudders through me. I cried out to the only source I knew, to God, Who would listen.

"Dear God, how could you permit the two girls to be captured? I cannot understand this. You have never let me down! Have I been sinful, indulging in reading instead of spending time in silent prayer? Please, don't let the cruel Russians murder my sisters! Please, God, have mercy!" I silently pleaded. The strength I gained through prayer enabled me to give Mother a calm explanation. In this sudden chaos, the two girls evidently had not taken the time to write.

I assured her, they would be on their way. It would take them a few more days to arrive.

Two days later, on January 29, 1945, Mother received a telegram from Ursula. She had arrived safely in Rendsburg, Holstein. She was on her way to Aunt Erna in Hamburg, but Ursula did not mention a word about Herta. Mother's heart was glad about Ursula.

"But where is Herta?" she cried. It was gruesome to think about it. A few days later, a long letter from Ursula explained what had happened.

The official evacuation notice for the city of Roessel, where Ursula had temporarily worked, was given too late because the Russians had advanced very rapidly during the night. Trying to telephone Herta in Lautern, only five kilometers farther south, in the morning, she was unable to get through. The operator told her the cold fact: the wires had been cut. The Russians had already occupied Lautern. Ursula was panic-stricken. Realizing she had acted too late, she could not risk traveling to Lautern. She had to get away fast before the Russians moved into Roessel. In her distress, she grabbed a small bag of clothes and stopped a German military truck to find out whether the rumor about Lautern was true. The German soldier confirmed the fact and told her that East Prussia was about cut off.

"There is no use heading for Danzig because by now the Russians could be there," the soldier told her and, instead, urged her to try to get to the harbor of Pillau. Helping her climb on the truck, he suggested that she hitch-hike to the harbor and evacuate by boat, the only chance left to get out of the province. Dropping her off approximately half way, Ursula fought her way through by hiking or begging the military for a ride until she finally arrived in Pillau the night of January 25, 1945. She was relieved to learn that the overseas steamer, the *Ubena*, had been assigned to evacuate as many civilians as possible. Luckily, Ursula was admitted to the ship, which she boarded with an immense number of people. Late at night, under the cover of darkness and patrolled by several warships, the *Ubena* left Pillau harbor. All operations, locating of sleeping facilities, eating, and walking around were ordered to be done in total darkness, a precautionary measure taken not to attract enemy planes.

The location of the ship was kept secret. All Ursula knew was that it was moving westward. At that moment, it was the only fact that mattered. During the next day, an alert was sounded. Everyone was ordered to put on his life jacket. But the planes flying high overhead miraculously disappeared without attacking the ship. It took two nights and two days to cross the Baltic Sea and to pull in safely at the harbor in Rendsburg, a city located in the northern province of Schleswig-Holstein.

Once Ursula had disembarked, she telegraphed Mother and immediately boarded the next train to Hamburg. At this point, she did not worry about the nightly bombings in Hamburg. She had gotten out of East Prussia; she was safe. Ursula assumed that Herta had arrived in Dievenow by now.

When Mother replied to Ursula informing her that we had not received a word from Herta, Ursula was upset. Aunt Erna again urged Mother to move to Hamburg. However, Mother did not dare risk Herta's arriving in Dievenow on foot one day and not being able to find us. It was a maddening situation.

Therefore, Maria and I faithfully walked to the bus stop each night, hoping, praying that Herta might arrive. By now, we hated to return home with another disappointing "No." Each time Mother's heart sank. But we did not dare give up hope. No matter how bad the weather was, Maria insisted on walking with me. During January and most of February it was bitter cold. The snow, sleet, and icy rain added to our despair.

"Where in the world is Herta?" Maria asked in desperation and I did not know the answer. I asked myself whether she was alive or captured by the Russians. But when these thoughts of horror entered my mind, I dismissed them quickly.

"Bring her to us safely, please, dear God." I silently wrung my hands in prayer to him. She had to come. I refused to believe differently.

Meantime we watched Elsa Barock sew herself a new winter coat from green army material which her father had evidently purchased from the depot at the *Fliegerhorst* on Wollin. Elsa had time to think about fashions while we were frantically waiting for Herta's arrival.

In early February we had given up our boat trips to Cammin because the weather had turned bitter cold and clammy. Furthermore, we had to be prepared for at least one air raid during the day. Therefore, Mother kept us close to the house. Reading the paper, she was not sure whether or not she could believe its reports. She did not know the actual position of the Russian front. Although our own front, thinned out over the last few years in Russia, bravely tried to fight back the enemy. The Soviet armies were positioned approximately 250 kilometers away from Berlin.

We civilians had long since given up on winning the war. We were tired, tired and disheartened. The worry over our men at the front, the loss of them, the fear of being bombed, the fear of being murdered, and the chicanery of our own Nazi party had undermined our faith in our country. Father had been right. He had recognized the downfall of our regime from the beginning. He knew that an atheistic government denouncing God and the Law of the Universe could not exist. Its misuse of energies had to result in destruction, the destruction of its very own existence.

Contrary to our opinion, Dr. Goebbels was still shouting victory. It was unbelievable. Did he not know that Schlesien with its vital coal resources and steel industry was lost? Did he ignore the fact that the Ruhr area was now a heap of rubble? He must have held on frantically to the last straw—the promise that Hitler's new weapons, the V-2 and the new electro-driven U-boat, would turn the tide.

Even if Dr. Goebbels held on to his own threadbare promises for dear life, the German public knew the bitter truth. It was only a matter of time until Germany would be totally occupied by her enemies. We held the one hope, however, that the Western Allies would not permit the Soviets to capture Berlin, our capital. Everybody watched the front movements closely, like a chess game, knowing our own lives were at stake. Fearfully, we watched the Russians advance faster than the Allied forces in the west. Our soldiers at the eastern front fought bravely, knowing that once the beastliness of Bolshevism was upon us, we would have to write off our lives. Everyone envisioned the two grim possibilities—either to fall into the hands of the Russians, those bloodthirsty Cossacks, anxious to mow down anyone who crossed their paths, and suffer under the tyranny of Stalin, a dictator known to be even more brutal than Hitler, or fear the deadly prospect of being sent to Siberia, from where no one had yet returned alive to tell his gruesome tale. In both cases, these prospects were worse than death, and I believe that our soldiers, realizing this fact, fought on fiercely until the bitter end.

Mother's distress had increased over the last weeks. She was on edge, nervous, worried. Spending half of our nights in the dank bunker only aggravated the situation. Yet in wind, rain, sleet, and snow, Maria and I faithfully made our trip to the last bus, each time returning sad and disappointed after having carefully checked each passenger's face.

"No, Herta was not on the bus," Maria whispered, looking tired and disappointed.

Meanwhile the situation around the Stettiner Haff grew steadily worse as even smaller cities, including Cammin, were bombed. Heading for the bunker during the nightly raids, we worried. We saw the soldiers, stationed at the army and air force base on Wollin, evacuate the island and walk along the beach in small groups. What did this mean? So far, the *Fliegerhorst* had not been bombed, although it could happen any day.

"It is a precautionary measure. To keep eventual losses at a minimum, the men stationed on Wollin are evacuated," Mr. Barock explained.

One night Mother thought it would be safer to stay at the beach during the air raid but, when we appeared there, we were firmly ordered to take shelter in our bunker—fast! A few nights later we had a weird experience sitting in the bunker. We heard the rumble of bombing and this time it seemed closer than Stettin. Trying to control Maria's violent shaking, I had not looked up. Yet in the faint light that our flickering candle offered, I noticed to my horror that the upper beams of the bunker were swaying. It felt like being on a boat and we knew that the bombs were falling very close. Time crept by so slowly. When the siren sounded to call off the danger, we were anxious to check whether the air force base was on fire. But the *Fliegerhorst* across the channel lay dark and motionless; it had not been bombed.

"What could have been hit so nearby?" Mrs. Barock wondered. Later in the morning we heard that Swinemuende, the city from which the mysterious V-2 was launched, had been severely bombed and the harbor area around it had been heavily mined.

Danger was closing in on us. Still we had received no word from Herta or from Father. To ease her tense mind, Mother continued to write to Father, using his Unit number. My nerves were at the breaking point, but I did not dare let the fact be obvious. Had Herta been with us, we would have started to pack our few belongings. It was maddening.

"Dear God, have you forsaken us? Am I not praying often enough?" I cried out in silence. My routine had been to pray while we were sitting in the bunker at night. Holding on to shaking little Maria, assuring her that everything would be all right, I prayed silently and earnestly that Herta might find us, that Father would be safe. Did God hear me? My agonized heart was crying for help, but sometimes it doubted.

Once again, late at night Maria and I stepped outside to walk to the bus stop. Drifting new snow blew into our faces. This sign indicated a change in weather and, within days, the frost would break, giving way to an early thaw. Pulling our collars around our necks, we walked off briskly to the bus stop located a few blocks east, close to the docks. We were early to make sure we would not miss the bus. Stomping our feet in the rapidly accumulating snow, we tried to keep warm. The sharp east wind was raw and cold and we turned our faces away from it. After a while, Maria complained about cold hands. At that moment, I saw the dim lights of the approaching bus as it slowly turned into the stop. We watched each person climb down and silently disappear into the night. We were ready to leave, thinking the last passenger had disembarked, when I heard someone behind me call my name. Turning around, I saw Herta! Embracing her silently, I started to tremble as streams of warm tears rolled down my cheeks. I was unable to utter a word.

"Thank you, dear Lord; you have answered my pleas." I shot a silent prayer of thanksgiving up to the One I had learned to trust and rely on. Maria regained her composure more quickly.

"Come, let's go," she said, pulling at Herta. She was anxious to get home and tell Mother. This time we arrived with good news—at last! A stone rolled off my heart. Herta was alive; she was safe! Now we could move on.

* * * * * *

Mother had seen us from the window and, although it was dark, she had noticed three dark figures approaching instead of two. Flying down the stairs, she greeted Herta in the yard, her words choking in sobs. She held her tightly as if afraid to let her go.

Finally, the nightmares of fear and uncertainty had ended. Allowing the darkness to hide our tears, we slowly went upstairs.

"This was our last walk to the bus stop!" Maria shouted joyfully. Herta had found us!

When we entered the warm room, I realized why I had not recognized Herta, except for my own red knitted shawl which she wore in turban fashion around her head. She looked exhausted. Helping her out of her coat, it felt heavy and damp.

"It has been exposed to snow, sleet, and rain for several weeks. I had no umbrella, no rain cape," she explained. Dropping her two heavy bundles in a corner, Herta looked at her hands. They were covered with blisters and cut in places from carrying her baggage.

Frederick ran downstairs to pump a pail of water so Mother could heat it for Herta to clean up. Tired as she was, she insisted on washing her hair, although it was late. Maria and I tried to help her take off her boots.

"Oh, please be careful," she cautioned us. Apologetically, she explained they had not been off her feet for over a month and she felt her soles were one big blister. I cringed. How could we get those boots off without hurting her? It was cruel but, after an hour of careful peeling and pulling, the last boot finally came off. Her socks were wet and crumpled. When she took them off, I cried. Both feet were covered with one whole blister all the way to the heel. It was incredible.

"How could you walk on those feet?" Mother cried. Bravely, Herta asked for a needle to puncture the blisters. Reluctantly, Mother handed her one, lighting a candle in which she could disinfect the point. Herta insisted that she do this delicate job herself as we stood around watching, holding our breath. It was amazing how much water drained out of her soles once the blisters were broken.

Meanwhile Mother had prepared a big pan of warm soapy water in which Herta soaked her sore feet. In a flow of words mixed with tears, Herta told us her story.

Toward the end of January, the weather had turned very cold in Lautern and, while most people focused closely on the position of the eastern front near Gumbinnen, the Soviet armies had broken through from Warsaw and were approaching very rapidly northward. By nighttime they had advanced so frighteningly close that Herta urged Gertrud Seefeld to grab their two bags and leave. This was on January 27, 1945. Gertrud, against the pleading of her parents to stay home, joined Herta and both left the farm at 8:00 p.m. They walked over to a neighbor named Wiedmann. As most of the farmers by then had soldiers of the German military stay over night, the two girls had been promised a lift by truck. Soldiers would take them to a station from where they could get away, using other means.

"The telephone lines had been cut. I was unable to inform Ursula of our emergency decision," she explained and continued her story. To their greatest horror, the military convoy stationed at the farmer Wiedmann had received emergency orders earlier in the morning to leave Lautern. All trucks but one had left the village. This last one, stuck in a huge snowdrift, had to be dug out. This delayed truck was the girls' good luck. After chains were hastily thrown around the gigantic tires, the huge vehicle finally moved and a lieutenant Kaiser packed the two girls on the truck to join the rest of the convoy. From this one, Herta and Gertrud were transferred to a different one because this convoy was to deliver supplies to the close front in combat.

It took a week until another truck dropped the two girls off at the city of Heiligenbeil, located at the Frische Haff. During this week they had seen the Russians as close as half a kilometer and, at one point, had found themselves directly in a combat zone where Herta described seeing freshly wounded, profusely bleeding soldiers scattered all over the area. Members of the Medical Corps, their own uniforms crumpled and discolored with dried blood, frantically collected them and rushed them away in a truck standing by. Herta shuddered, recalling how the white snow was splattered with fresh blood stains covering a huge field. Their truck was attacked and splinters flew all around them, but the Russians missed. Hurriedly, under the cover of a small wooded patch, the truck jostled them away across a frozen, ploughed field.

There was only one way to get out of Heiligenbeil: across the frozen Haff. Many civilians on foot or by trek had already gone this route. The deep furrows in the ice, furrows filled with blood from the many dead strewn along the way, made Herta's heart freeze. The Russians had been attacking these treks from the air with machine gun fire. Would they get across alive, the two girls asked each other. But they had to try. It was their only chance to pass Danzig before the last road was completely cut off by the Soviets.

Several civilians had warned them not to make the attempt to cross the Haff. In places where the ice was not thick enough and wagons had moved too closely together, whole treks had broken through, drowning horses, wagons, and men. Nevertheless, the two girls were determined to try.

"Those eleven kilometers were the most ghastly I have walked in all my life," cried Herta, recalling the sights of horror. Dead bodies of men, women, and children, along with dead horses and cattle, told a silent tale of inhuman treatment.

"I was tempted to bring along a baby," Herta continued, telling us how it was crying in one arm of its dead mother, who was still holding on to a loaf of bread with the other. But she had to pass, to move on, and prayed that God would send someone from the Red Cross who could take the tiny creature. Herta's hands and feet were blistered and, to relieve her aching arms, she occasionally had put her bundles on the back of a wagon, trying to keep up with its pace. Most of the time the trek moved very slowly because the horses had little rest, a minimum of feed, and the weather was bitter cold. Herta and Gertrud were afraid the Russian front might catch up with them. Therefore, both moved along the trek as fast as their feet would carry them.

The night they crossed the Haff, however, was overcast. The thick layer of clouds acted as a protective cover and they were relieved to get across without an attack from the air. Although tired and weary from walking all night, both girls did not allow themselves time for sleep. Grateful for the hot soup that compassionate civilians, who had decided to stay home, handed to them, they continued their walk at the western side of the Haff, along the Nehrung.

"We continued walking all the next day and by evening passed the city of Danzig." Herta sighed as she recalled the monumental task, the strain on her body, her hands, her feet. Only then did they stop for a brief rest, continuing their march westward in the graying hours of the next morning.

"That same day the Russians closed the circle around East Prussia by cutting off the last road for escape," she continued. Herta and Gertrud had made it by a hair's breadth. Meantime, on her long walk toward Dievenow, Herta worried about Ursula, accusing herself for not getting in touch with her sooner. Gertrud Seefeld was upset, knowing that her family by this time was under Russian occupation. Were they alive? Would they be permitted to stay on their farm, or would they be transported to Siberia? These questions haunted her. But her parents had insisted on staying at home, convinced that nothing could happen to them, that they could stay on their farm.

"I had told Gertrud the story you had heard from the soldier in the military hospital," she said to me. Its horrible contents had enough impact on Gertrud to make her want to move westward with Herta. Now she was glad about her decision, yet sad that she had not been able to persuade her parents to leave.

The weather stayed cold even throughout February and the trek moved slowly. The Russians were moving close behind them. Transportation was not available. Trains in those areas had stopped running. Along with hundreds of thousands of other East Prussian civilians, both girls had to depend on their own two feet. Herta and Gertrud had marched the two hundred kilometers from Danzig to Cammin.

When the trek leader decided to move around the Stettiner Haff, Herta had parted from Gertrud and walked on to Cammin, from where she finally got on the bus to Dievenow.

"Why didn't you bring Gertrud along?" Mother asked anxiously. Herta explained that Gertrud did not want to be a burden to us. In addition, she thought it safer to move on.

It had taken the two girls a month and three days to walk the distance and Herta's sore feet and tired face showed the strain. While Mother helped her wash her hair, Herta insisted that Mother check her head for lice. Herta had not been out of her clothes for over a month and had slept in the dirtiest corners, sometimes sitting or just standing up. Only after Mother confirmed that miraculously she had no lice, Herta ate lightly and then fell into bed half dead. Mother and I soaked her clothes, once she assured us that she had a change of clean clothes in her bag.

I took a closer look at the boots Herta had worn, the boots that had carried her over two hundred kilometers. They were military boots, heavy, stiff, and clammy from the rain, snow, and mud through which they had trudged. One of the heels was missing. Herta had told us that she lost it during the night she had walked those deadly eleven kilometers across the Haff from Heiligenbeil. Tomorrow those boots would be thrown away, although I felt they deserved to be kept at a museum as a commemoration to humanity's endurance and proof of the Good Lord's grace. He had again heard my silent pleas. He had marched with Herta. He had guided her through this ordeal and kept her alive.

Very late at night when I finally went to bed, I felt tears trickle down my face and soak my pillow as I recalled a phrase from the Bible: "...they shall walk and not faint."

Chapter X

Save Us! For Thy Mercies' Sake

As if the Lord knew that Herta needed her sleep, miraculously we had no alarm during the first night. The sirens kept quiet. It was a blessing.

After waking early, I had picked up my clothes and tiptoed out of the room not to disturb Herta's sleeping. Maria's body evidently was catching up with the hours of sleep lost. She did not even stir when I got out of bed. In the room next door, Mother had already started a fire in the stove and it was cozy.

"First I want to wash Herta's clothes, to give them plenty of time during the day to dry," she whispered. Even the weather was on our side and promised us a clear, sunny day. While Mother washed the clothes over and over, I prepared breakfast. At the same time I set up a pot of potatoes so they could boil and cool off during the day. Toward evening, I would mix a big bowl of potato salad for us. Food had become a very important item on our list of survival. As I was busy setting the table, I heard the sputtering of cutters leaving the harbor for another day of fishing.

"I hope they'll catch a big one for us today," said Frederick in a sleepy voice. The familiar noise of the cutters had wakened him and with his eyes scanning the table, he asked what we had for breakfast. The boy seemed to be forever hungry. Andreas, an early riser, had gotten up with Mother and, looking out the window, gave us an account of the bypassers down below in the street.

Shopping had become an all-day chore as it required standing in line for every item, especially butter and meat. As we had no infant in the family, our ration of milk was limited. Breakfast usually consisted of two slices of bread with a thin spread of margarine and brown syrup or, as a special treat, maybe an occasional fruit jelly. From left-over potatoes, Mother made home fries, frying them in cod liver oil. Substitute coffee was made either from ground roasted beans or roasted barley. Our family preferred the roasted barley. The brew did not taste quite as bitter as the one made of roasted beans.

When Mother was finally satisfied with her laundry, I took Herta's wet clothes downstairs and hung them on the line to dry. Returning to the kitchen, I noticed the relief on Mother's face. After two months of anxiety, she did not have to worry any more. Herta and Ursula were safe. Meanwhile, Frederick was ready to eat. Mother cautioned us not to waken Herta and Maria, and the four of us ate together. Frederick, usually not inclined to conversation, again mentioned Herta's incredible feat of marching over two hundred kilometers.

"If it were not for those boots in the corner, I would not believe it," he said. Ragged and soggy, they were stark proof of the truth. Mother told him to take them downstairs and drop them in the garbage pail. She had hurried through breakfast, while the three of us were lingering.

"I have to speed off a letter to Ursula," Mother explained, "to let her know Herta has arrived here safely." While the potatoes were boiling, the water for the dishes was hot. After rinsing the cups and saucers, I set them up again for Herta and Maria.

"Will she wake up at all today?" I wondered, realizing that she had been at a point of collapse the night before.

We could hear the Barocks next door. They were up also because the slightest noise and conversation easily carried through the thin walls of the house, a house that had been constructed for summer guests only.

When Mother had sealed the letter, Frederick took off to the post office, picking up Herta's boots ceremoniously to take them downstairs.

"Here they go, the faithful soldiers," he said walking out the door. Walter Barock joined him in the corridor. The two boys had been doing everything together for the last three months. Boys, twelve years old, they did not like to spend their days in crowded rooms and, usually glad to take care of their mothers' errands, stretched the time and went on exploratory walks.

The reset table was ready for Herta's and Maria's late breakfast. Quietly Maria tiptoed into the kitchen and, still yawning, told us that Herta had opened her eyes. She would be up shortly. Nobody in our family had ever managed to sleep later than noontime, no matter how little sleep we had gotten during the night. It was before eleven o'clock when Herta walked into the kitchen. She looked better, although the dark shadows under her eyes still indicated exhaustion.

"It felt like heaven to sleep in a clean bed again," Herta told Mother and Mrs. Barock who, having heard the news of Herta's arrival, came in to hear what had happened. Elsa Barock, tall and slender, her dark, curly hair neatly styled, curiously followed her in. While having breakfast, Herta repeated the details of her story. The two women became very quiet and Mrs. Barock, touched by Herta's dramatic experiences, sobbed bitterly. But Herta did not lose her composure. Instead, she stated optimistically that once her feet were healed, she would be willing to walk to the end of the earth.

"No Bolshevik is going to lay hands on me," she declared with emphasis. She would leave and walk again to make sure that she would not suffer beastialities. I was glad my closest ally was with me again. From now on, I was confident we would get away from Dievenow in time. Meantime, I was concerned about Herta's feet. As we did not know of a doctor in Dievenow, we had to use the home remedies available. Poultices soaked in camomile tea and vaseline creme were speeding up the healing process. As Herta examined her feet, I could see that the water had drained out of the gigantic blisters and the redness had diminished slightly. If she stayed off her feet a few days, she would be all right. Instead, Herta was determined to try on her shoes, the pair she had brought along in the bags. They hurt her feet but she assured us that, if need be, she would be able to wear them. This fact was very important to her.

While I prepared the potato salad, Herta volunteered to help me. Maria took Andreas for a walk along the beach.

"It worries me that you have not heard from Father," Herta mentioned to Mother. Under these chaotic circumstances in our country, however, she reasoned that Ursula's letter to him might have been lost. If this were the case, he did not know where we were. Mother told her she kept addressing her letters to Father's unit, hoping they will reach him. She mentioned also that Aunt Erna had invited us to come to Hamburg, but that she was undecided. Herta suggested that we wait for the official evacuation notice instead and leave with the first shift. Hamburg, at this point, was not a safe place to be. The harbor was bombed daily and repeatedly Aunt Erna had complained about the extreme shortage of food. While Herta and I cut the potatoes, onions, and pickles into small pieces, Mother added three hard-boiled eggs, making the salad a special treat. So far, we at least had something to eat every mealtime. Although it was only the bare essentials, it was better than going to bed hungry. Thousands of other people were suffering from hunger.

When we heard the noise of fast steps clamoring up the stairs, we knew Frederick and Walter had returned from their errand. Both had a surprise in store. Following their daily routine, they had strolled along the docks. To their surprise, they heard the sputtering of a cutter. It had returned early for repairs and, anxiously waiting at the dock, the two boys asked the men if they had caught some fish. They had.

"The men recognized us and when I told them that Herta had arrived home, they gave me this big fish, free of charge!" Frederick shouted. Walter had also received a large cod as a gift. Both boys were so excited and bragged all day about their good luck. Mother was overjoyed. She estimated the fish to weigh about eight pounds. It would be sufficient for two plentiful meals. Cod stretched her meager food supply because the fish could be fried in its own liver oil.

Frederick had taken over Father's job of cleaning the fish outside. While Mother was preparing lunch, I walked downstairs with Herta. Her clothes on the line were almost dry and we walked to the bunker where we had spent many nights.

"We will never get away from here by train," I told Herta, mentioning that I had not wanted to bring up the subject in Mother's presence. The closest station was Cammin and it was over an hour's distance away by boat. Herta was not surprised at my comment. The thought had occurred to her the night of her arrival. We decided to take a walk to map out the surrounding territory.

"This is the reason I insisted on trying on my shoes," she told me. As the boots had gone into the garbage, she wanted to be cerain she had a pair of shoes on her feet. If need be, we had to evacuate on foot, but she realized immediately that it was still the middle of winter and the three younger ones could not walk very far. I suggested to Herta that we take a walk around the peninsula to give her a better picture of the geographical location of Dievenow.

As we were about to go upstairs, Maria and Andreas returned from their stroll. The blustery wind had colored their cheeks pink and both announced that they were hungry. The smell of fresh fish in the kitchen told us that Mother had lunch ready and we were anxious to eat. It was a feast to have a full-size meal with plenty for everyone. Mother had taken over Father's function of saying grace.

"Come, Lord Jesus, be our guest and bless what Thou hast graciously given unto us. Amen." We were indeed grateful, not only for the plentiful food but also for Herta's safe return.

* * * * * *

Mother decided to take advantage of the sunny day and visit Mrs. Gander, who lived in a two-room apartment on the eastern side of Dievenow. She would take Andreas along, and urged Frederick not to venture too far away from the house in case of an alarm. Assuring her that he would only go for a stroll along the beach with Walter, he left.

While Mother helped Andreas into his coat, Herta and I washed the dishes and Maria volunteered to straighten the rooms. It was late in the afternoon when we finally started on our exploratory walk. The clean, cool air felt good on my face. Maria insisted on giving Herta an official "sightseeing tour" and I gladly let her have the fun. She guided us over to the sea.

"You have to see the water first," she told Herta and walked up the steep climb to the boardwalk. The stiff breeze and the incoming tide whipped the waves up high, throwing them far up on the low, white beach. In the distance, the water was a deep greenish-blue, a picture that captured Herta's fascination. A few fishing cutters were still out but, because of the heavy sea, closer to the shore than usual. Herta was still limping; therefore, we did not dare risk her getting sand in her shoes so we stayed on the cement walkway. Nevertheless, it took us far enough to the west so Herta could see the tip of the peninsula.

"Now we will walk across the main street to get to the channel," Maria told us authoritatively, playing the role of the perfect guide, and, like curious tourists, Herta and I followed her obediently. In less than two minutes, we arrived on the southern side of Dievenow and walked in an easterly direction back toward town.

"The bridge you see ahead is the only connection to the island of Wollin," Maria continued, enjoying our full attention. Momentarily a low-flying plane drowned out our conversation.

"Where did that plane come from so suddenly?" Herta asked and promptly Maria had the answer. Pointing toward the plane as it headed toward the sea, Maria explained that this type, a Focke-Wulf, with its peculiar double fuselage and swimmers, was stationed at the *Fliegerhorst* and most likely was on its way to clear a minefield in the Swinemuende harbor area.

"How many planes are stationed on Wollin?" Herta inquired, but Maria, our guide, advised that this was a military secret and no civilian knew the exact number. Meanwhile we had passed the bridge leading to Wollin and Herta gave me a knowing glance.

"If this narrow bridge is our only way of escape, we'd better be on guard," she told me. Coming closer to the harbor area, we had to pay attention again.

"From these docks a small fishing fleet goes out to sea every day; that means, weather permitting," continued Maria. Most of the boats were still out; therefore, we climbed over heavy ropes and looked into the oily water.

"Across the bay to the east, you can see the city of Cammin," Maria pointed out and Herta wondered how far Gertrud Seefeld had walked by now. She thanked Maria for the informative tour and slowly we strolled back to the house. I mentioned to Herta that I had the feeling the people in Dievenow resented us, a resentment I had noticed the day we had arrived. Herta reminded me of the same attitude we had met in the farmers in Lautern.

"Gertrud Seefeld never believed she would be a refugee until she crossed the Haff with me," she said thoughtfully as if in reflection. "Experience is a harsh but sure teacher."

As the sun was moving close to the western horizon, we felt a sudden chill in the air and we stepped up our pace. It was unusual that we could enjoy a clear sunny day without the disturbing howl of the sirens. Arriving at the yard, I touched Herta's clothes and took them off the line. The wind had blown them dry.

"Within a few days I have to report to work again," Herta mentioned as we slowly climbed the stairs. I was aware that she was part of the work force. Nevertheless, I urged her not to volunteer because Elsa Barock, the same age, had not reported for work. Elsa was well, I reasoned, whereas Herta was still limping on her sore feet. This was a legitimate excuse not to register for work.

It felt good to step into the warm kitchen and I quickly threw a few logs into the stove to rekindle the embers that were still red from lunchtime. Just before dark, Mother returned with Andreas. Not finding Frederick at home, she worried about where he could be so late. But her famous statement held true.

"Hunger drives them home," and soon we heard fast footsteps run along the corridor. On her way home, Mother had bought some milk, planning to cook a hot oatmeal cereal. It would warm us quickly. In addition, the two slices of bread for each would fill our stomachs for the night. Obviously, Mother missed our house, especially the variety of vegetables she had stored away in glass jars.

"The potatoes you dug are probably feeding some Soviet soldiers," she mused, regretting that I had spent so much energy in completing the task. But she realized it was not wise to live in the past. It did not change anything. So far, God had provided sufficient food for our family and we were grateful. Times would hopefully change again for the better.

Mother suggested that we go to bed early to get as much sleep as possible. It was a good idea because after midnight the monotone of the siren sounded an alert and wearily we got into our clothes. By the time we were dressed, the alarm sounded. Mother hurriedly grabbed her bag, checked if we were in our coats, and together we rushed down the stairs. The Barocks were following us. Herta, obviously troubled about Maria's shaking, assured her not to worry. But no matter how insistently Maria claimed that she was not afraid, she could not control the trembling of her slender little body. Herta and I crammed her between us so she could hardly move and then gradually she calmed down.

* * * * * *

As our family's concern had focused around Herta's full recovery, we had not heard any news about the front for the past two days. Therefore, Mother was shocked when Mr. Barock pointed out that the personnel at the *Fliegerhorst* had received an official alert commando, notifying all men to be ready on a one-day basis. Mother anxiously asked what this indicated.

"In case of an emergency, the army and navy will be put in charge to evacuate civilians," he explained. Upon Mother's question as to how soon this was expected, he answered that he did not know. No immediate danger seemed to exist at the moment. The sudden swaying of the bunker, however, betrayed his statement. Judging by the loud rumble we heard, some place nearby was heavily bombed, possibly Cammin across the Haff, perhaps Swinemuende.

"If the *Fliegerhorst* is ever going to be bombed, this bunker will not hold up," Mother stated worriedly. It had never swayed as badly as this.

"Maybe the navy base is being bombed," Mrs. Barock held her breath in panic. After a fearful hour, the waves of planes stopped coming and the rumble subsided. The monotone sound of the siren indicated once more that the danger had passed, that we could resume our sleep.

What usually kept me awake after these raids was the clammy bed and my ice cold feet. Often it took me an hour to fall asleep again. In the big room where Herta, Maria, and I slept, we had no stove. The three big, drafty windows made the room almost as cold as the outside. It had been a grim winter for us, spending the last three months at this summer resort in a house Mother referred to as a big matchbox. Enormous in size with its ten or more rooms upstairs, it was built of wood and was without heat. Maria and I had spent many nights shivering in bed until we were warm enough to fall asleep. Thank God, Mother had brought the two feather beds; otherwise, the three of us would have gotten frostbites even in bed.

The next day was foggy and overcast again, a change that was conducive to stay inside close to the stove. Herta decided to go through her clothes in the two bags and start ironing, including those she had worn on her long, weary walk from Lautern to Dievenow. Having lost my drive for reading, I went across the street to return the book I had borrowed. The bespectacled man in the store looked as lame as the weather and only grumbled when I handed him the book. By his questioning glance, I could tell that he was surprised that I did not ask for another book.

"I have given up reading for a while," I answered his silent question and left the store. He only nodded and buried himself in his own book. Mother appreciated my returning empty-handed and resumed her conversation with Herta.

"Karl Gander had also mentioned the special alert on the Fliegerhorst," she mentioned, having visited Mrs. Gander the day before. The situation in Dievenow was growing critical. Herta was concerned that we, as refugees in this small town, might not receive the evacuation notice in time. Therefore, we agreed to keep a close eye on the news and check the main street for activities.

As it had been a dreary day, we felt sleepy and went to bed early, hoping not to be wakened by the cruel sirens. But this night it was not the harsh sound of the siren that wakened me. I heard shouts and noises below in the street which jerked me out of my sleep. It was the persistence of voices, accompanied by a noisy commotion, that forced me out of my warm bed and made me rush to the window. As it was dark outside and the sky overcast, it was difficult to grasp what was happening down below. By now Herta and Maria had joined me at the window and Herta immediately clarified my confusion.

"Oh, it's the trek; it has caught us with us. The narrow bridge is holding them up," she shouted, her anxious voice betraying worry.

"I know what this means. The Russians will be right on their heels." Understanding the grave implication, we decided to start packing early in the morning to make sure we were ready once the signal for evacuation was given. As we listened, it seemed that no one in the room next door was stirring and we agreed not to waken Mother. As we could not do anything at the moment, the three of us went back to bed. I tried to envision the means of our escape from Dievenow but nothing logical or acceptably efficient came to my mind. Then tiredness overcame me and I fell into a troubled sleep.

Early in the morning, Andreas stormed into our room, urging us to look out the window.

"What are the cattle doing in the street?" he demanded to know. Herta explained to him that these were farmers with their wagons moving westward trying to save their families from being captured by the approaching Russians. As they had not wanted to leave the valuable cattle behind, they had driven them along. Usually one or two villages had joined in a trek and after electing a leader, who mapped out the best route westward, they followed in their wagons, one after the other. Their cattle followed the trek, guarded and directed by a few men or women on foot. Herta explained further that the persistent mooing of the cows was a cry for help. They needed to be milked and were in pain if milking time was overdue.

By now the street was totally congested with horses, wagons, cattle, and people. It was a sight of confusion and despair. I felt the desperate tugging at my mind again: to get away from Dievenow as fast as possible. But how?

* * * * * *

The question haunted me. As soon as we finished our hurried breakfast, we heard a knock at the door and, not waiting for Mother's "Come in," Mrs. Barock rushed into the room.

"What are we going to do? It is getting dangerous again. How will we get away from here?" she worried, consulting Mother. Not waiting for Mother to reply, she added that her husband had given her strict orders to keep her family in the house. He would rush home for lunch in case he heard news which needed to be acted upon immediately. Herta told her that we had decided to start packing as soon as we had cleared the table and would be ready to leave at a moment's notice. Tears welled up in Mrs. Barock's eyes again.

"Will we ever stop running? Will we ever be safe?" Realizing that she really had no time to spare, Mrs. Barock left, agreeing that she and Elsa should also hurry with their packing. Mother called behind her, telling her that Mrs. Gander and Mrs. Adomeit had asked to be informed if we decided to pack and that Frederick and Walter should rush over to relay the message. Imploring Frederick not to linger but to return promptly, she dismissed the two boys.

While Mother took charge of the cooking, Herta and I moved our packing into the large, cold room. This arrangement prevented us from getting in each other's way. As long as we kept busy, I felt that God would provide a way out of Dievenow. Although we did not need the baby carriage for Andreas, we decided to pack it again. It would come in handy if Frederick's or Maria's arms got tired from carrying their bags they could drop the bundles on the carriage. It was a practical device, something that had wheels. By now, having had experience in packing, we put the linens and towels on the bottom, almost filling it, and the duffle bag, stuffed with the two feather beds, we tied on top. We had to carry the other baggage, except that Maria and Frederick had their little knapsacks.

Mother wished she had more food in reserve and, taking stock, she estimated that we had enough for only two more meals, a loaf of bread, some margarine, and a small piece of the smoked ham. She urged Herta to pack the salt.

"Salt? Why burden yourself with such nuisance?" Herta demanded to know. I explained to her that in Dievenow we had experienced a critical shortage of salt and that we had not liked to eat our food without it. Obediently, Herta packed the salt, shaking her head in disbelief. Jokingly, Herta remarked that she should have left her bags packed because it was only four days ago that she had arrived here. Realizing the trauma we would have experienced had she not come by now, I sent a prayer of thanksgiving to my beloved Lord, adding my urgent plea that He show us a way to get out of Dievenow quickly and safely.

Across the stripped beds, we lined up coats, shawls, hats, and gloves for everybody. This meant that I was going to wear my triple layer again. Ready to wear Father's trousers under my dress, the jacket over it, and his winter coat over mine, I did not treasure the thought of my project, but I felt it was my duty to rescue some civilian clothes for him.

"Dear God, where is he now?" I asked myself. We had not heard from him since we had left Lautern. My thoughts were suddenly interrupted by Frederick's and Walter's noisy arrival. They shouted their message across the hall.

"Mrs. Gander has been packing all morning. We didn't have to run over and tell her." Mother realized that Karl, Mrs. Gander's son, must have suggested her packing, having heard the news about the special alert at the *Fliegerhorst*.

Shortly after Mr. Barock came home for lunch, a bit out of breath from rushing, he informed us of very important news as we gathered in the corridor. Tonight all civilians were urged to move with their baggage across the bridge to the *Fliegerhorst* because of the danger that Russian troops might advance during the night as close as Cammin. Bombs had been laid across the bridge to Wollin, ready to blow it up if the situation grew critical enough to demand it. At least we were not caught by surprise. Although the idea of spending a night at the base did not sound promising, the military must have planned a way to evacuate us, Herta and I reasoned. Therefore, we would follow these orders to the letter.

After a long and busy day, Herta checked over our baggage in the evening and found everything in order. In the meantime, Mother had prepared our last warm meal to bolster up our energy. Uncertainty lay ahead of us. Mrs. Gander and Mrs. Adomeit with their children had walked over to us, leaving their baggage in the yard. Sitting around, we waited for Mr. Barock and Karl Gander to return from the *Fliegerhorst* to give us further instructions.

"We have completed our three months in Dievenow, as we had in Lautern. It must be time for us to move on," remarked Mrs. Barock in retrospect. I felt it was high time to leave and was glad to see the two men finally arrive. With them had come Heinz, a new friend and co-worker of Karl, also from East Prussia, volunteering to help us carry our baggage. Mother appreciated the extra pair of hands and watched the two young men handle the baby carriage with ease.

"Quite a heavy baby," Heinz joked, commenting on its weight. His light-hearted comment eased Mother's tension. Having donned my three layers of clothes, I felt as if I were carrying all the burdens of the world. One thought was a consolation. I appreciated that it was not raining and that the weather was cold enough so I would not perspire. We did not have to walk far to get to the bridge, but to squeeze through horses, wagons, cattle, and a confused and excited crowd was not easy.

"Hold on to me, Andreas. Let's all keep close together," Mother said excitedly, anxious not to lose any of us. Mr. Barock steered the crowd and the two young men secured the rear of our weary little trek of four families. Herta noticed that, for the time being, the trek of farmers was stopped before the bridge. The halt explained the accumulation of people, the milling congestion in the street. But confidently Mr. Barock marched forward and approached the guard in green army uniform who was controlling traffic moving across the bridge. Showing his passport, Mr. Barock explained that we were familes of those employed at the base—only a half truth—and, like a robot, the stocky soldier motioned us to cross. Not hesitating a moment, we hurried across the bridge. Passing the soldier, I breathed a sigh of relief. I had feared this stone face, staring at the bayonet mounted on his gun, would create a problem. But, thank God, he let all of us pass. Mr. Barock silently motioned us to glance at the steel rails. Spaced three meters apart lay the bombs, ready to be exploded within a moment's notice. Careful, as if stepping over a keg of gunpowder, we tiptoed by.

"Were will we sleep?" asked Mrs. Barock when we reached the other side. Mr. Barock explained that we had to be brave this night. We would not sleep at all. With this statement, he led us to an old pier facing the bay, explaining that the passenger boat which usually shuttled between Cammin and Dievenow would be chartered to evacuate civilians in the morning. For docking purposes, this old pier was to be used. Mr. Barock suggested that we stand in line, to be the first four families to board when the boat arrived the next morning.

Although Mother looked troubled, wondering how the children would get through a night without any sleep, I was glad about this announcement. God had again heard my pleas and found a way for us to escape from Dievenow. If my faith in Him would only grow stronger, if I could realize that I could always rely on Him, I would not need to be so fearful. Again, I gave my silent thanks to Him, praying that He might see us through this ordeal, this evacuation. Mother's fears of having to spend a night at the fringe of the air force base were somewhat lessened.

"We will stay here with you until you board in the morning," promised Mr. Barock, Karl, and Heinz so that we did not have to be frightened of the darkness, of the mob of frantic people who were lining up behind us. Mr. Barock had also heard of another possible way to evacuate. The Focke-Wulff planes had been put into action for this purpose. The men decided to take turns in checking this newest development. In the meantime, we had piled our luggage in one heap and sat on it as comfortably as possible. As time moved on, the line at the pier grew longer. Many East Prussian refugees who had arrived in Dievenow with us had received the same evacuation notice: to wait at the pier for the boat. Knowing that our little troupe was first in line, Mr. Barock and Karl had walked over to the air strip to check our chances of leaving by plane. Both came back, confirming the possibility, but cautioned the women that baggage was strictly limited, permitting hand luggage only. Anything heavier had to be left behind. Mother was undecided.

"I don't know what to do," she fretted over and over. The factor of restricted luggage could have been only a minor concern but I sensed that she was terrified of flying.

The night wore on with different rumors passing from every side. It was difficult to keep a cool head. Finally, to clarify Mother's confusion, Herta and I suggested that we check the plane situation. Afterward, we would decide whether to wait for the boat or evacuate by plane. As we headed into the darkness, we discovered something had been hidden behind a thicket of tall reeds, from our view at the pier. The City of Cammin across the bay was in flames! Standing still for a moment, Herta and I heard the rumble in the distance. An enormous pink hue, against which the black silhouette of a burning church steeple was clearly visible, covered a large half moon area against the dark coastline of the bay. It did not seem to be a bombing and Herta voiced her frightful suspicion that the Russian artillery were most likely firing heavily into Cammin.

"Do you realize what this means?" she asked, and I knew this fact indicated the front was less than eight kilometers away.

"My God, how will we get out of here?" I prayed aloud in panic. It had to happen fast because the Russians might be in Dievenow by morning. Herta and I rushed over to the air strip. The situation looked worse here. People were frantically packing and rearranging their few belongings. It was one mass of confusion, people shouting, pushing and fighting, children crying. One woman was leaning on another, sobbing in the darkness.

"They went down; they are all dead," she moaned. Checking further as to the reason for her hysteria, we learned that those people waiting in line at the air strip had counted that almost every fifth plane crashed into the bay. They had been overloaded with panic-stricken refugees. Frantically men of the army tried to control this mass of hysterical people, shouting—screaming snappy commands at them. Herta and I fought our way back to the pier, almost getting lost in this dark, terrified mass of humanity. The fire in Cammin had spread panic among them, which even the military had difficulty in controlling. I walked slowly, hampered by the many layers of clothing but, more so, because I needed to think, to think clearly, to think fast. At one point, I leaned against the cold cement wall of a huge hangar, staring in the direction of Cammin. One soldier had confirmed our suspicions: the front was before Cammin, only a stone's throw away.

"God, what shall we do?" I almost screamed my prayer out loud. In order to be able to concentrate, I closed my eyes. Herta urged that we leave by plane; I was suggesting that we risk waiting for the boat in the morning.

"But will it come? Will it get through?" Herta asked fearfully. If we missed it, we were lost—that I knew. Silently, each one fighting with her own decision, we walked back to the pier. We had agreed on one thing: to tell Mother the truth. With all the calmness we could muster, we told her that Cammin was under artillery attack and burning.

"Oh, my God!" she stammered, panic flashing across her face. When we mentioned that we had a chance to get away by plane, but that a great number of casualties had been reported because of crashes, she firmly decided to wait for the boat. What shook her decision a few moments later though was that Mr. Barock persuaded his wife and family to evacuate by plane. Mother anxiously watched them hurry over to the air strip. Mrs. Gander worried, and consulting Mother was no help. Her son Karl appraised the emergency.

"If the front gets as far as the bay during the night, the Russians might shoot into Wollin and the boat, being in full view, might not be able to dock," he reasoned. We were fully aware that we might wait this entire night in vain, only to find the Russians in Dievenow at dawn.

"Please, dear God, make this decision for us; we are too confused," I pleaded. It was a decision of life or death, of freedom or captivity. Being captured by the barbaric Russians almost guaranteed that we would all be murdered. Staring into the blackness of the night, I prayed. No, I pleaded, and then I made a promise.

"If You will take all of us out of Dievenow safely and alive, I will serve Thee and Thine Creation for the rest of my life! God, I pray, have mercy! Hear me! Please!" Then, feeling somewhat calmer, I stepped over to Mother and suggested that we should wait for the boat, no matter what the others decided to do. She looked relieved and I was glad Herta now agreed with me. It might be a call as close as a hair's breadth but evacuating by boat was the safer way to leave. Only a short while later, Mrs. Barock and her family returned from the air strip.

"No, if I am to die, I might as well die on the boat, but I will not drown in a plane crash," Mrs. Barock cried determinedly. Her decision settled the matter also for Mrs. Gander and Mrs. Adomeit. After three hours of turmoil, our crowd became strangely quiet and I had the comforting feeling that I was not the only one praying feverishly throughout the night. I did not feel hungry or tired. The only way to control my inner panic was through continuous prayer. Only God knew how many cries, pleas, and prayers reached out heavenward this night, but the thousands of fearful souls frantically held on to one promise: God's mercy.

When, almost unnoticeable at first, the darkness turned into a deep gray and then the early dawn announced a new day, a feeling of hope lifted my anxiety. The Russians were not yet in Dievenow and the fires in Cammin had died down to faint smoke against the early morning sky. When someone announced the fact that the boat was on its way to the pier, a middle-aged soldier posted himself at the entrance, a bayonet on his gun. His function was to assure that boarding of refugees took place in an orderly fashion. Mrs. Barock and her family were first in line and we were standing behind her. Lining up behind us were Mrs. Gander and Mrs. Adomeit and their children. We had the best chance to get on. After another hour of anxious waiting, the boat was finally visible as it slowly moved along the channel and then it made a right turn to dock at the pier. The weary crowd perked up. But something happened when the crew of the boat threw the wooden bridge on the outer end of the pier. A stream of people coming from the left side broke a portion out of the flimsy, wooden railing and climbed onto the pier, only ten yards before our noses, and boarded the boat. It took us a few seconds to grasp the sudden change in our situation. "What is this!?" Mrs. Barock let out a scream of fury that turned the armed, fat soldier around on his heel. She stormed up to him, demanding an explanation, but did not wait for an answer. As the boat filled quickly, she tore at his collar, pounded her fists on his chest, screaming, yelling.

"Where do you have your wife and children? Let us pass this second or I'll push you into the bay, you beast!" she threatened, her hands grabbing his throat. The tumult, quickly turning into an open revolt, made the guard fear for his life as we pushed him full force against the railing and almost stampeded over him. He had not had a chance to utter a word or use his weapon. When we arrived at the boat within seconds, it was almost filled. But the Barocks, Ganders, Adomeits, and Mother with Andreas, Frederick, and Herta got on. As if a phenomenon had happened, the boat was fully loaded within five minutes. Hurriedly checking where Herta had found a seat on deck, I heard terrifying screams from the pier. To my horror, I saw that it was Maria. Dutifully watching the bag with the bedding, she was still standing on the pier and Mother had momentarily forgotten her in this frenzy, this chaos. The deck hands were about to pull in the wooden bridge. I jumped back on the pier.

"Hold the bridge!" I yelled at them, grabbing Heinz by his sleeve, and dragged him to the front of the pier. Only then did he realize the crucial situation. He flung the duffle bag over his shoulder while I frantically tore Maria along. We flew down the distance to the boat and jumped onto the bridge just as the men grabbed the ropes, pulling it in hastily. My heart pounded as if it were going to jump out of my throat. I trembled so hard that I had to force my back against the cabin wall to steady my knees. "You can't afford to collapse," I puffed to myself. The triple layer of clothing had made it almost impossible to walk, not to mention flying down the pier. When I finally regained my composure and steadied my trembling knees, I realized that I was still gripping Maria's hand as if by a steel clamp. Yet she stood next to me, not speaking, not complaining, only staring at me. Letting her small hand go, it looked white from my tight grip.

"I hope I didn't break your fingers," I apologized but, massaging them, Maria assured me they were all right. Then, slowly, I pulled away from the cabin wall to find a way downstairs where the majority of people sat tightly cramped together. I had to locate Mother and the two boys. Within the second that Maria and I had jumped aboard, the boat had moved away and headed back for the channel to get out of the open view of the bay, out of the shooting range of the approaching Russians! While we climbed over tightly seated people, someone shouted.

"What is this? Look at the trees! They are bending down to the ground!" One of the boat hands, with a trained eye, explained that it was Russian artillery shooting into the southeastern outskirts of Dievenow. I wanted to push the boat, to move faster, to get away! Finally, it made its way safely around the bend and into the narrow channel and was heading for the tip of Dievenow, westward. Standing at the top of the stairs, I saw the captain of the boat climb down from the helm and, to my amazement, he smiled. As he carefully made his way down, trying to avoid stepping on those people sitting on the stairs, he told us that the Baltic Sea was rough today and had been mined the night before.

"Usually the boat is not permitted to go out on such a rough sea," he informed us but, under these chaotic circumstances, he had taken on the responsibility of steering it. He assured the crowd of worried women that the boat was structurally sound and should be able to handle the rough sea. The high waves might be our luck, inasmuch as they made it easier to spot a mine, allowing him to change the course of the boat if necessary. Although his comments indicated that we still had to surmount a number of grave obstacles, the obstacle we had just overcome was the worst of my life. By a hair's breadth, we had got away from the Russians, from Dievenow! The captain's confident smile lifted a heavy load off my anxious mind. In passing us, he suggested that we rather not eat, no matter how hungry the long and sleepless night had made us because, if we did, we would only feed the fish.

By now I was confident that we were on our way to safety as the boat moved between Dievenow and the island of Wollin, sputtering its way through the channel, toward the rough, open Baltic Sea. I walked Maria down the narrow, crowded staircase to the only floor under deck. The odor emanating from the mass of people packed together on the lower deck made me feel faint, but I insisted that Maria stay with Mother.

"You almost forgot me! You left me behind with the duffle bag," Maria broke out in tears. Mother's face turned white, but I assured her that we were all on board and all right now. Telling her about the captain's suggestion, I mentioned the possibility of seasickness and she promised not to let anyone eat. I was not hungry. The tight band of anxiety around my stomach did not permit me to eat until we had crossed the Baltic Sea, until I was certain we were out of danger.

Giving Mother a description of Herta's and my own whereabouts on deck, I left. The closeness below deck would have added to my anxiety. Therefore, I preferred to sit under the open sky, despite the sharp, cold wind whipping across the water. I had taken only a few steps when the boat jerked wildly, as if it had hit something hard. A few women screamed. Holding on to a post, I felt the boat roll from side to side. I soon realized it was fighting its way through the first breakers along the steel pier to get out into the open waters. I assured Mother that this swaying would subside and she should not be alarmed about the violent rocking of the boat because the sea was rough. Climbing and stumbling my way back to the stairs, I noticed the first signs of seasickness and I moved quickly to scramble on deck. The odor downstairs had drawn my throat tightly shut and I was glad to feel the crisp breeze on deck. Even here, seasickness was spreading. Wherever I looked, people were vomiting and I had to move quickly and carefully to keep Father's coat clean.

Stopping on an unoccupied square foot of space, I looked for Herta and spotted her sitting on a pile of ropes, the duffle bag beside her. Walter Barock was frantically holding on to Elsa's coat as she was leaning over the railing to feed the fish. The heavy swaying of the boat had almost thrown her overboard. So far, no one in our family had ever been seasick and I wondered how we would weather this storm.

"How does your stomach feel?" I asked Herta. She assured me that she felt fine except that she could not watch the crowd spit up.

"Thank God, we have not eaten anything," I said and, watching Elsa's struggle, Herta agreed that following the captain's suggestion had been an excellent idea. While we helped Walter in his efforts to hold on to his sister, Elsa turned her green face toward us.

"There went my breakfast," she said, a trouble she would have saved herself by fasting. Walter promised to get some water and Elsa sat down next to us. As she pointed to a baby carriage in front of us, we noticed that even the tiny infant was seasick.

"The poor creature," said Elsa compassionately. Its carriage rocked back and forth with the rolling of the boat. Walter, having fought his way back through the throng, held up a glass with water, of which he had spilled half trying to balance himself on the rocking boat. Elsa drank it with relish. It perked her up immediately and her face took on her normal complexion.

While searching for drinking water, Walter had heard another piece of news. Downstairs, a young mother was in labor, delivering a child. In a two by three meter compartment, a midwife who was among the crowd of refugees was giving her assistance.

"What timing! The poor woman will remember this agony for the rest of her life," Herta cried out. She was right. A different thought, however, crossed my mind. It was miraculous; even amidst chaos, life would not be subdued; life had a force of its own, a very powerful force.

When the boat was far out at sea, I heard the distant sound of a plane. Scanning the sky, I noticed one flying very high overhead. Worriedly, I pointed the speck out to Herta.

"I hope it is a German plane, if not, God help us!" she said. Sitting down on the duffle bag, I silently started to pray. I was convinced that prayer and my cries to God had gotten us this far. Therefore, I had to hold on to Him. He was the only One Who could assure us a safe crossing of the heavily mined Baltic Sea. He could send this plane away, even if it was Russian. I prayed that He would and, keeping my eyes open, I followed its direction. The plane seemed to move with the boat at a slow speed as if watching or following us. After each prayer, some long and some short, I checked the position of the plane. Finally, after a seeming eternity, it changed its course to a northerly direction, away from us.

"Thanks, dear Lord, for hearing me," I prayed with a grateful heart. He had graciously averted another danger.

The boat labored heavily through the fury of the waves and often it looked as if the raging sea would swallow it but, after sinking almost to the bottom, it was spewn up again like a ball dancing up and down. Tumbling sideways like a drunkard, it fought its way forward ever so slowly, a brave soldier indeed. From the helm of the boat, word came that the captain was trying to route the ship safely through the heavily mined ocean before Swinemuende and, if we passed, head for the channel between the island of Usedom and Wollin and aim for the west bank of the Stettiner Haff. Once we had passed Swinemuende, leaving the choppy sea behind, the rest of our weary journey would be less hazardous. Within approximately a half hour, the boat would be steered through the heavily mined harbor. On hearing this news, I resumed my feverish prayer. The boat had to make it through. We were several hundred people on board, people trying to escape from Bolshevism, a life and death matter.

Soon the boat swayed violently as the captain changed its course landward. In the distance I noticed several church steeples which I assumed were in the city of Swinemuende. Judging by the position of the sun, it was past noontime.

"I guess we will reach our destination before dark," Herta estimated. I wondered how far south we would be taken because we were told that our journey would continue by train from the western shore of the Stettiner Haff.

Slowly the boat approached the mouth of the channel, careful of each move, as if trying to avoid a blow-up by a mine lurking in the deep. When the creaking boat braced itself to battle the violently breaking surf at the mouth of the channel, I knew it would take only a few more critical minutes. For a moment it felt as if the captain had lost control over his ship as it tumbled around in the raging sea, but then it slowly steadied its shuddering body and finally nosed into the calm channel.

"Thank God!" I let out an audible sigh of relief as we passed the first docks at the gray and battered harbor of Swinemuende. From the boat I could see that an entire area had been destroyed during the last bombing attack. Black, charred beams stuck out of a heap of rubble, bearing witness to a raging fire that had destroyed the buildings. The Soviets must have gotten wind of the V-2 missile installation and had savagely bombed the area, putting it out of operation.

As the boat moved farther south, the channel widened into a bay and the coastline of the western island of Usedom grew narrow against the northwestern horizon. We were crossing the Stettiner Haff at a southwestern angle, steering toward the coast of the province of Mecklenburg. It was a relief to know that the boat was under control and had doubled its speed now that it had left the churning Baltic Sea behind. I sent up a fervent prayer of thanks to my gracious Lord, Who had safely cloaked the boat and had protected us from being blown up.

As the captain was now positive that his heavy load of precious souls was safe, he entrusted the wheel to one of his mates and climbed down from the bridge to make an announcement: he had received orders to dock and unload at Ueckermuende. This small harbor at the western shore of the Stettiner Haff was considered safe, safe enough to shelter us for a night, and in the morning we would be moved westward by train. He explained that the fast approaching darkness would provide a protective cover and he was confident that we did not need to fear bombing of the boat. Pointing westward, he added that the steeples and buildings in the distance belonged to Ueckermuende. Within an hour, he expected to arrive.

"I'll go downstairs and tell mother," said Herta. Walter Barock also got up to relay the encouraging news to his mother. With a grumbling stomach, hunger was making itself known after a night and a day of fasting. For the first time I became aware that I was tired, exhausted, but I would not give in to sleep until we had arrived at our temporary destination. The shoreline moved closer and closer and when the sun touched the horizon, I saw the harbor of Ueckermuende. I estimated the city to be approximately the size of Cammin, perhaps fifty thousand inhabitants. When Herta returned, she told us that during our rough ride on the Baltic Sea the expected baby had been born.

"The brand new citizen is feeling fine," she reported with a smile, but the woman who had acted as a midwife had mentioned that the young mother felt weak. A stretcher had been moved into the small compartment to allow her to lie flat.

"Not one of our family has been seasick," Herta proudly added. It appeared as if we were the only seafast family on the boat. Herta told me that Mother appreciated the news that we would soon dock and put the baggage in order to disembark quickly. She was curious as to where we would sleep tonight as the three youngest ones showed definite signs of fatigue. Only Andreas had fallen asleep during the day.

Finally the boat slowed down its speed and the harbor of Ueckermuende was in full view. As no lights were permitted, the black silhouette against the darkening sky made the city appear like a ghost town. Herta was ordered to get up from the pile of ropes and a strong seaman hurriedly untied them while the captain maneuvered the boat sideways against a high, cement dock. Evidently members of the *Volkssturm*, a civilian reserve, were in charge of guiding the arriving refugees. When the hard-worked engines finally stopped puffing, two seamen shouted a signal and, with a labored swing, flung the ends of two heavy ropes onto the dock where two burly men fastened them around enormous steel spools. Quickly a wooden bridge with flimsy side railings was lowered from the dock onto the side of the boat and the weary crowd started to disembark. Herta and I posted ourselves at the side of the bridge until we saw Mother climb up the narrow stairs with the three children. When they had scrambled on to the dock, Herta and I followed, tugging along the duffle bag and the baby carriage.

"Land under our feet again!" Mother called over to Mrs. Barock. "What relief!"

Chapter XI

Thy Rod and Thy Staff...

Although I was dead tired, my heart felt free; free of panic, free of tension. My Lord had escaped with us. He had accompanied us every step of the way. Through this close call, He had held us by His firm, loving Hand. I loved Him, I trusted Him. He would take us to a safe place. I was certain.

As the weary, exhausted assemblage walked in a given direction, numbly following the men of the *Volkssturm*, an order was passed along.

"All heavy baggage must be stored in a warehouse overnight." This announcement made Mother uneasy, although the men in uniform accompanying the stream of people assured her that it would be safe. Our troupe of refugees was scheduled to leave by train early the next morning and the baggage was to be loaded during the night into the last few cars. Mother was reluctant to part with the luggage, especially as she feared losing the linens in the baby carriage. But she had no choice. Herta suggested that we securely tie the heavy duffle bag on top, leaving our name and home address clearly visible. A *Volkssturm* man rounded up a piece of rope and helped Herta with the job. It was a funny sight to watch the man shuffle off with the baby carriage. In the darkness and confusion, it took us a while to realize where we were taken until word again travelled from the front that our load of refugees arriving from Dievenow was scheduled to spend the night in the town theater. It was the only public building available to accommodate such a big crowd.

"Of all places!" Mother called out good-humoredly, "I never

imagined that our family would sleep in a theater." Mrs. Barock laughed, and giving her simple attire a searching glance, remarked jokingly that she felt bad, not being dressed properly for the occasion.

The warehouse was nearby and as many women loudly protested against parting with their few belongings, the confusion and noise was incredible. Convincing Mother that our baggage would be safe in the warehouse, she stopped fussing, especially when I mentioned that God would watch over it.

"If He wants us to have it, we will; otherwise, we should appreciate that we have gotten away with our lives," I heard myself say. Even Mrs. Barock agreed that humanity lacked a trust in God and, instead, frantically held on to things. Maria and Frederick were permitted to carry their small knapsacks, which would serve them as pillows during the night. Mother held on to her handbag and the meager food supply which she carried in another. At times I felt my head spinning, but I forced myself to stay awake and remain alert. Soon we would be able to sleep, I consoled myself.

When we arrived at the entrance of the stately looking theater I glanced inside. A feeling of shame came over me. Our motley crowd, looking worse than beggars, filed into a hall covered with straw. Each family was ordered to take as little space as possible. It bothered me to see walls covered with deep red velvet and the most elegant and elaborately designed crystal chandelier hanging from the dome of the theater. How the walls must cringe in disgust at the sight of us, I thought and, mentally apologizing, I entered, feeling like an intruder. We had to spend this night somewhere. Besides, it was an official order, I excused myself.

In a sense, I was glad that by the time our troupe scrambled in, the main floor was filled. A man directed us upstairs to the balcony. The balcony would lend a trifle more privacy than the ground floor. Glancing up, I saw that the theater had two balconies. Slowly we climbed up the creaking wooden stairs, shuffling over plush carpeting, forward and upward. When we reached the first balcony, it, too, was already filled. This meant our family would spend the night in the second balcony. Looking down over the beautifully carved mahogany banister, I saw that the seats had been removed in order to provide as much seating and sleeping space as possible for this throng of homeless and fleeing humanity. Puffing under my triple layer of clothes, I followed the rest of the family, securing the rear to make sure we had everyone accounted for. From now on, I was not going to take any chances. A slow halt at the top of the stairs allowed me to look around. As well as circumstances permitted, one family at a time settled at the far end of the second balcony. It took a while until our group finally found some space. Mrs. Barock, Elsa, Walter, and little Martin were first. Mr. Barock and Karl Gander had been ordered to stay behind at the *Fliegerhorst*. Mother, with the five of us, climbed up closely behind the Barocks. Mrs. Gander and Mrs. Adomeit and their children had been squeezed into the first balcony. Mother was glad that we slept next to our neighbors, people we knew, but those following us were strangers. The *Volkssturm* men, however, ordered us to move together as closely as possible.

"We will be packed like sardines if everybody stretches out during the night," Herta said. Although the scene repulsed me, making me feel sick at heart, I had to secure enough space for myself to be able to sit down. God knows what tomorrow might bring, I thought, knowing that my body demanded sleep desperately. Taking off my two coats and folding them neatly, lining out, I put them down on the straw, knowing this spot had to serve as my bed for the night. We were safe, at least for now; we were alive; that was all that mattered.

Glancing over the banister down to the ground floor, I saw a cloud of dust, stirred up by the crowd, milling around the gorgeous chandelier. The air was dry. Holding on to a polished post, my eyes rested on the scene for a moment. My empty stomach, the dizziness, the subdued light from the chandelier, all made me wonder if this scene was real or only a bad dream. I blinked my eyes deliberately and tapped my dizzy head against the post to assure myself that what I saw, was reality. It seemed insane, but it was true. If Father ever saw us here, he would not believe his eyes, I thought. "Where is he?" I wondered, "while our country is falling apart and we, his family, have sunk to a state lower than gypsies." We did not even have a wagon. Knowing it was not right to allow my mind to wander into despair, I pulled myself up, sizing up our situation coolly. Having noticed the two long lines downstairs, I turned to Mother.

"Let's forget about using the bathroom facilities. They are on the ground floor," I suggested. She was aware of the problem we would have in climbing over this multitude of people stretched out like sardines, heads to the wall, feet to the banister. In the dimness of the light, one could not avoid stepping on someone's feet. For myself, I decided it was safer not to eat but Mother insisted that I at least take a small drink of water. It amazed me how well she managed to feed everyone, sitting on one of the knapsacks and handing out a dry sandwich. For our family it was the first meal after a long sleepless night and a strenuous day. Mother knew it would be useless to try to persuade me to eat once I had decided to continue my fast.

The crowd in the second balcony soon stretched out as well as the tight quarters permitted. Standing and waiting at the pier during the previous night and the long, hazardous boat ride had taken the last bit of energy out of everybody. Yet I did not hear one word of complaint from anyone. Each person must have been grateful to have pulled through alive. Before our family retired, Mother took a roll call of the three young ones.

"Who needs to go to the bathroom?" she asked. As I had feared, all three raised their hands. Consequently, the troublesome climb downstairs could not be avoided and, as I was closest to the stairs, Mother asked me to go with them. We formed a chain by holding hands at the left and balanced ourselves against the banister with the right. After countless times of saying "Excuse me" and "I'm sorry," we finally made it down the stairs. Judging by the lines in front of the two doors, I estimated our waiting time to be approximately an hour. The very thing I had tried to avoid had happened. As the line moved foot by foot, I glanced at the crowd spread out on the huge ground floor and recognized the faces of a few people who had lived in Dievenow all their lives. Only three months ago, they looked down on us, had considered us as second-class humanity but, tonight, they shared our fate.

What were their thoughts at this moment? I wondered. Did they realize they were refugees now, or did they think it to be a bad dream? Experience was a hard but sobering teacher, making one aware that nothing in life was guaranteed, especially not life itself. Therefore, every person lived by the Grace of God and by no other reason. This was an uplifting realization because, through my recent experiences, I had learned to talk to God, to trust Him with everything, including my life, and He had not failed me once. His guiding hand, although invisible, had carried our family this far; therefore, I could be confident He would take us far enough to the west, to safety.

"Help me to realize this more often, dear Lord," I prayed, knowing this awareness would make me calmer, enable me to think more clearly. For the first time, a feeling of compassion, of understanding for those who had resented us crept into my mind. Two ladies from Dievenow had taken only a handbag and a pillow when they left, positive that the whole evacuation was a nuisance, not realizing they would never return. Never, unless they were willing to live under Soviet tyranny, which I considered equivalent to death. Had those poor ladies fully grasped their situation?

Amidst the crowd and commotion, I recognized the young mother who had given birth to her child only a few hours ago. Someone had donated a baby carriage, as it was the only one on the floor. The newborn baby gave his first thin cries, while the mother prepared a bottle to feed it. What a way to start a life, I thought and prayed that God may hold His hand over both.

From the women standing in line, I tried to find out what our next destination would be, but no one knew.

"Far enough west, I hope," said one of them, and I agreed with her. We had finally shuffled to the door and Maria went to the bathroom. The line for boys was shorter and Frederick and Andreas had already returned. When Maria joined us again, I noticed that each one looked exhausted. I was glad I had not passed a mirror and seen my own face. The sight of myself would have horrified me. Having been awake all night, having been in constant panic, having had no chance to wash or change clothes, it was wiser to avoid a mirror and I was glad that, except for our neighbors and my family, nobody here knew me.

As we struggled up the many stairs, I wondered where my classmates were and my beloved teacher, Miss Zahn. It seemed eons ago that I had lived in Gumbinnen and gone to school. And where were Aunt Ina and Uncle Oskar, Oma, and Aunt Maria? Did they evacuate in time? We had lost contact with all relatives, and we had not received a word from Father. Neither did we know what was happening at the fronts, other than that the Russians were right on our heels. With this move I was certain we would be taken far enough west to escape the Bolsheviks. I did not care which army overran the west after we were safe. I knew the Americans were the most humane of our western enemies but, if the British occupied our territory, it was all right with me.

I did not fear the Americans or the British. Both countries were inaccessible to our armies and therefore had not been invaded by Hitler as was done in Russia. From the many wounded soldiers who had returned from the Western front we learned that the Anglo-American troops were honorable in their warfare. No cases of murder or cruelties committed against civilians had been reported. Their countries' leaders and their generals were considered to be fair men. What neither our military nor we civilians could understand, however, was the fact that Britain and America had signed a pact with Stalin, a man whom Father considered to be as raw and brutal a character as Hitler, if not worse.

Therefore we civilians knew that the Russian army, under Stalin's direct order, would carry out their commander's instructions, and we had the feeling that Stalin and Hitler tried to compete in bestialities and outdo each other in viciousness.

Mrs. Gander, our neighbor, had also confirmed this feeling. She had told Mother in one of their over-the-fence conversations the reason why she had returned from the Ukraine to Germany.

"My parents are originally from the German province of Sachsen. They had moved to the Ukraine and owned a farm near the city of Odessa under the Czarist regime," Mrs. Gander had told Mother. The Czarina, a German princess by birth, had generously invited German farmers to Russia, invited them to till the thousands of acres of the fertile soil of the Ukraine. After the family of the Czar had been brutally murdered at Sarajevo and the Bolsheviks had forced their way to power, German families living in Russia were harrassed, their farms set on fire, their owners forced to leave. The Gander family therefore had decided to return to their homeland, Germany, but instead of moving back to Sachsen, they settled near Gumbinnen.

"My husband and I were born in Russia," Mrs. Gander had stated, a fact which accounted for the slight flaw in their German language. The Ganders knew the resentfulness of the Russians, had witnessed their cruelties, had experienced their harrassment. Therefore Mrs. Gander had stated that they would move to the end of the earth, if need be, to escape Bolshevism.

Although not every German family had experienced eyewitness accounts, there was a fear, a distrust toward the Russians, that no one was going to take a chance on their lives.

Being aware of the threat, of the danger and having heard the wounded soldier's story at the military hospital in Gumbinnen, I was driven by panic: we had to get away.

Although I realized that the British and Americans, after winning the war, would treat us Germans as the losers, I was certain that they would not deal unfairly with civilians.

As a matter of fact, seeing Hitler's power destroyed, was a great relief to me, having suffered under its chicanery.

Once our family would be captured by the Anglo-American troops, we would be free, free from tyranny, free to speak and free to live again. Oh, how great it would feel to be free, free of Hitler and his cohorts, and free of that witchy Mrs. Thorne. God would deal with those dangerous fanatics in a just manner, I was certain. Neither would I have to worry any more about the beast of the Jungmaedel who had ordered me to see a Nazi doctor when I had not felt like sacrificing my precious summer vacation. God knew even this girl's blindness, her errors, and He was in charge of her life. And I remembered the phrase from the Bible.

"The revenge is Mine, saith the Lord." Father was right, trusting in God and keeping one's own hands clean had been his motto. God had proven to me today that we were still in the palm of His hand and, as He had promised, He would not permit anyone to harm us. I realized that my faith in Him had made me grow strong so that I was able to keep my emotions under control. Only this discipline had prevented me from panicking, and I was grateful to know an Almighty God, Someone Who I could hold on to. This Someone knew me as an individual and, moreover, He loved me. I gladly submitted my life to our Creator, Who had room in His heart for everyone, for each and every human being. What an exciting adventure it would be to see where He would guide me in order to have me fulfill my promise: to serve Him and His Creation!

When the four of us again finally reached the second balcony, cautiously climbing over a multitude of legs, feet, and shoes, I was glad to sit down. Complete fatigue was overcoming me. Arranging the two coats closer to the wall, I sat down, leaning my back against the plush velvet wall for support. To my right, our family had settled for the night. Maria, Frederick, and Andreas had stretched out flat on their coats and Mother arranged a narrow spot for herself next to Elsa Barock. Herta had followed my example, propping herself up against the wall in a sitting position.

My eyes wandered to the left; these people were all strangers. Two young boys had stretched out next to me and close to them, an elderly man. Probably noticing the questioning look on my face, the boy nearest me explained that this man had traveled to Germany from Windhoek in Southwest Africa, where he had lived for many years. When he saw the danger that East Germany could be over-run by the Soviets, he hurried back home by boat in order to visit his family, to persuade them to move to Southwest Africa. When he arrived in Germany, the Russians had already occupied his home town and he found himself caught up in the stream of refugees, not knowing where the members of his family might be. His graying head rested on a small leather briefcase and his beige, prominent Southwestern hat on his stomach, while his hands were folded across his chest.

What caught my attention was the man's face. Covered with long, graying bristles, evidently from not shaving for days, a stream of tears flowed from his half-closed eyes, soaking his face. He must have been praying, pouring out his heart's agonies to God, the only One Who in these hours of destitution would lend His ear to hear, Who would comfort a wretched soul with His love. A feeling of compassion welled up in my heart as I watched the man for a while. He, although alone, had also found a Hand to hold on to, a God to cry out to, a God he could trust. We were all the same: God's children, young and old alike, regardless from where we had come. I prayed for the mass of refugees down below, including this man, a lost and lonely soul, and added a practical request that the balconies might not break under their heavy loads.

Although tired to the point of exhaustion, I could not relax sufficiently to fall asleep. The dim lights of the chandelier were kept burning during the night and did not let me sleep. Neither did my cautious mind permit me to faint; it was a troubled state of desperation.

"What will we do in case of alarm?" Herta asked sleepily. Moments later the announcement came over the loudspeaker that only in case of the danger signal would we move out of the theater. As if our merciful God recognized our tight situation, the alarm never sounded. The rest of the night I remembered only as a vague blur, waking early the next morning when someone climbed over my feet. I had fallen asleep and found myself in a crumpled-up position on the floor. As most of the crowd was still sleeping, I carefully got up to climb down to the bathroom. A splash of cold water on my face would feel heavenly and I wanted to wash my hands. I felt cruel having to step over so many sleeping people, but I saw no other way.

Having taken off my shoes, carrying them by their laces, I tiptoed toward the stairs and managed with relative ease to get by. The line to the facilities was short and within minutes it was my turn to get to the bathroom. Miraculously, I found a strip of toilet paper which I used as a towel after splashing handfuls of clean, cold water into my face. With a scrap of soap, I washed my hands and the foam was dark gray. I quickly combed my hair, avoiding the mirror. I felt better; now I would be able to handle this day.

Passing the big entrance hall on my way back, I saw that something was being delivered in huge steel milk cans. It was warm milk for the infants, I learned from the conversation of two men. While I speedily climbed to the second balcony, a voice over the loudspeaker ordered the crowd to be ready and outside the theater within an hour. Food would be served in the open because people were too tightly packed inside. Immediately the commotion started and I was glad to get back to our family.

* * * * * *

Meantime everybody had wakened and aimed for downstairs. As the crowd thinned out in the main hall, people started to file down the stairs. When the Barocks and our family, the tail end of our troupe, stepped outside, I took a deep breath of clean, fresh air. Following the move of the crowd in the food line, I was glad when my turn came. I was famished. The dry sandwich and the milky cereal tasted heavenly. Feeling stronger after this hearty breakfast, I was able to handle my triple layer of clothes with relative ease. A *Volkssturm* man ordered us to follow the main stream of people to the station, assuring Mother that our luggage had already been loaded. Quickly assembling with our neighbors, we stepped up our pace, having located the Ganders and Adomeits as well as the Barocks. It was only a short walk but, to our dismay, we discovered that all refugees were to be loaded into freight cars, cars without windows, without seats.

"What a disgrace!" Mrs. Barock cried out, but the men urging us to hurry left her no time for protest, for emotions. We had to move quickly to secure sufficient space for our four families because loading went fast. A man in uniform assigned us a car toward the second half of the train. The children had no trouble climbing on, but the adults had to be helped up the two narrow, widely spaced steps. Five families were assigned to our car. Besides our three neighbors, a woman with two small children joined us. The floor of the car was covered with straw and the distinct stench of herring inside repulsed me.

"They must have transported fish with this car," said Herta, holding her nose. It was obvious. The man running past outside told us that Russian prisoners had been transported with the train recently, but he assured us that the straw had been renewed.

"How sickening!" I cried, feeling my hair stand up straight in disgust. Mother gave me a glance of understanding. She knew my sensitivity in regard to odors, to uncleanliness. Herta reminded me that the ride in this cattle car was our only chance to freedom and I had to accept it gratefully as such. Hoping we would be out of here before nighttime, I appraised our situation from this point of view. Although it was cold outside, we had to leave the big, heavy sliding door open in order not to suffocate from the stench of herring. To make sure no one would fall out while the train was in motion, we had to crowd into the sides of the car. We settled the small children in the back where they would not be exposed to the cold draft. It was not easy but we managed.

"This is far better than walking," said Herta assuringly, helping me to appreciate even these primitive means of transportation. She explained that by train we had a chance to get far enough away from the forward-pressing Russians. This fast move would guarantee our being captured by the western armies. I agreed with her and this fact alone helped me reconcile myself to our most uncomfortable situation.

When, with a sudden jolt, the train started to move, I was glad we were on our way westward again. Mrs. Barock took a head count of the people in our car and arrived at a number of twenty-one children of all ages and five adults, a large crowd for only one car. What we did not know, however, was our destination. The man in charge of the train had breezed by, saying it would depend on the safety of the cities we passed and how quickly open tracks could be obtained from the railroad net to move us. It could take two days or a week. He himself did not know, but would keep us informed.

Having been told that Russian prisoners had been transported in our car, I was petrified that we might pick up lice. I tried desperately to avoid this problem by standing up, leaning against a wall, not sitting down in the straw. It was maddening. The thought of a sleepless night in this cold car, however, was the worst. The stench and the sight of uncleanliness made me itch already. I decided to stand up as long as possible and, as it was a sunny day, I held on to the open door, watching the countryside slip by. It was such a peaceful scene, farms strewn here and there, and patches of deep green pines in the distance; no outward signs of war or danger.

Is it true then? I asked myself. But the jolting of the train, its rattling noises, confirmed the stark truth. A mad war was being waged and we were refugees, trying to escape to freedom with little more than our bare lives, escaping from Bolshevism, an idea of horror that devoured people. It devoured them by way of raw murder, slow starvation, and forced demoralization, all three a sure death of body, mind, and soul. So far our family had been deeply humiliated but we were still free, free to think, free to believe. I realized that under the Hitler regime, our freedom was greatly limited. Therefore, I hoped that soon, perhaps very soon, we would be free, truly free.

As my mind rushed forward, envisioning a better future, our train moved slowly, ever so slowly westward toward an unknown destination. As it crawled in a huge curve around a wooded area, I noticed its length. It must have been more than fifty cars long, a heavy load to pull for the one locomotive.

"It looks endless," commented Frederick, who leaned against the other side of the door. "Small wonder that we move at a snail's pace."

Sometimes, for no apparent reason, the train stood in one area for hours. Questioning the man in charge about these long delays of the train, we learned that a large city was being bombed and, to remain unobtrusive during daylight, it halted at a wooded area, taking cover. After the first day of this routine, we used these long waits to escape into the brush for lack of toilets on the train.

"Don't run away too far," Mother cautioned us, afraid that the train might move, leaving us behind. Only under cover of the night had the train stopped at larger stations. Hence, the lack of food became a problem. Inventive Mrs. Barock suggested that at our next long stop, two women should run to the nearest farm and ask for food.

"It will be risky, but we have to feed the young ones," she insisted. Mother agreed because our own meager reserves had run out. Herta mentioned that a potful of boiled potatoes would fill our empty stomachs.

When the train stopped on the third day of our aimless journey westward, Herta spotted a big farm close by. We both jumped off and ran toward the buildings. Apparently many others had the same idea. When we arrived at the farm, the kitchen was crowded with women asking for or preparing food. The farm lady gladly allowed us to boil potatoes.

"For this reason I keep a huge pot of boiling water going all the time," she told us. I kept my eyes on the train and Herta kept hers on the pot of potatoes. We counted the minutes. They needed an hour to boil. Would the train stop that long? Meantime we were lucky to buy a loaf of bread and a few boiled eggs. Finally, after what seemed like eternity, the potatoes were cooked. Pouring off the water, we promised the lady of the farm to return her pot but, in case the train started rolling, we would leave it close to the tracks. Herta and I dashed back to the train, each holding one handle of the huge pot. With still some hundred yards to cover, to our horror, we saw the train make a sudden jolt, as if starting to move, but then it stopped short again. We scrambled up the two steps and quickly handed out the boiling hot potatoes, a difficult task without plates, and realized that the train had started to roll. Once more, it jerked to a halt. We let the pot slide down the gravel slope, hoping the farm lady would find it.

Enjoying my hot potato, I felt the inside of my body warm up. Mrs. Barock had received a pail of fresh milk, an old ladle, and a few broken cups. The liquid felt good in our hungry stomaches. Silently, after giving thanks for my food, I wondered how much longer this train ride would take.

The previous day we had passed the city of Schwerin in Mecklenburg and today we had entered the area of Lueneburg. Obviously, we traveled on local tracks, avoiding big cities. In the afternoon Frederick spotted planes overhead and the train stopped with a sudden jolt. Mother had heard rumors that other trains, packed with refugees, had been bombed or attacked by low-flying British Spitfires.

"I hope they won't see our train," Mother worried, afraid that our train might be attacked. But as fast as the planes had approached, they disappeared and the train cautiously crept on westward. Judging by the position of the sun, we now steered in a southwesterly direction. But nobody recognized the names on the small stations we were passing.

As another night fell, we closed the heavy door to shut out the cold and draft. We had slept only a short while when loud noises and hard knocks at the door wakened us. Demanding that we open the door, a man of the Red Cross asked if anyone in our car needed a shot against dysentery. He explained that a number of people in the front cars were suffering from the disease. This news alarmed Mother.

"How much longer will we be on this train?" she asked the man and he assured her that we would soon be at our destination. The disease evidently had started with the newborn infant and spread to many others whose bodies were weakened from lack of food. A moment later, women handed out small bowls of soup. Taking one look at its gray, clear color made my stomach twitch; I decided to pass it up.

The next morning when everyone had rubbed the sleep from their tired and dirty faces, Mother suggested that the women should go on a food hunt the next time the train stopped. She was determined that no one in our car would get dysentery from lack of food. The train halted before noontime and the three women jumped off, leaving Mrs. Gander, Elsa Barock, Herta, and me in charge of the children. After an hour they had not returned.

"How far could they have run?" Herta wondered. If they had gone to the nearby farm, they should have returned by now. We worried. Then, to our horror, the train jolted and started to roll slowly. We saw Mrs. Adomeit come running toward the door. She was tiny so that we had no trouble pulling her up. Coughing and choking, trying to catch her breath, she told us that Mother and Mrs. Barock had climbed on the next car when they realized that the train was picking up speed. We were lucky! Mother and our neighbor had been able to jump on the train. Had the two women been left behind, they might never have found us. Later in the afternoon when the train stopped again, Mother and Mrs. Barock rejoined us.

"This will never happen again," Mother promised over and

over again. Mrs. Barock told us excitedly that the farmer had directed them to a small store nearby where the owner, recognizing the emergency among refugees, sold food without food stamps. But the line had been so long and, once she and Mother got close to the counter, they were determined to wait a little longer. They had bought bread, butter, milk, cheese, and some apples. Frederick was happy about their precious purchases.

"I did not believe my eyes when I saw the train start rolling without warning," said Mrs. Barock. Running as fast as they could, they had reached the train but had to jump into a different car. Mother was still in a state of agitation over the possibility of having lost us. When she heard later that some women had indeed missed the train, including a young mother, leaving an infant unattended, Mother recovered quickly and was grateful for having caught the train in time. A whole day later, those missing women rejoined our train by jumping on the next one following us. They finally caught up with their frantic families.

News had come from the front, from the chargé of the train that if tracks were freed, we would arrive at our destination the next day. One more night in this jolting, stinky cattle car, I thought to myself. Thankful that our gypsy life would end soon, I prayed that God might prevent us from having lice. Later I fell into a fitful sleep. Four days and nights we had spent on this train. It seemed like an eternity. Tomorrow perhaps we would find clean water somewhere and a bed to stretch out in.

* * * * * *

When early morning dawned, I was anxious to find out how far westward we had traveled. We passed a small city, Diepholz, and another with the name Bohmte, Kreis Osnabrueck, "Kreis" meaning suburb. Having no map to consult, I tried to remember where Osnabrueck was located. At long last, we passed it, via retracking maneuvers and after another long halt.

"When will we get off?" asked Andreas, as anxious as everyone else. But the train was rolling again, passing one station after another.

Finally, when I had almost given up hope, we pulled into a small station called Dissen and received orders to disembark. Cold, tired, stiff, and hungry, our four families huddled together, waiting for our luggage to be unloaded. A man assured Mother that it would follow us and urged us to get on the waiting bus. Quick! he ordered. Reluctantly, Mother did so.

A short ride took us to a small place and the bus stopped at the schoolhouse in the village of Aschendorf. Here farmers had assembled, according to given orders, and picked a family suitable to the space available on their farm. Obviously, no one wanted to take a large family.

"Feels like a cattle trade," Herta whispered to me after a woman had asked her how old she was and if she could work. Glancing also appraisingly at me, the farm woman told Mother to follow her. While I did not promise anything, I was glad that we were finally given a destination. Nevertheless, the cold-blooded attitude of the woman troubled me. I sighed deeply, realizing that after a five-day ordeal in a cattle car, none of us looked presentable. Too tired, too bedraggled, too sick to defend us, I quietly walked to the farm wagon. To my relief, Mother had secured our baggage, including the baby carriage with the duffle bag.

I appreciated the fact that it was getting dark, because Herta motioned me to look across the street where curtains were moving, evidently hiding someone curious, someone giving us a scrutinizing appraisal. Each of our neighbors was taken to a different farm in the village. The explanation was logical. Here in the country, the refugees from the east would be safe from the bombing raids and, hopefully, would get enough to eat. No refugees were officially permitted to settle in large cities like Hamburg or Osnabrueck.

"Let's go," said the woman, Mrs. Mueller, brusquely, and the young man accompanying her took charge of the horses. It would not be far to the farm, she explained to Mother; we could walk the short distance. Only Andreas, Maria, and Frederick sat on the wagon. Quickly we waved our neighbors goodbye, promising to keep in close touch, and off we went into the darkness along the village road. Mrs. Mueller became talkative and, although I tried to get used to her accent, I had difficulty understanding her.

When the wagon rolled into the slightly sloped yard, Herta pointed out how differently the buildings here were arranged than in East Prussia.

"A farm without stables?" she asked. But Mrs. Mueller had walked ahead, showing us the house. The animals were under the same roof with the farmer! We could not believe it. Entering a cemented area with stables on either side, cows to the right and horses to the left, Mrs. Mueller opened a wooden door with a latch on the right side and explained that this would be our kitchen and the adjoining room our bedroom. Explaining that she had taken on more people than she had intended, she ushered Mother across the *Diele*, the stable area, and showed her another tiny room, suggesting that Frederick use it.

"I have not yet heard from my husband, but he will join us later," said Mother, to give Mrs. Mueller the correct number of our family. She mentioned Ursula, who temporarily lived in Hamburg. But Mrs. Mueller paid no attention. For the moment, she had her hands full. Walled off and behind a big glass door were the living quarters of the farmer. Yet, worse off then we, was the Polish family who lived in a room next to the hayloft. The young man, a Polish prisoner, who had picked us up complained openly that he could not walk in the room without hitting his head.

At the moment, we were glad to have a roof over our heads and beds in which to sleep. After shedding my excess clothes, I tapped water on the *Diele* to get cleaned up. As a precautionary measure, Mother suggested that we leave our clothing in one corner; she wanted to examine every piece closely in the morning.

It was the evening of March 11, 1945. Our gypsy life had ended.

"Check our heads right now," Herta insisted and, to my great relief, Mother found no lice. Herta and I lamely unpacked and put clean white covers on the two feather beds. The two enormous and old-fashioned beds had stuffed straw mattresses, but we did not let that trouble us. Mother quickly assigned our sleeping space. She would sleep with Maria, Herta with me, and the two boys would share the bed in the room across the *Diele*. It was tight, but nobody had to sleep on the floor.

Mrs. Mueller, commenting that we looked tired and hungry, whisked in with a huge bowl of vegetable soup with potatoes. Mother thanked her and we enjoyed our first decent meal after a week of flight from the Russians. God had carried us through. It was a miracle. After a hurried clean-up, I crawled under the cold, clean cover. I was in a bed again, I was a human being again! Thank God!

In the morning, Herta, having examined our clothes in the corner, made a quiet announcement.

"We have lice in our clothes," she said calmly. I shuddered.

"What are we going to do?" I asked frantically. But Mother and Herta had already prepared a kettle with boiling soapsuds to give every piece of underware a cleaning and delousing treatment. To get the plague out of our dresses was more difficult because we could not boil them. Nevertheless, after a week of continuous washing and scrutinizing, Mother finally declared that we had overcome the problem. Addressing me, she said jokingly: "It proves that you can live even through this disaster."

* * * * * *

Herta started to work on the Mueller farm the next day with the hope that the Muellers would sell food to Mother. But Mr. Mueller resented the fact that our family had been forced to live on his domain, was furious about our intrusion and, eventually, on one occasion a few months later, even called us names. Mother hoped our stay here would be only temporary. Several months had passed, however, and we still received no order to move on. Slowly we came to the unnerving realization that we were there to stay.

The war was in its final stages. I was confident that in this area we would be captured by the western front. It was only a matter of time until it would pass us, a fact that had never occurred to the Muellers. A few weeks later, in early April, we heard distant rumbles in the north. We learned from the local paper the next day that the city of Osnabrueck was heavily bombed.

The morning of April 5th, the early spring sun felt warm and promising. I had walked out the huge door to the yard to look for Maria. From the west I saw figures approaching as they walked across the neighbor's field, peculiarly spaced, about six to ten feet apart, forming a line. In a flash I realized that these were either British or American soldiers combing the countryside, marching forward to the east. Calling out to Maria, who was sitting in the sun on an old carriage, that I saw soldiers approaching, I noticed her freeze in terror and scream hysterically.

"Come over here," I urged her, assuring her that she did not need to be afraid any more. But, petrified, she was unable to move. Calmly walking over to her, I took her trembling arm and explained that she did not have to be frightened.

"These soldiers are not vicious like the Russians," I assured her, "we can trust them." As if in disbelief, she tightly held on to my hand and, when the dozen soldiers arrived at the farm, she still looked panic-stricken.

"German soldiers here?" one of them asked in broken German, questioning if the farmer was hiding any. Although we assured them that we were civilians only, he took no chances and followed us inside to check out the farm. Their search was thorough, going through the basement and checking under the beds. With a grin, one soldier picked up a German mark on our dresser, explaining to the others that it was money. Dropping it where he had found it, he tipped his hat and they left.

In the afternoon Walter Barock came running over, asking Mother if they could spend a night with us. They had been assigned to live at a farm close to the main highway and, having seen heavy American trucks and guns move by, Mrs. Barock was afraid of shooting, of artillery fire.

"When will this panic be over?" cried Mrs. Barock, after spending two nights with her family in our tight quarters. I assured her that it would not take much longer, pointing out to her that we had reason to be grateful to have landed far enough west. This very day, as the Anglo-American troops passed through Aschendorf, guaranteed us that we had escaped Bolshevism. Mrs. Barock could not share my gladness. Instead, she hoped that our German army might be able to recover, throw back the enemy. But we saw no German troops in the area. As a matter of fact, none were left. To our family, the war was over.

We were free! We were alive! I was grateful. The losses of war did not trouble me. I did not bemoan the loss of our home. Now I prayed for only one thing—that Father might be alive, wherever he was.

When on April 30, the news spread that Hitler was dead, I was neither touched nor moved. This very day he had been called to stand before his Maker and account for his life, for his ruthless actions, for ruining a nation, for the countless millions of lives he had on his conscience. God was his judge and He would deal with him justly.

"As a man soweth, so shall he reap." Father had been right from the beginning.

The official capitulation of our country was announced on May 7, 1945. It would be a difficult start for our battered country, but I was certain God had a new life in store for us. Chaos would turn into order again.

Chapter XII

Gathering Them Together

It was a few days after the final collapse of our country. Most people had overcome their initial fear of the occupational forces and dared to venture out of their houses. Our hometown neighbor, Mrs. Barock, visited Mother to evaluate the situation. The two women had mixed feelings. Mrs. Barock, emotional and easily excitable, was upset that Germany had lost the war. She asked Mother if she had noticed the crass change of tone in the media. With bitterness in her voice, she said:

"Our country's *Befreier*, our liberators," she referred to the Western Allies, a term against which she took special offense.

"They have freed us from everything, our homes, our possessions, our men," she mocked bitterly. Furthermore, she resented the fact that we as a people now totally depended on the mercies of our former enemies.

"Most likely we will be treated like slaves," she moaned.

"Besides, the Americans had nerve to steal Wernher von Braun! Our intelligentsia is now split between the Russians and the West. Our liberators have robbed us of our finest minds and now they most likely will use them against us." Our neighbor poured out her anxieties, her frustrations, while Mother tried to change Mrs. Barock's point of view, explaining that we, as the losers, had little choice in the matter. But our neighbor pursued her line of argument, pointing out the many arrests of our former Nazi leaders. She insisted it was unfair that every one, including Hermann Goering, whom she believed to be a mild-mannered man, was treated like a criminal and that all had been jailed.

Another fact that outraged her concerned the photographs and detailed newspaper reports about concentration and extermination camps that had existed in our country.

"I do not believe these headlines. It could not possibly be true. Not a word of such ghastly places was mentioned to us under the Hitler regime," she hotly pursued her argument. Although Mother agreed with Mrs. Barock regarding the fact that we, as civilians, had no knowledge of the mass killings of Jews and anti-party factions, she pointed out the possibility of the existence of these places, places like Dachau and Ravensbrueck.

"Remember the incident I had with Mrs. Thorne?" asked Mother, refreshing Mrs. Barock's memory. Mrs. Barock remembered well that Mother had been watched and followed by one of our fanatic Nazi neighbors in Gumbinnen; nevertheless, she thought that Mrs. Thorne's intentions had possibly been to get Mother jailed, nothing more. Mother was not sure what Mrs. Thorne had had in mind but, knowing now that she could have possibly been sent to a concentration camp, or worse, to an extermination camp, she shuddered.

"I could have been killed, starved or worked to death, or exterminated in a gas chamber," Mother told her, voicing the opinion of our entire family: we were indeed glad that the Nazi party had been totally eliminated. She referred to the Nazi regime as the cancer that had suddenly befallen our nation and, like a galloping disease, had stretched out its deadly fangs to possess peoples' minds, those minds who had strayed away from acknowledging God as the ruling force of their lives. Now the core of the disease had been eliminated, a painful process for our nation, and it would take years until the sick parts of the body would recover, would be healed. What Mother disapproved of were two facts: that men of the capacity of Freiherr Dr. Wernher von Braun were treated as prisoners and most likely would be forced in the United States to apply their brilliant minds and continue to produce weapons and, secondly, that Germany as a whole was condemned of the murder of the millions of Jews, including those people who were innocent and had no knowledge of the crime.

As mother defended her point, I wondered if Mr. Beinert had come out of the war alive. He was one of our neighbors who had refused to commit the crime of murder, disregarding the order of the S.S. We did not know where the Beinerts lived now, because at the moment it was difficult to locate a relative or friend. After the frenzy of fighting a losing battle, our country was in a state of forced calm, as if quietly licking her wounds.

When Mrs. Barock left, still unreconciled with her new lot, but anxious to get home before the newly posted 8:00 p.m. curfew, it was late and dark outside. Mother breathed a sigh of relief. Our family's position was not easy either but Mother was confident that if Father returned home alive, we would build a new life again, even starting with nothing.

* * * * * *

Mrs. Barock's visit and emotional outburst had stirred my mind and I lay awake for a long time. Although I disliked the fact that my East Prussian idol, Freiherr Wernher von Braun, had been taken as a prisoner to America, I had great faith in East Prussians. Once hostilities had diminished, giving way to trust, Dr. von Braun could be influential in building a bridge of understanding between America and Germany. Our country desperately needed to build again instead of wasting her feeble energies in harboring hatred and resentment. In my prayers I asked for Wernher von Braun's protection, that God might use him as a peacemaker. Realizing that our country needed to atone for its sins, I offered up the loss of my home, my lost privileges, for those innocent souls who had lost their lives under the cruel hands of the S.S. The dead could not be made alive again, guilty and innocent alike but, knowing that all had returned to their Maker, I prayed that God might bless them and forgive those among the living who had committed their crime in ignorance, in false obedience, in fear of losing their own life. Humbly, I asked for Father to come home safely. Some day, I hoped Germany would be at peace with the world again.

The next morning, Mother mentioned, in retrospect of Mrs. Barock's visit, that if Mrs. Barock were given the option of returning to East Prussia to live under the Bolshevik regime, she would in all probability refuse it, preferring to live under the present limited circumstances.

On the third day under the Anglo-American occupation, Herta and I ventured to Bad Rothenfelde, spurred on by the rumor that one of the major appliance distributors was selling household utensils without special purchasing tickets. Although Mother was anxious to buy a new ladle, she cautioned us to walk through the woods instead of venturing along the major highway.

"I hope we won't make the trip in vain," said Herta on our way. Agreeing with her, I was glad that she was not afraid of the Western Allied troops.

The long line in front of the store proved that something was on sale. We were not the only brave ones; many people had ventured out of their houses, evidently trusting the British and American soldiers. Listening to conversation while standing in line, I realized, however, that some had mixed feelings. I overheard one woman say:

"What will they do to us? Will they take away our homes?" But another woman answered her, saying:

"Hermine, as long as you can prove that you were not a member of the Nazi party, you should have no reason to be afraid."

Herta glanced at me. The two women were strangers to us and we could not predict their lot; as far as our family was concerned, we had no home to worry about, neither had we been members of the party. We had nothing to fear.

When the sales clerk finally asked us about our wishes and, to our surprise, sold us the desired ladle, Herta smiled encouragingly.

"Did you hear? For the first time in the three months we have lived here, the man has changed his tune. The 'sorry, we don't have it' has changed to 'yes, please,'" she whispered.

Was the owner of the store afraid that the occupational troops might plunder his warehouse? Herta told me that she had overheard a conversation between Mrs. Mueller and her husband that they stored dozens of cartons with brand new merchandise in their barn for this store owner. One of the farm hands had discovered the huge pile of boxes hidden under bales of straw and had curiously investigated the contents. He had found brand new meat grinders, bread cutters, cutlery, sets of dinnerware and expensive glassware and had helped himself to a meat grinder, mentioning to Herta that his mother had been trying to buy one for several years.

Glad not to return home empty handed, Herta and I gingerly jumped down the flight of stone steps. At the street crossing, only half a block away, we saw a column of heavy armored tanks, bearing the American insignia, roll by, heading eastward, roaring along noisily.

"Let's rush back home through the *Wellengarten*," urged Herta and we speedily headed for the woods connecting Bad Rothenfelde with the village of Aschendorf. The close encounter of such heavy foreign war equipment had shaken our confidence somewhat.

Half an hour later and slightly out of breath from rushing, we approached the crossing of the main road leading in a south-north direction through Aschendorf. Herta pointed to the number of parked armored trucks at the roadside ahead.

"Do you dare pass them or should we go back and take a different road across?" Herta asked me, looking a bit unsure of herself.

"Naturally, we won't go back. Just slow down and don't look so fearful," I told her and we passed them as casually as we could possibly pretend. As soon as we had the crossing behind us, Herta whispered into my ear:

"Did you see that the soldiers smiled at the children? They gave them chocolate—I saw it! That proves that we don't have to be afraid of them, they are civil, they are friendly."

I was glad that this close encounter and her positive observation had convinced Herta that the British and American soldiers were people we could trust as I had intuitively known; we did not have to fear them.

It was difficult to judge which fact made Mother happier: that we bought her the long desired ladle, or the news that the Americans were friendly soldiers.

As long as troops moved along the highway and up the village road, school had been suspended for the children. The school house, located in the center of the village of Aschendorf, was being used by the occupational forces as temporary sleeping quarters. One afternoon, as Herta and I accompanied Mrs. Barock back home, we experienced an incredible shock. On the steps of the school house, obviously enjoying the warm spring sun, sat a row of soldiers with pitch black faces, their pearly white teeth glistening in the sun as they smiled at us.

"Oh, my God, Africans!" wailed Mrs. Barock, starting to run. "The Americans must have signed a secret pact with an African nation."

"Don't run!" I hissed at her, "It would only betray your panic." I did not dare admit my own feelings: I was frightened too. But determined not to reveal my shock, I felt my heart pounding, and Herta asked fearfully:

"Where could these black soldiers be from? They wear American uniforms." None of us knew the answer because at that time we were not aware of the fact that Americans could have either black, white, yellow or red faces and could all be born in the same country.

As a result of our ignorance, we were afraid and Herta and I cautiously took a side road to get back to the Mueller farm. Learning about our shocking discovery, Mother ordered us to obey strict rules: none of us should leave the house alone or be out after dark until the African soldiers had left the village.

* * * * * *

The troops of the Western Allies were occupying our country and those soldiers on the move often stopped by a farm to trade cigarettes, coffee or pepper for eggs. Mrs. Mueller, petrified of them approaching the farm, usually ran out, knees shaking, to offer her trade outside the house and was always glad when they left. Due to the encouraging words of her son, however, over the weeks, her fear diminished and she permitted the American soldiers into her kitchen. One day as they were involved in their usual exchange, the big grandfather clock on the foyer sounded out the full hour in a loud ding-dong. The soldiers looked panic-stricken and, with their guns pointing to the foyer entrance, kicked the door open, only to find the clock sound out its last stroke. Realizing their error and unnecessary suspicion, the Americans broke out in hysterical laughter and the very nervous Mrs. Mueller relaxed. There was no enemy in sight, there was no reason to be fearful, to be suspicious.

A different fear, however, developed over the weeks regarding another matter. All Polish and Russian prisoners had been automatically set free, including Polish families who had worked on German farms during the war. Full of hatred and revenge, they returned during the day or at night and armed with guns harrassed the farmers who had mistreated them. Often the revengeful mob gathered to plunder a farm. One day, in their hatred, they had shot the old Mr. Kamp. He had tried to approach them, to reason with them. He had paid with his life for his bravery. For this reason Mrs. Mueller had asked Mother if we could take over a shift of the regular night watch.

"Naturally," Mother agreed. It was on one of these dark, long night watches that Mother and I heard a loud clear gun shot resound in the huge, tiled foyer, a shot fired from the direction of the outside door. Peeking carefully through our window next to the door, we saw nobody. Nothing moved. It was pitch-dark and quiet outside.

"I have the terrible feeling as if Uncle Anton has been shot somewhere," said Mother, her face full of fear. She seemed to have an inner knowing and I did not question her intuition, having clearly heard the shot hiss through the hall. But curiously, no one else in the hosue had heard it nor stirred. Many years later, Mother learned from Aunt Tina that eyewitnesses told her of having seen Uncle Anton get shot by the Russians in Koenigsberg. He had been arrested and separated from her. Could it have been the same shot Mother and I had heard that night?

Mr. Mueller had not heard anything that night, although he showed signs of nervousness whenever a stranger approached the farm. Therefore Herta was positive that Mr. Mueller would not be brave enough to provide shelter for any of the straggling German soldiers, who hid from the Americans and usually walked lonely country roads at night to return to their families.

Mr. Mueller's son, however, had received such risky shelter on his own walk home to Aschendorf. A West German farmer had given him an old set of civilian clothes and burnt his uniform. Handing him a pail with white paint and a big paint brush, the farmer had mentioned:

"In case you encounter the American military, get busy painting the milestones along the road. Pretend it's your job—and good luck." Equipped with this practical advice, Mr. Mueller's son had set out to walk several hundred kilometers, often joined by one or two other men. He had arrived safely at his father's farm with an empty pail and a stiff white paint brush.

"The milestones in Germany never looked so white and clean," he commented to his father good-humoredly, when he told his story.

Another young man from the village, Albert Berger, had a similar report. Once the American forces over-ran his unit, he threw away his passport, hid at a farm, where he cut off the legs of his trousers—only boys under age wear shorts in Germany—and ran as many kilometers as he could during the night, carefully avoiding big intersections, where the American military had set up check points. During the day, Albert slept in the barns at farmers, who also fed him secretly. By walking home, he had avoided the red tape and long waiting period involved that he would have experienced had he been released as a German prisoner.

When the former Polish and Russian prisoners were finally transported to their own country, calm was restored among the villagers. In spite of the fact that the farmers had armed themselves with forks and clubs to ward off the threatening, plundering mob, many a pantry had been emptied out, and one man in the village was cut down by the bullets of the revengeful prisoners.

"I'm so relieved that the Poles have been shipped back home," Mrs. Mueller said one day, her hands stemmed against her hips. She had been petrified during the last few months, petrified that the Polish family, who had worked on their farm, would return and take revenge. Now she breathed a sigh of relief. Maria and her son were on their way home to Poland; Mrs. Mueller could relax.

It had been an embarrassing incident, when Herta told

Mother one day, as the denazification procedures were under way, that the Muellers had received a form letter, charging them with a penalty of two thousand Reichsmark. Despite Mrs. Mueller's insistent denial, they had been paying members of the national socialist party and Herta heard the lady of the house balk over the penalty for days.

During the last few years until now, money was plentiful, yet it was a worthless currency. People living in large cities were willing to pay exorbitant prices for staple foods: bread, potatoes, eggs, milk. A popular joke was circulating, stating that farmers had enough money to wallpaper and carpet their stables. As a matter of fact, Mrs. Mueller charged Mother fifty Pfennig, half a Reichsmark, for one egg. Instead of complaining about the Black Market price, Mother appreciated that she was able to buy additional food items.

In addition to her worry about feeding us, another matter was foremost on Mother's mind. Her greater concern was to locate our relatives with whom we had lost contact during the last eight months of chaos and constant move. She hoped that through the newly established service of the Red Cross, registering all refugees in their new locations, adding their home residence in 1944 to the statistics, we might find our relatives and friends. Mother was anxiously waiting for mail from Aunt Erna. By writing to her address in Hamburg, Father would have a chance to locate us, in case he had not received the letters Mother had sent to him. We knew the task the Red Cross had undertaken was enormous and it would take years to locate anyone through its service.

The many weeks of uncertainty and waiting put a strain on Mother. Therefore, I was glad that at least our three hometown neighbors, the Barocks, the Ganders, and the Adomeits lived in walking distance. They consoled each other, lending moral strength when one was in despair. Despite her worry, Mother seemed to be the strongest of the four, reminding the women to appreciate the personal freedom we had gained. We could talk freely now. We did not have to fear being arrested if we voiced our honest opinion about politics. Mother was especially glad that she was rid of Mrs. Thorne who had haunted her during the last few years in Gumbinnen. Our country was freed of a very destructive force, National Socialism. Although millions of lives had been sacrificed, billions in value of materials had been lost, from the remnants, even out of the rubble, Germany would begin to rebuild. A nation, having been purged of her cockiness of desiring to rule the world, had gone down on her knees, forced to do so by a just and loving God, teaching her people a lesson. Obviously, the first lesson to learn was: I Am The Lord, Thy God. Those who had regarded Hitler as their god now had to do some very earnest soul-searching. Hitler was dead. Their god had been removed, his empire had collapsed. Whom would they serve now?

Although these questions might have been whispered only in long dark nights by a confused and searching soul, the outward signs were obvious. Churches were packed again. People flocked together in the houses of worship, searching for answers, for hope, for strength. Their souls knew that only God, their eternal and loving Father, could comfort them, help them back on their feet, rebuild their battered nation.

Even the bridges that needed to be built between East and West Germans, between refugees and those people forced to accommodate them, had to be built in the house of God. Here both parties sat closely together, worshipping the same Lord.

* * * * * *

One Sunday morning, sitting in church, my mind wandered. I wondered where Helga, my former classmate, was, and Miss Zahn, our beloved teacher. Did they evacuate from Gumbinnen in time? Where might they be? But I had to wait many more years to learn the answer to these questions.

When Ursula paid us her first visit in Aschendorf, she gave us a full account of her narrow escape by ship. She was grateful to be alive. Although the food and shelter situation in Hamburg had reached a critical point, she told Mother she would stay in Hamburg until we had room for her in Aschendorf. Ursula had secured a job with the city authorities. Giving us a description of Hamburg, she said the center of the city was a pile of rubble.

"Rescue teams are still pulling dead bodies from it, trying to identify them to give them a decent burial," she told us. Mother was glad she had not accepted Aunt Erna's invitation to move to Hamburg. She was positive we would suffer from hunger if we lived there now. Being aware of this fact helped her appreciate our tight and uncomfortable quarters at the Mueller farm. Ursula had also brought news of Aunt Marie and Uncle Wilhelm, Mother's brother. Both lived in a refugee camp in Denmark and were reported to be in a dire situation. Kept behind barbed wire as a retaliation measure for the Danes who had suffered under the German occupation, they were housed in cold and drafty barracks. Due to her frailty, Aunt Marie had developed pneumonia and suffered from fainting spells. Mother hoped they would soon be transferred to Germany.

Aunt Erna had had another surprise visitor—our cousin Christa from Koenigsberg. Mother was delighted to hear that she was alive and inquired about the rest of the family.

"Christa reported that she left Koenigsberg alone, taking only her infant son along," explained Ursula, because Aunt Tina, Uncle Anton, and Trude stayed in the city, trusting Uncle's conviction that Hitler would not permit the Russians to occupy any German territory. Christa had evacuated at the last minute, boarding a huge overseas steamer, getting away across the Baltic Sea to Rendsburg. She had not yet heard from Aunt Tina and was not sure they were alive. Having received the notice that her husband was missing in action, her mind was tortured not knowing whether she should consider him dead or alive.

"The poor girl! What a load to carry at such a young age," cried Mother in compassion. She insisted that Ursula invite Christa to visit us as soon as she returned to Hamburg. Mother packed a bag with potatoes and vegetables, the food we could spare, so Ursula and our "Hamburger," as we called them, would not go hungry. Living on the Mueller farm had its advantages as we had at least the basic foods—potatoes, flour, milk, and some eggs.

Mrs. Mueller had also sectioned off a small piece of land near the road where Mother could plant her own potatoes and vegetables. Frederick could hardly wait until they matured, ready to be eaten. The food shortage in the country was nearing a crisis. The humor, however, had not died out. One day the paper carried a small sketch in the corner, depicting a middle-aged man who stared at some sprouting weeds. The question underneath read: "Is it edible?" The food problem was the greatest in large cities like Hamburg, Duesseldorf, and the entire Ruhr area.

Every weekend train loads from the crowded Ruhr section arrived in farm areas with people begging, buying, or trading for food. Many women traded their precious jewelry, even their wedding bands, in order to obtain food for their hungry children. And the farmers, hard-hearted, took everything they could get. Our currency, the German Mark, was worthless and food available on the "Black Market" was outrageously high. Mrs. Mueller was not too generous in selling Mother extra food, overcharging her for a pound of flour and some eggs, but at least we did not have to go hungry. We had enough to eat. Herta, now working for a different farmer in the village, insisted on getting a portion of her pay in food items.

When Mrs. Gander visited us one day, she told Mother that she went on a weekly tour visiting neighboring farms, begging or, rather, trying to buy food. She persuaded Mother to go with her. Although I was apprehensive about this venture, Mother was determined to try it because Frederick was growing and forever hungry. When she returned in the late afternoon, she looked exhausted and defeated.

"Begging is not for me. I cannot do it," she said, sinking tiredly on a chair in the kitchen. Her experience of being turned away with a flat "No" by fat farmers who had everything including luxuries, had been degrading. Mother's experience had also made her painfully aware how much we refugees were resented. We were intruders; we did not belong here. Mother promised she would never go begging for food again. Silently I prayed that God might provide the necessary food for us.

A few days later, Mrs. Werther, the neighboring farmer, came to see Mother. She asked if I could work on their farm. Mother was reluctant, knowing my frail physical nature, but I gladly accepted the offer with the one stipulation that I receive a portion of food daily for our family in addition to the meager, worthless wages. Mrs. Werther agreed to my request, needing a replacement for the girl who had recently left. Here was God's way to provide food for our family; I gave thanks for this opportunity. Now Mother did not have to go begging any more.

* * * * * *

Farming was a rough school. It was quite different from my lessons in middle school. So far I had not given up hope of completing my education, but at the moment it was impossible. I had no books, I had no shoes, and the closest middle school was located in Dissen, a small town about eight kilometers away. Worst of all, I had no bike. Therefore, I had to postpone my own interests and concentrate on the most important need—to feed our family.

Amazed at my own ability, I learned to milk cows, a strenuous job for my thin arms. Mother laughed when I told her that the smelly animals had a way of whipping their dirty tails around my head.

"Why don't you tie their tails with a string?" Frederick suggested, trying to be helpful. It proved to be a good idea and eliminated that particular problem. I did not mind the cleaning aspect of the job. Twice a day I scrubbed a battery of huge steel cans, in which the milk was taken to the nearby dairy. I proved to be handy with the broom. But when the men asked for a hand during the haying season, I realized I had gone beyond my strength. The stinging heat, the prickly dust, and the fast hard work had rushed the blood to my head, causing my nose to bleed profusely. Nothing helped. Lying down made me sneeze and started the flow all over again. Ice packs on my neck and forehead finally brought the problem under control. My face looked green and I felt dizzy and weak. Mrs. Werther, therefore, told the men that I would not work in the fields.

"She is too young and too frail; besides, I need her around the house," she explained insistently, settling the matter in my favor. As promised, she cooked an extra large pot of vegetable soup each day so I could take a big bowl home to my family each night. Frederick always waited anxiously for my arrival. Watching him devour the food with relish, was worth my every effort.

One night, however, I had an accident. It was pitch dark outside when I passed the open gate of the Werther farm. Carefully, I balanced the bowl of hot soup, feeling my way along the short road, with one hand fumbling for the iron railing on the tiny bridge that led over the creek to the Mueller farm. Grasping it firmly, I took a confident step forward—right into the water, spilling most of the soup over my dress.

"How stupid can you be, Marianne?" I scolded myself. Instead of stepping on the bridge, I had slipped into the creek on the wrong side of the railing. When I entered our kitchen and told my sad story, Frederick was dismayed. He investigated what remained in the bowl and said regretfully:

"You didn't have to decorate yourself with the soup, did you?" His remark made me laugh and Mother helped me wash my clothes and dry my shoes. Telling Mrs. Werther of my mishap the next day, she gave me an extra portion to make up for the loss. She was a good and compassionate soul. Even her husband, an older man, tall and frail, had understanding for people in need, especially those people in the cities who were suffering from hunger. One evening in early fall, his younger son reported that a corner of the potato field had been dug up and the potatoes stolen. Mr. Werther, in his slow manner of speaking, surprised him with a rather philosophical answer.

"If you were hungry, you would do the same. God has given us plenty. They're welcome to the potatoes." With this remark, he ended his son's complaint, leaving him to ponder his attitude.

Mother appreciated even the small harvest our vegetable patch had yielded. She was able to store some potatoes, hoping they would carry us through the winter. She regretted not having been able to bring her canning equipment for the excess vegetables she would have liked to can. But the carrots, turnips, and cabbages would last for a while. Mother had stacked them in our little corner in the barn where Mrs. Mueller permitted us to store our supplies.

As heating supplies, especially coal and briquets, were available on a very limited basis and required ration tickets, we had to find a different means to get through the winter. Mr. Mueller owned many acres of woodland over a kilometer away on the sloping mountain. He permitted Mother to gather dry branches, those that had fallen off the trees, and use them as heating wood. Mother had obtained a used hand-wagon and the five of us, including Andreas, set out for the woods. It was a hard job. For over a month we collected wood. Then Mother and Frederick chopped it into pieces small enough to fit the stove and stacked it neatly in a dry corner in the wagon shed. Only when the heap was big enough and the weather turned cold and rainy did Mother call off the project.

When early snow and sleet set in, we got busy repairing our worn and shoddy clothing. Made of recycled, poor quality fabrics, they had suffered greatly during the months of our evacuation. One day Mother surprised us with a new idea. She had the opportunity to buy raw lambs wool from a farmer. A few days later she rounded up an old spinning wheel and, having watched one of the neighboring women, taught herself to spin wool. Fascinated, Maria and I sat close and watched her. Herta one evening was determined to try her hand at this new craft and proved to be quite proficient in it. Mother spun spool after spool, sitting up until late at night. Frederick was anxiously watching his new sweater take shape.

"You have to knit faster," he urged Maria and me because he had outgrown most of his clothes and, being very active, had ripped them beyond repair. Herta had been given a few used sweaters by her farm lady. One in a bright red attracted Maria's fancy.

"I'm going to unravel it and make a new sweater for myself," Maria announced happily and, with enthusiasm, she went to work. Within two weeks she had finished her new sweater. The inside looked hairy from the short threads knotted so many times but it kept her doubly warm in the cold, damp northwestern climate of Aschendorf. Mrs. Mueller was astounded at Maria's talent and complimented her on the achievement. When Frederick's lambs wool sweater with a Norwegian design was finished, we started one for Andreas. While Mother was spinning, Maria and I kept busy knitting.

We regretted, however, that we could not manufacture one

item: shoes. The one pair with which each had left Gumbinnen was worn and almost beyond repair. Now and then shoes were available in a store. The tops made of dyed sack cloth and the soles of wood, they did not last. When Mother mentioned the possibility of buying shoes on the Black Market in Bielefeld, Herta and I discouraged her.

"We are not shrewd enough; besides, we do not have enough money to pay the exorbitant prices."

Mrs. Gander, the lucky one, had heard from one of her distant relatives in the United States and received regular CARE packages with food and clothing. How much I wished that we knew someone overseas, someone who could help us, but we had nobody. We had to manage with what we had, although it was painfully little. Nevertheless, we were still able to share our meager food supplies with Ursula and Aunt Erna's family in Hamburg.

Ursula's recent letters were disheartening. She explained that she sat in the office at the *Rathaus* wearing her winter coat because of lack of heat. Her fingers were so stiff that she could hardly type. Worse yet was the food situation. Many of her colleagues complained about dizzy spells; some girls fainted while sitting at their desks. Their supervisor who lived in the outskirts of Hamburg and had a garden brought in the food he could spare, vegetables, potatoes, and fruit, but his meager supply did not go far among a hungry crowd. Faithfully, Mother sent a package with potatoes every week, adding some bread or butter, those rare items which Herta or I had obtained from the farms where we worked.

Mother had also received mail from our cousin, Christa in Hamburg. She was anxious to visit us. Upon arrival, she was happy to see us well and surprised at the adequacy of food. Most of the time Mother cooked a vegetable soup with potatoes but without any meat and, to Christa, it was a luxury. Five slices of bread and a tiny ration of margarine had to last her a whole week. For supper she often boiled one potato, nothing else.

"Often I have eaten my weekly ration in one meal, just to feel full once," she told Mother, apologizing for her lack of control. Then, for the rest of the week, the gnawing feeling of hunger would churn in her empty stomach, making her feel dizzy and sick. Although starvation was bitter, she said the worst blow for her to overcome was the loss of her baby son. He had died from dysentery and malnutrition. She cried bitterly when she poured out her heart to Mother.

"I never wanted to be alone. I hoped to raise him so I would have company when I get old. Now I have no one again," she sobbed and we cried with her, knowing she had not heard a word from Aunt Tina, Uncle Anton, or her sister Trude. Herta and I showed her around the farms to cheer her, to console her. When Christa packed to return to Hamburg, she had gained ten pounds, one pound for each day she had stayed with us. Mother happily noticed that her hollow cheeks had rounded out. Christa promised to come back soon and hoped by then to have located her family through the Red Cross.

* * * * * *

By spring of 1946, after a hard and dreary winter, Mother received a letter from Aunt Marie and Uncle Wilhelm. They had been released from the camp in Denmark and lived in a small city near Stuttgart in the southern part of Germany. Several months later, a letter from Oma, Father's mother, was in the mail. She, Aunt Marie, and Aunt Ina had been in Berlin in May of 1945 at the time of our country's collapse. Having taken shelter at Uncle Willi's, Father's brother living in the outskirts of Berlin, they had been over-run by the Russians. My cousin, Suzanne, and one of the *Schuster's* girls were with them at the time. Recently Aunt Ina had located Uncle Oskar who had been released from the army to a small village near Flensburg in the province of Holstein, where Hans had been stationed. She would join them shortly, taking the little *Schuster* girl along.

Contemplating this news for a moment, a sudden revelation hit me. How incredible God's guidance was! He had foreseen the necessity for our family's evacuation from Gumbinnen. To prevent me from being over-run by the Russians in Berlin with Aunt Ina, He had in time taken me back to the Beethovenstrasse, causing the incident of Hans' confirmation. Then, knowing of Father's reluctance to leave our house in Gumbinnen, He drafted him into the army at the last minute when our situation became critical. He guided me to the military hospital to portray a picture of the raw truth, using the soldier who had told me of his gruesome experiences at the front, to evacuate our family from Gumbinnen. My Lord's ways were incredible! This realization kept me awake for a long time, giving thanks again for His loving care and guidance. His promise had held true: "... and no one shall pluck them out of My Hand." This phrase assured me that Father would be alive and join us some day. He, my beloved Lord, would gather all of us together again, family, relatives, and friends.

* * * * * *

215

During the summer months, Ursula's letters indicated that the severe food shortage in Hamburg was giving rise to friction in Aunt Erna's household. The tight living quarters aggravated the situation. Therefore, Mother suggested that Ursula join us in Aschendorf. We would manage to weather the times and she would feel more secure, knowing that all of her children were in close reach.

Using Herta's birthday as the occasion, Ursula moved into our cramped quarters on August 12, 1946. Two weeks later, the lady who owned a small variety store in the village asked Ursula if she would be willing to work for her. The task of keeping track of food stamps was overwhelming. Ursula, extremely well organized, managed her new job well. She even found time to handle some of the household chores.

One day Elsa Barock and her mother paid us a visit. Elsa told me that she was contemplating work at the shoe factory in the village. The Barocks, having been assigned to live with the owner of the factory for several weeks, had heard of the working conditions. Mr. Niemeyer, one of the proprietors, had told Mrs. Barock that every employee received a monthly contingent of one pair of shoes as part of his wages.

"Shoes! We all need new shoes!" exclaimed Mother excitedly, and I realized that here was my chance to get Frederick out of the wooden clogs he had been wearing for lack of fitted shoes. Discussing the matter with Herta and Ursula, we agreed working in the shoe factory would be more suitable for me than working on a farm. My body was not strong enough to handle hard farm work. Quietly I wondered how I would hold out doing factory work. Having never done this type of work, I did not know what to expect. When I inquired about the work, I was hired on the spot. Ursula was lucky too. Word had spread in the village that she had secretarial and administrative abilities and the mayor of Aschendorf hired her as a secretary and assistant. It was a modest position, but much closer to her previous occupation than household and clerical work.

On October 10, 1946, we both started our new jobs, Ursula working for the mayor, and I working at the Niemeyer shoe factory. My reports from the factory were not as enthusiastic as Ursula's from her modest office job. Nevertheless, I consoled myself that with each completed month, I would receive a pair of new shoes for one member of our family. Frederick was first, naturally, and, enthusiastically, he drew an outline of his foot standing on a piece of paper. As his feet had grown so fast, we were not sure of his correct size. At the end of the month, as if handed a treasure, he inspected his first new pair.

"Shoes! New leather shoes!" he shouted, trying them on anxiously. They fit perfectly. His happiness compensated for my hard and dirty work at the factory. It also compensated for the double talk, the nasty remarks, made by one older man when he passed me. He had been born in Aschendorf and lived all his life in the village. I could feel that he resented me, a refugee. I did not dare complain about this problem to Mother because she would have urged me to quit. Instead, I avoided the man and focused on the reward of my work—a pair of new shoes every month.

Both of the Messrs. Niemeyer were straight-forward men of the old school. They were brothers and had been paying members of the Nazi party until the end of the war. Although neither had a much higher education than I, they managed the small shoe business jointly. Frederick Niemeyer, the older of the two men, supervised production and the younger, Ernst, managed the financial and accounting aspect of the firm. Both families had lived in a handsomely constructed villa across the dirt road from the factory but, under the Anglo-American occupation, their houses were occupied by the British military. The Niemeyers had to move out. This measure, taken by the western allies, was part of a general punishment meted out to former Nazis. Business went on, however, and, apart from a slight physical change, their comforts were not greatly impaired. Now the two families lived in the old house where Mr. Niemeyer, Sr., the founder of the firm, had lived.

Frederick Niemeyer had three attractive teenage daughters. Ernst, by his first marriage, had three sons and one daughter. After his wife died during the delivery of the youngest son, Ernst, Jr., he remarried and had a daughter by his second wife. The children of both families were on friendly terms. The two women were engrossed in caring for their families, and absorbed in their own interests.

The factory, the only one in the village, appeared to be an extension of the two families. A cousin of the Niemeyer brothers, Mr. Henry Niemeyer, held the position of foreman in the factory and acted as the right hand to Frederick who was in charge of operations. It was a big family affair. All personnel referred to Henry Niemeyer as "Uncle Henry," and he knew it was meant in a respectful, fond manner.

"Uncle Henry" had assigned me to the finishing line and I waxed and polished shoes, a dirty, dusty and odorous job. But knowing that I would receive a new pair of shoes at the end of each month spurred me on. I regretted the fact that the firm did not produce women's shoes, but was only equipped to manufacture workmen's and boys' boots. "Uncle Henry," however, promised to round up a skin of soft leather and make a pair of casual walking shoes for me.

In the meantime, a farm woman from the neighborhood had stopped Mother and asked if I could sell a pair of shoes to her son, knowing I received a monthly contingent from the factory. Mother suggested that I do so with the stipulation that, in addition to the money, she had to give me something useful. Mrs. Halter offered a large, used dress which she had received in a CARE package from her relatives in America. At the end of the month, she promptly came over to pick up the shoes and brought a large size woman's dress of a light woolen texture in a bright, flashy hot pink. The color stood out like a beacon. None of us had ever seen such a vivid color. During the long years of war, all clothes had been dyed in drab colors, in black, brown, gray, or navy mixed with either white or red. Having recovered from my initial shock, I accepted the dress and Mrs. Halter and I settled the matter. Obviously, Mother did not like the color.

"You will stand out like a checkered cow," she joked, but admitted that the material of the dress was almost new and of a very good quality, sufficient for a short-sleeved dress. Immediately I went to work on it, tearing out the seams with a razor blade, then brushing and ironing the pieces. I decided to let the seamstress in the village sew it for me because I intended to wear the dress on Sundays and to church. The seamstress's reaction to the bright pink color was similar to Mother's.

"My goodness, where did you get this?" she called out. Ignoring the seamstress' curiosity, I was happy about the prospects of a new dress, and had already decided on the style. It was to be cut in a simple A-line pattern, with short sleeves, and the collar was to be trimmed with white flaps. It would be an outstanding color combination. Several weeks later, I picked up my new, bright pink dress, the first after years of deprivation. Everyone in the family liked it, including Mother.

Wearing the dress to church, I attracted a great deal of attention and received a number of compliments. I acknowledged these, yet I attached a different meaning. To me, my new dress was silent proof that Americans were not our enemies any more. They were people who cared and tried to help our nation overcome our losses, the aftermath of war. This pink dress, sent in a CARE package to our neighbor, proved it. I loved the color because the deep, rich pink to me indicated love. Someone in America, probably unaware of it, had sent to me a symbol of love, assuring me that the battle axe was buried. Were we willing to do the same? Although I could account only for my own feelings, I knew I had never regarded the western nations as our enemies. History had taught us that they were educated, religious people, the descendants of God-fearing pilgrims, who had founded their great nation. Suddenly, a strong desire to emigrate to the United States surged up in me. At the moment, however, we had to wait for Father to return home. We had still received no word from him.

It hurt Mother to see so many other men released from prison camps. Only a few weeks after the country's collapse, Mr. Barock and Karl Gander had joined their families. The two Werther sons had long since been released from the liquidated German army. Mr. Mueller's young son, no older than twenty, had walked home right after the end of the war. Although his rank of lieutenant was then obsolete, his father had not been able to conceal his pride.

"How are you, Mr. Lieutenant?" Mother had overheard Mr. Mueller greet his son as he had entered the yard. Mother was puzzled. Did a rank mean more to the man than his own blood? Did he have no feelings, no emotions to see his son return alive?

Finally, after two years of uncertainty, Mother's time of anxious waiting and worrying came to an end. A letter from Father was in the mail! He had received some of Mother's letters, but obviously his replies, addressed to us, had been lost. We had been on the move for over six months. To her amazement, Father's address read: Alexandria, Egypt. Mother tore open the envelope and flew over the lines, tears streaming down her face. Father was alive! He expected to be released by July of 1947, approximately three months hence.

"Read the letter out loud," demanded Maria and each one of us inspected the two small black and white photographs he enclosed, showing him standing in the blazing Egyptian sun, his face thin and his work clothes much too big. But the familiar smile on his face indicated that he was optimistic, as his letter stated: soon he would join us in Aschendorf. The second photograph depicted an Arab family of four, dressed in little more than rags, exposing their thin, bare legs.

"Why do they cover their faces?" Andreas asked curiously and Father, evidently anticipating this question, had noted on the back of the picture that Arabs dress in a lot of loose clothes to shield themselves against the hot sun. As Moslems, the women wear the traditional black veil over their faces.

Father wrote that he had been captured by the Anglo-American forces in Villa del Conte, near Vicenza, Italy in May of 1945 and with thousands of other German prisoners was taken by truck and railroad to a temporary camp in Tarent, a city located in Southern Italy. Two months later, he was shipped with a big transport of prisoners across the Mediterranean to Alexandria, Egypt and onward from there by train to El Daba, a small railroad station close to the Mediterranean. Located between the coast and the station was an enormous prison camp and the rumor spread among the German men that here the de-nazification was supposed to take place. By November this huge camp was liquidated and Father was taken to an Allied Forces transit camp in El Amirya, located close to Alexandria. Here all prisoners were assigned work and because of his experience, Father's lot was to work in the field bakery for the British military.

"His face looks so drawn," Mother wailed, "I wonder if he gets enough to eat." But Father had not mentioned a word about provisions at camp.

"I have to speed off a reply immediately," said Mother and Maria and I gladly took over the household chores. Mother was so glad to report to Father that each member of our family had safely come through the war.

It was a thick envelope when Mother had finished and Frederick volunteered to walk to Bad Rothenfelde to mail it at the post office.

Before falling asleep, I thanked God for keeping His promise: . . . and no one shall pluck them out of My Hand. He had held His protecting Hand over Father. He had shielded him from danger, He had kept him alive. Soon he would join us.

* * * * * *

The next day Mother inspected Father's clothes. She aired and brushed them and Herta offered to give them a thorough pressing.

"The suit almost looks like new," Mother complimented her, when the pants, vest and jacket were neatly on a hanger.

During the following weeks, Mother kept busy airing the bedding, giving the tiny apartment a spring polish.

For Mother, time did not move fast enough and as soon as the calendar showed July, she expected Father any day.

To earn a few loaves of additional bread, Mother had been helping the neighboring farmer, Mrs. Werther, with her heavy load of laundry.

Having returned home after one of those hard days, she heard a light knock at the kitchen door and without waiting for her "come in," Father stepped in. Too bad, most of us had missed

Father's arrival. But when I came home from the factory, Mother was still all tears and smiles. Herta, the last one of the family to drop in, found the kitchen bursting with people, conversation and laughter. Although Father rarely wasted words, he gladly answered our multitude of questions and the shine in his eyes showed his happiness, happy to have found us well and alive.

"So, luckily, you were captured in Italy and not in Russia," Frederick recalled Father's previous letter, "How did this happen? Were many soldiers killed? Was it a fierce battle?"

"Yes, I was very lucky," Father started to answer the many questions. "I was drafted at the end of July 1944 to the infantry and was shipped to the city of Braunsberg, East Prussia. Our training in the use of weaponry was supposed to be completed within three months. But I developed trouble with my teeth toward the end of this period and had to have several teeth extracted. As a result I had to remain at the barracks for several additional weeks. During my time of recovery new orders were issued, stating that the younger men, holding administrative positions, were to be replaced by older men. Born in 1901, I was almost forty-three years old and my military passport indicated that I had served at the East Prussian Field Bakery in 1919 after World War I. This experience came in handy. As soon as I received the replacement of my teeth, I was shipped with several other men my age to Gruenheide, near Berlin. We were so glad not to be sent to the front, to Russia.

"At Gruenheide we served at the field bakery and at the end of October 1944, our troop was sent to Italy. Several of the men stayed in Verona and I was stationed, with the rest of the field bakery unit, at Villa del Conte, near Vicenza. As part of the infantry, we operated approximately one hundred kilometers behind the front."

We had followed Father's story with great interest, when Andreas asked a curious question.

"How can you transport an oven? Where did you bake the bread?"

Father's eyes rested on the youngest of the family. He could not believe that his "little one" was now almost eight years old. He had been away from us for over three years.

"In the army, the field bakery is on trucks, the huge, mobile ovens stay at a fairly safe distance behind the front to bake the bread."

"Interesting," said Andreas and listened attentively to Father continuing his story.

"In April 1945 our front in Italy was on a fast and steady

retreat. Our baking unit had moved back as far as Feltre, a small place in Southern Tirol. Our troops further south were in such a state of confusion and obviously needed bread desperately. Therefore, several men and one truck load with ingredients remained in Feltre, and the rest of the unit moved south to feed the German-Italian troops in Italy."

"Again, I was lucky, I was ordered to stay in Feltre. Using a private Italian bakery, we immediately set out to work and, hot from the oven, the bread went to the fast approaching front."

"It all happened so quickly. Because we were baking until the last minute, we were delayed in Feltre and all of a sudden found ourselves at the tail end of the retreating front. Frantically we tried to get to Austria. Instead, only a few hours later, the British caught up with us. At Belluna, they fired at the only escape route available to us. To make matters worse, low flying Spitfires attacked our columns with gun fire and blasted us with small bombs."

Frederick's eyes were glued on Father's face, re-experiencing with him the close call of battle, a battle between life and death.

"How did you get out of this hell?" he wanted to know, asking the question all of us had on our minds.

"Our truck was stuck in a deep trench alongside the road and a few feet from it I spotted a huge cement drainage under an overpass. Immediately I crawled in there, tightly packed against my comrade, taking cover from the furious shelling."

"By noontime our officers negotiated the capitulation of our unit and imprisonment with the British military. Just before we were taken prisoner, a curious incident took place. From the mountains, Italian partisans approached, heading directly for us. Dressed in civilian clothes, a big red kerchief around their necks, they were anxious to take us prisoner. Very close to me were several German soldiers from a Flak-unit, who had captured one British soldier. Immediately, the partisans freed him and gave him arms. That very moment we were prisoners of the British and the partisans had to leave with long faces. I am certain that we would not have fared well, had we fallen into their hands."

"Where were the Italian civilians when all this happened?" asked Herta curiously.

"After the battle was over, they came out of their hiding and lined the streets while we were taken prisoner and led away. Turning back, I saw them dive for the material we had left behind."

"At first we were taken to a temporary camp which was sectioned off by strips of cloth. Naturally, we were searched several times. The British took my pocket knife and the gold watch I inherited from Grandfather. At Villa del Conte I had purchased material for a light print dress; they took that from me also."

"Too bad," sighed Mother, "but I'd rather have you back than a new dress."

"A few days later we were taken by truck and train to Tarent in Southern Italy," Father continued. "Located outside of Tarent was an old prison camp where we stayed. All administrative buildings of the camp were constructed of corrugated sheet iron. We prisoners slept in our own tents."

"Wasn't it cold to sleep on the ground?" asked Andreas.

"No, by then it was May and warm in Italy. I had the feeling that the British were determined to stuff us. For dinner we could ask for as many helpings as we liked. Usually we were served soups, cooked with too much fat. Perhaps they did not want the big supply of bacon to go to waste."

"Obviously the British were also overstocked with flour, because several times a few of us bakers were ordered to the camp bakery to bake Danish with crumbs."

"You must have been happy about the order," said Ursula laughingly, knowing that Father's favorite Sunday breakfast was danish with butter crumbs.

"Right," agreed Father, "it was like getting a birthday present. The bakery was in the center of the camp and consisted of several clay ovens, holding approximately three to four baking sheets. We heated the ovens with scraps of wood but it served the purpose."

"By the end of July, after a two months stay, we were transported by ship to Alexandria, Egypt. Upon our arrival, Arab children were standing by, pointing their thumbs downward, a sign that they wished us bad luck. From Alexandria, we were shipped westward by rail. El Daba, a very insignificant railroad station, close to the Mediterranean, was our destination. This enormous prison camp, consisting of several camp units, was located between the railroad and the coast. Here, as we learned from rumors, the Nazis were supposed to be re-trained, de-nazificated. Obviously, our Anglo-American captors had been under the false impression that every German was a convinced Nazi."

"That is unbelievable," said Herta, shaking her head in amazement. "I assume you were treated according to this assumption."

"In the beginning our activities resembled army training, or rather stiff drills," Father explained. "Every morning started with inspection. Duffle bag, blankets, towels and utensils had to be cleaned and lined up neatly in front of the tent."

"Sounds like a regular army drill," said Frederick.

"Oh, yes, after each inspection, our few belongings had to be put back in the tent. In the afternoon we rested and in the evening we were permitted to walk within the camp confines."

"We received a bare minimum of food and in this camp I suffered from a severe case of dysentery. Weakened from the disease, I felt dizzy as I lay on my cot. I was hungry. Then I simply prayed that God might feed me. I had barely finished my brief prayer, when one of my comrades asked:

"Would any one like to have my bread? I can't eat it tonight."

"Since no one asked for it, I told him that I wanted it."

Father's eyes filled with tears as he recalled the event and so did ours. God's loving care was incredible, so spontaneous, He was there at the immediate moment of need.

"Were you expected to work in such a physical condition?" Ursula inquired worriedly.

"In this camp we did not have to work. Therefore, the minimal amount of food was sufficient to keep our bodies functioning."

"Not sufficient enough, if you suffered from dysentery," declared Mother. But Father did not complain. Instead, he filled us in with more detail on his years in prison, the years in Egypt.

"Several times the British accompanied groups of us to the beach at the Mediterranean. We enjoyed the swim, if only our walk back to camp along the hot desert road would not have covered us with dust again."

"Didn't you get bored, having nothing at all to do?" inquired Herta, knowing that Father had never sat idle.

"At camp various activities were available where we could spend our leisure hours. The prisoners, who had occupied the camp before us, had built an outdoor theater in ancient Roman style, where we could see a show, attend lectures about a variety of subjects, including astronomy, get entertained by a comedian or even watch someone swallow razor blades."

"Wow!" cried Andreas, "I would have liked to see him." Father smiled, he obviously would have rather been home with us.

"It is amazing how much talent surfaces in a crowd of thousands of men. A group met regularly to sing folk songs. At one time we set up a boxing rink and even the British authorities were invited to watch the match. After the two men had fought for a while, the taller of the two, landed a hard blow on his opponent's jaw and with one crack, the false teeth broke in two; a serious mishap to a prisoner." We laughed.

"Did the poor man ever get his teeth repaired?" asked Mother.

"I don't remember," said Father, "because by the end of November this big camp was dissolved and we prisoners were distributed to several work camps. A few groups were transported to Cairo, others to the Canal Zone, but I was taken with a great number of others to El Amirya, a camp located not far from Alexandria. El Amirya had a railroad station and close to it was a transit camp for the Allied troops. In this camp of the Allies, we had to perform a variety of jobs. We prisoners kept the huge tent and the recreation grounds clean. For several weeks I was assigned to help out in their field bakery. In the evening, when our job was done, we returned to our own prison camp."

"Was the work very hard?" asked Mother curiously.

"No, I really enjoyed having something to do; it made the time pass quickly."

"So you worked for the Allied forces almost three years free-of-charge," commented Ursula, the practical administrator in our family.

"Oh, no, we received a minimal pay for our work in Egyptian currency, one half we were paid in cash and the other half was credited to us."

"What happened to the credit?" asked Ursula, in a tone as if having detected something fishy.

"It is still in Egypt," Father said with a grin, indicating that he did not care about having been fleeced this way.

"Could you buy anything for the money you received?" Maria inquired curiously.

"Yes, the canteen in our prison camp was supplied by the Egyptians and we were able to buy salami, smoked meats, wine, coffee, tea, shoe polish, even ladies' stockings."

"And what would you do with those?" Andreas wanted to know.

Father laughed and mentioned that they interpreted this fact as an indication that their release must have been contemplated by the British. Stockings would make a nice gift for their wives at home.

"While we were waiting for the official word to be announced, we spent most of our spare time on crafts. Several men used their talents to make cigarette cases, cigarette lighters, others sewed caps with big peaks, to shield our eyes against the bright Egyptian sun."

"As soon as the rumor about our release circulated, the men

built wooden suitcases, using the empty tea crates as material. I ordered one myself and paid for it in Egyptian currency."

"When you worked for the Allied troops, were they still under the impression that all German soldiers were fanatic Nazis?" asked Herta, curious to know if the British ever realized their error.

"No, after a few weeks, working closely with us, they became aware that only very few of the men had been total believers in Hitler. They observed us at work, they came to see our entertainment, they greatly admired our crafts and paid generously for them, they began to trust us. We received an adequate amount of food and could freely visit men located in other camps. As transportation we were permitted to use British army trucks. Usually the drivers were German prisoners anyway, we could move freely.

"During these two years in prison, I made new friends from different parts of Germany. Most of all, these two years have strengthened my faith. Furthermore, I learned to respect the faith of others, those of a different religion than ours," he added, illustrating it with another story.

"Christmas of 1945 was the dimmest for us men. Most of my comrades were German and longed for their families and the green Christmas tree. We were then at El Daba. One prisoner, a very quiet, subdued man, and a devout Catholic, worked as a carpenter around the barracks. He had a surprise in store for all of us. From the mess hall he had obtained sheets of paper which he painted dark green. Using a pair of pliers, he cut barbed wire in small pieces and built several Christmas trees of it, over which he put more green paint to give them a life-like effect. From scraps of paper he made papiermache and molded the Holy Family. The stable he made from hard cardboard and painted it white. Giving his figures an artful coat of paint, our comrade single-handed had created an altar, converting a table by covering it and enclosing the legs with green paper. In the center was a crucifix, flanked by Christmas trees, with the Nativity on one side. Presenting his masterpiece quietly to us fellow prisoners on Christmas Eve, the crowd fell silent and many of us had wet eyes. Our camp chaplain, reading from the Bible and delivering his Christmas message, renewed our spirit, our hope. As word about the altar spread around the camp, all men lined up to see the wonder made of barbed wire. Even the British soldiers were moved by so much compassion." Father showed us a picture one of the British officers had taken of them at Christmas. "This event brought us men at camp closer together and had removed all feelings of hostilities between our captors and us prisoners."

"Were the camps guarded?" Mother inquired.

"Most of the guards in our prison camp were German. Only at the entrance did we have a British soldier as a guard," Father explained.

"How did you spend your spare time?" Mother asked curiously.

"A generous supply of reading material in camp had been donated from Switzerland; we could buy books, Bibles in all languages, New Testaments, Hymnals and a variety of scientific literature. Therefore, I read a lot."

"You mentioned a chaplain at camp. Was he a German prisoner also?" Mother inquired.

"Yes, he had been a chaplain in the German army," Father told her. "Once a week I joined with a number of my comrades for Bible study in the Church tent."

"Did the British question you if you had been a member of the Nazi party?" asked Herta with great interest.

"Oh, yes, right at the beginning when we arrived at El Daba. I had a clean conscience, I had no problem. Except for my automatic membership with the *Arbeitsfront*, which had substituted the former union, I had no affiliation with any political organization. Obviously, those men, who had not been party members, had no problem being released."

"At the beginning of July 1947, a troupe of us men was taken by truck and then by train to Port Said. We knew we were on our way home! Here we boarded a troop carrier. A substantial number of British soldiers and their families boarded with us. Before Gibraltar we anchored to take more British on board. Crossing the Biscaya we hit a storm and most of the passengers were seasick. I was lucky, it did not affect me."

"Our family must be seafast," said Herta, recalling our crossing of the Baltic Sea in a storm.

"The Channel was calm, but heavy fog lay over the water. Before Southampton a pilot came on board and steered the boat in to the harbor. Here all British families disembarked. The next morning we continued our trip to Cuxhaven, Germany. We were back home. From Cuxhaven we travelled by train to Camp Munster, located in the Lueneburger Heide. Here we received our luggage and I was handed a train ticket to Bad Rothenfelde.

"Asking a man in a railroad uniform for directions to Aschendorf, he told me that he lived in Bad Rothenfelde and we travelled together to the station. He took turns with me carrying my suitcase to Bad Rothenfelde. Although the man had given me directions to Aschendorf, I had to ask several times until I located the Mueller farm. My heavy luggage was bearing me down. I stopped several times to rest my arms, to catch my breath. But, thank God, I found you at last."

"The suitcase is very heavy," commented Andreas, trying to lift it. Father opened it and to Mother's delight, handed her precious items: two canisters of Egyptian cottonseed oil, one bag of black pepper, one bag of raw coffee, one bag of seasoning and a set of clean work clothes."

"The oil will carry us through a long period of time," said Mother overjoyed.

The chicken dinner, a generous donation from Mrs. Mueller, had turned cold on our plates. Finishing it with half closed eyes, we realized that it was passed midnight and time to go to bed. Father did not complain having to sleep in the tiny room across the *Diele* with Frederick and Andreas. He thanked God that he was home.

* * * * * *

The next morning Father asked us about possibilities for work in our area. Except for the Niemeyer factory, we knew of no industry within a radius of five kilometers. Despite the fact Father was hopeful and determined to find a job, Mother suggested that he allow himself a few weeks of rest because his face looked drawn and tired.

"Your cheeks are so hollow; they should fill out first," she tried to persuade him but, instead, Father donned his clean clothes the next day and walked to Bad Rothenfelde, a small spa nearby. Here, he was determined to locate a job until the prospects were brighter. Ursula had given him the address of the town administration, where Father registered and filed a job application.

Returning home, he told Mother that although at the moment there was no opening, the clerk had earmarked his application, according to his own suggestion, that he would be willing to accept any work, even if it was out of line with his experience. In the meantime he collected a small amount of money from his unemployment insurance. Mother was glad to have Father at home, glad that he would get a few weeks of deserved rest.

But after the second week of leisure, Father returned from Bad Rothenfelde late in the afternoon, with a smile on his face.

"The Lord will not desert His own," he assured Mother,

telling her the good news that he had located a job as a superintendent with the British Air Force which had part of its personnel stationed in Bad Rothenfelde. The military personnel and their families lived in private German houses, houses confiscated temporarily from former Nazi members, which needed maintenance. The few words of English Father had learned during his imprisonment in Egypt came in handy. Having never known the word "enemy," he got along well with the four British families he was serving. Although Father's job was to maintain the heating, electrical, and water systems in these houses, he often volunteered to work in the garden, trimming hedges, cutting lawns, or weeding the flower beds. As a result, the British men liked him and gave him food and anything else they could spare. Mother welcomed the powdered eggs, milk, and the canned meats. Our diets improved and, with the yield of our rented garden patch, supplying potatoes and vegetables, we were fed adequately.

One family from Glasgow, Scotland, asked Father if he knew anyone who could speak English who could baby-sit for their eight-year-old daughter. Father, recalling my having taken English lessons in middle school, volunteered my services and our family grew very fond of the Methvens, especially Helen, my new young friend.

Mother decided that Frederick, now in his formative years, would be better off working at a farm, thus assuring him plenty of body-building foods. Consequently, Frederick worked on a farm in the village, literally for his daily bread.

As all Polish and Russian prisoners, including the many civilian workers, had returned to their own countries shortly after May of 1945, laborers were scarce. The desperate food situation in large cities of the Ruhr area had forced many people to the country. To escape starvation, they hired themselves out as maids and farm hands. Farmers had to relearn to treat their personnel with respect and dignity, obviously a difficult lesson for many, after having grown accustomed to treating prisoners as slaves for many years. The farmers also had to learn to tolerate us, the refugees from the east, because our country was not in a position to provide better housing for us.

Herta could never understand why the Western Allies, after having captured most of the southeastern territory of Germany during the war, voluntarily retreated, allowing the Soviets to occupy the area and pronounce the Elbe river as a demarkation line between East and West Germany.

"Some day, the Americans will regret this step," she said

accusingly. Father believed in a different philosophy.

"If the Americans willfully divided our country, separating the people of one language, then God will do the same to their own country, cut it in two, divide the people among themselves. But since we don't know the intentions of the Americans, we cannot judge them. It is up to a just God, Who can see in to the hearts of men. Let us not be resentful against anyone. Let us be grateful to be alive."

I was amazed how easily and without complaint Father adjusted to our crowded and uncomfortable living quarters. He never bemoaned the loss of his house, his garden, his privileges to go fishing at the pond. What he did miss, however, was the church he had so faithfully attended and the men he knew from the Bible class in Gumbinnen. The pastor of the small church in Bad Rothenfelde did not appeal to him because he preached from the scholarly point of view rather than from his heart.

"I wonder where our dear Pastor Preuss is now," Father said and suggested to Mother that the two read the Bible daily in order not to lose touch with the Christian teachings. Our activities usually halted at the end of the day and many times I listened to the ancient texts from the Holy Book. At the close, Father said a brief prayer, encompassing anyone who needed help or attention that day.

So far, no one in the family had received word from the two men missing in Russia: Uncle Karl, Father's youngest brother, and the "Schuster," Father's brother-in-law. Faithfully, Father included them in his daily prayers, asking for their protection, offering them up to God, the One he trusted, the One Who could gather even these two last ones together.

Chapter XIII

A Stranger in His Own Country

During the years of 1946 and 1947, our currency, the German Reichsmark, had lost its value. A rampant running black market had drained away its last bit of stability. Wages were meaningless and our family considered these two years a free service, free labor to our nation. In these two years an immense amount of rubble in the severely bombed cities had been cleared away. When in 1948 a new currency, the Deutsche Mark (DM), was issued to replace the outdated and worthless Reichsmark, it was a great step forward. The German people, their spirit undefeated, optimistically stepped forward to rebuild their battered nation.

Every person, regardless how much of the old Reichsmarks he held in his savings account, received a modest starter of DM 40.-Deutsche Mark. Surprisingly, a variety of merchandise, especially hardware, appeared in the stores the same day. Hoarded by merchants during the previous years, these items were expected to produce hard, stable cash. It took several months, however, until the average family had saved enough money to shop freely as every mark had to be spent wisely and economically. The situation regarding cheap farm labor also changed overnight. As the manufacturing industries began to fill the desperate needs of the nation, jobs became available. Anyone who had learned a trade or skill returned to his own field. The times of laboring for one's daily bread on a farm were over.

Farmers, suddenly short-handed, were forced to till their own soil. Not accustomed to hard work and gaining no extra help from refugees, who lived on their domain, many farmers showed open hostility toward them. Nevertheless, since Father's return, our life at the Mueller farm had become less troublesome. Mr. Mueller, a tall, flat-footed, and boisterous man, respected Father and stopped causing arguments.

The Niemeyer factory stepped up production and we worked ten hours a day, including Saturdays. It seemed as if the demands of the public could not be satisfied. With the new currency, the food stamp system was automatically abandoned and trade was done in hard cash. The Niemeyers offered me a job that necessitated itself. It consisted of controlling stocked merchandise, assembling, finishing and boxing shoes, and handling shipments. During the war, none of this extra work had been required because the merchandise was purchased in any acceptable condition. Now with the competition factor playing a new role, close attention was given to the appearance of the finished product.

I also detected a drastic change in attitude of the firm's main customer, a wholesaler named Mr. Pauling. He scrutinized his order painstakingly before releasing it for loading on his truck. Poorly manufactured shoes rejected by his customers, he promptly returned and fired his noisy accusations at Mr. Niemeyer.

"Don't try to sneak your junk into my order, Niemeyer, I'll throw it right back at you," he shouted. Those rejects soon received their appropriate name; "Ladenhueter," the keepers of the store, and, to Mr. Niemeyer's distress, the pile in one corner increased rapidly. He blamed "Uncle Henry," his cousin and right hand in production, for sloppy workmanship. But after a few bull sessions with the factory workers, hammering into them the need for flawless merchandise, he got his satisfaction. The quality of the shoes improved.

Fortunately, several local shoemakers were hunting for bargains. Watching me reduce the pile of rejects this way, Mr. Niemeyer accepted my rule-of-thumb pricing and allowed me a free hand in the matter.

The stockrooms, located above the factory, separated me from the main crowd and I appreciated my new privilege. In my own territory I did not have to listen to nasty gossip but instead enjoyed my freedom in the spacious rooms. Opposite from the stockrooms across the small landing was the office. Between the two was Mr. Ernst Niemeyer's office from which he could watch my work area through an enormous window. I enjoyed being part of a growing business and hoped that some day I could transfer to the office to be trained as a bookkeeper.

Prospects for my brother Frederick also looked brighter. As

the building trade expanded, and housing was in desperate demand, he located a job as an apprentice with a builder. It was hard physical work but, during the two years of farm work, he had grown over a foot and developed strength. Now he was ready to put it to constructive use.

Mother and Father had hopes of building another house in the future in order to move us out of our crowded, primitive quarters at the Mueller farm. Another troublesome factor spurred them on.

"It is a shame that Herta cannot live with us because we have no room," Father remarked. Our tiny apartment had only two small bedrooms and the kitchen. Mother often pointed out that Herta had many talents and loved people.

"She would be a very devoted nurse or an efficient business woman," she used to say, but since we could not accommodate her in our inadequate quarters, she still worked on the farm. In the meantime, the two younger ones, Maria and Andreas, had completed their public schooling in the village of Aschendorf and, to Mother's dismay, had not received an adequate education. It had not equipped them sufficiently to attend the middle school in Dissen. Ursula explained to Mother, however, that without bus service it would be irresponsible to let them travel such a distance, even if the school would admit them.

Therefore, after graduation, Maria worked in the stockroom with me at the Niemeyer factory. After a year she located a job as an apprentice with a tailor in Dissen. Although she would have preferred to serve her apprenticeship with a dressmaker or a fashion house, we as refugees did not have the required connections. Nevertheless, Maria made the best of her opportunity and became very proficient in her trade. While she was engrossed in tailoring her own first suit, I watched her with fascination. Happy about her accomplishment, she modelled it with great pride before the assembled family. Pattern making was part of her training and in early spring I made a suggestion to her.

"Let's design our own dresses," and she agreed enthusiastically, telling me to tackle the job of designing. Quickly I sketched a design on paper, a new style that had struck my fancy, and, after her enthusiastic approval, watched her with great curiosity first measure, then calculate, and finally cut out the pattern. Sewing was easy and the next Sunday we proudly wore our new dresses to church. Mother mentioned that our neighbors were taking notice.

"Your girls always are so well dressed; even during the most difficult years after the war, they looked neat," Mrs. Halter had told Mother, stopping her at the grocer's. It was no secret. The fact that we kept our fingers busy knitting during the two years after the war and now spent most of our spare time sewing accounted for the results. We never looked ragged. It had been a frantic effort then, and now it enabled us to save some money, savings which would enable us to build a better future.

The year 1948 was also a milestone for our Gumbinner community. As soon as the Allied occupational forces permitted public gatherings, our most respected and admired representative, Mr. Hans Kuntze, arranged the first Gumbinner meeting in Hamburg where he and his family now lived. Mother and I attended, hoping to find our relatives, our friends, our neighbors. Two ministers who had survived the war were present. Our dignified Superintendent, Konrad Klatt, and Pastor Bruno Moritz attended the meeting. The senior of the two, Superintendent Klatt, opened the agenda for the day with a brief church service. Then Mr. Kuntze took the podium and thanked the two men for their outstanding work in establishing a register of all Gumbinner families in East and West Germany. By this means, about forty thousand lives of the original fifty-five thousand had been accounted for but, sadly, many of these were registered as dead. As this count included the neighboring villages of Gumbinnen, it had been a monumental task to set these data up on file.

Although at the end of the war dancing was again permitted, no one at the meeting was in a gay enough mood to dance because thousands of our people from Gumbinnen had died in the ravages of war. Instead, I could hardly wait for the official speeches to end as I had spotted several familiar faces in the attending crowd. As soon as the applause died down and time was allowed for people to get together, I rushed over to Christa Pasling. She recognized me immediately.

"Oh, it's Marianne!" she cried, embracing me tearfully. Settling in a corner where we could talk, she gave me an account of many of our classmates. Waltrud Gerber, Ilse Kahn, and Christel Frees lived in or near Hamburg. Lilo Schlaechter was somewhere in West Germany and Lilo's cousin, Rita Schuler, lived in East Germany.

"Miss Zahn and Trudel Brauer were murdered by the Russians, and 'Stinker' died at the front," she reported sadly, adding to tell me that the Director of our Middle School, Dr. Bruch, a former Nazi, worked in East Germany and was now a member of the Communist party. Then Christa steered me across the hall milling with people, often laughing and crying at the same time, to meet Mr. Kluge, our gym teacher. He wore dark glasses, explaining apologetically that his eyesight was failing; therefore, he had difficulty recognizing faces.

Heading back for my seat, trying to locate Mother, I met the two Schwan brothers of our parallel class and Hardy Preuss, the son of our beloved pastor. Hardy told me that his father had stayed in Gumbinnen with the remnants of his flock and, not wanting to desert them, had died from hunger. This news made me sad. Pastor Preuss had been a typical shepherd, staying with those who needed him. He had refused to eat the food that people had taken from the fields because the Russians let them starve. Realizing the food was taken without permission, Pastor Preuss had refused to eat it, saying that it was stolen. Therefore, he died of hunger and malnutrition. His wife and children had escaped to West Germany. He had insisted upon their leaving. My notebook was now showing a long register of names and addresses. As I walked across the hall searching for Mother, a girl stopped me.

"Aren't you Herta Schmeling's sister?" she asked curiously. When I agreed, she told me that she had been one of Herta's classmates and she asked me to give Herta her regards. Adding the girl's name to my list, I was happy to take some good news home to Herta. Finally I located Mother. She was involved in a heated conversation with one of our neighbors and told me the news she had just learned:

"Mrs. Thorne, my number one adversary, lives somewhere in West Germany," she told me. Having lost her husband, Mrs. Thorne now had no friends. Mother pointed out to me that because of her active participation in the Nazi party, Mrs. Thorne could not dare attend any Gumbinnen meeting. Her guilty conscience and fear of any possible legal action would not permit her to come and, for that reason, she had shut herself off from the people of her home town. I was amazed that Mother held no resentment toward Mrs. Thorne but, instead, felt sorry for the woman, knowing how desolate she must feel.

"Did you notice that none of our active Nazis are present?" asked our neighbor and only then did Mother realize this fact. While I followed their conversation closely, another girl stepped over to me.

"I know your sister Ursula," she said and I immediately recognized her. She was Liesel Baumann, one of our Hitlerjugend leaders in Annahof. She told me how many of them, especially those who had discarded their belief in God under the Nazi regime, had difficulties coping with the loss of their homes, their possessions, and, most of all, their prestige. She had kept in touch with several, mentioning to me the name of the girl who had forced me to visit the Nazi doctor. She was alive and Liesel was willing to give me her address.

Here was my chance to get even with this vehement individual. Then a statement flashed across my mind! "The revenge is Mine, saith the Lord!" Father had said it years ago at the burning of the synagogue. My suddenly welled-up anger subsided. It was true. Throughout these years, my beloved Lord had proved to me that all power belonged to Him. He was a just God. While He had graciously protected us and guided us through the most difficult times of evacuation, millions of others had died. I could always trust Him and put my life in the care of His hand. Our family of eight, although scattered, was gathered together. No one had suffered as much as a scratch. I was surprised that Liesel had the courage to talk with me as she must have been fully aware of my difficulties with the Hitlerjugend and with its leaders. But I realized she had recognized her error and was willing to rectify it. I was glad she evidently had never abandoned her faith, even during her time as a Hitlerjugend leader.

Another observation I had made at the meeting. All of our attending members from Gumbinnen had openly admitted their faith and, judging by the enormity of the crowd, I knew that our country was back on the road to godliness. With this realization, the feeling of security, which I used to have as a small child, filled me again. National Socialism was dead; our country had freed, purged herself of this disease, this haunting nightmare. We, her people, could breath freely again.

At the close of the meeting, our representative expressed hope that some day we might be able to return to East Prussia, to Gumbinnen, and till our own soil again. But at this time, in 1948, no peace settlement between the occupying forces and Germany had been reached.

When Mother and I were on the train heading back to Aschendorf, I took stock of what I had learned. Christa Pasling had married at the age of eighteen and had a one-year-old daughter. Her husband was East Prussian, one of the few men who had returned from the war. Having examined the ranks of our young men from Gumbinnen at the emotional and tumultuous meeting, I realized that at least eighty per cent of eligible men between the ages of eighteen and twenty-one had been killed during the war. My chances of marrying an East Prussian were slim. Knowing I could not marry someone from Ascendorf, out of the people who so openly resented us, I had to search a wider circle. For the moment, our family had to be reestablished before I could concentrate on such selfish endeavors as marriage. To serve my family was of foremost importance to me.

While Maria was serving her years of apprenticeship in Dissen, she heard of a church that had a very active young adult group. Under the sponsorship of Pastor Georg Baring, the group engaged in Bible study and discussions.

"Let's join them," she encouraged me. Attending its weekly meetings, our restricted lives took on a brighter scope and we were received warmly. Here East and West Germans, boys as well as girls, joined harmoniously in a group to discuss the Word of God. Happily we got on our bikes each week and pedaled the many kilometers to the church house. As a result, every Sunday we both attended Pastor Baring's church service.

* * * * * *

Time passed quickly and the four years I had worked at the Niemeyer factory had slipped by almost unnoticed. Nothing outstanding had happened in our family, except Herta had confided to me that she was secretly dating a young man from the village. She knew it would be difficult for Mother and Father to accept the fact that he was an "Aschendorfer" and not a refugee. He lived with his mother and sister in a *Kotten*, a house owned by one of the large farmers. This type of farm system was unknown to us in East Prussia. In the west farmers owning many acres of land built houses, including stable facilities, on a small parcel of their property and rented this out to a family. The rent from the tenant was due to the farmer in labor and the farmer took the privilege of dictating the days and hours agreed to. Usually, families living under such a contract spent a lot of time at the farm, especially during planting and harvesting seasons. Most of the men held a factory job and, as a rule, their wives performed the work agreed to at the farm. Herta knew that Albert's parents lived under such an agreement and she was fully aware that Father abhorred the system.

"This is a remnant of slave labor," he had said one night when the subject was under discussion. For this reason Herta wanted to keep her dating a secret until she was sure whether she would marry Albert Berger. Secretly, the two had been attending the popular barn dances sponsored in the neighboring villages. Having been introduced to Albert at one of these dances, I found him to be a tall and handsome fellow with a quiet disposition and a great sense of humor. Since his father had died, Albert had taken on the responsibilities of performing the work due to the farmer. Therefore, he had not been able to learn a trade. But he was young, having returned form the army only a few years ago, and life still had possibilities in store for him.

When Herta arrived home one evening to announce her engagement, I was not surprised and Mother and Father, to my amazement, had no objection to their marriage. Mother surprised me with a positive philosophical comment.

"The most important thing in a marriage is that both agree in making decisions," and, knowing Herta's clear head and insight, Mother knew they would have no problems.

At the small engagement party held at the *Berger-Kotten*, we met Mrs. Berger, Albert's mother. She was a quiet and pleasant lady. Slender and slightly bent from her life's hard work, she was easy to get along with. Albert's older sister, Laura, was married and lived in the Westphalian city of Guetersloh. Lena, his younger sister, still lived at the *Kotten*. The party was a happy occasion, especially since I sensed no prejudice, no resentment, no hostility. Mother easily worked out the wedding details with Mrs. Berger. Herta, modest in nature and envisioning a better future, insisted that costs for the wedding be kept at a minimum. Five years after the war, with only a small amount in her savings account, she did not intend to splurge on a new wedding gown. Uncle Karl, Father's youngest brother, who, shortly after the *Schuster*, had returned from Russia, had married recently. Herta was positive that his young wife would lend her the long, white satin gown.

"But you must allow us to buy you the veil," insisted Maria, since we had chosen this as our wedding gift. One weekend we bought a beautiful lace veil, several yards long, in Osnabrueck. The delicate lace would dress up the plain white satin gown and transform Herta into the prettiest, most slender looking bride.

* * * * * *

Until November our family was busy sewing dresses for the wedding. The dressmaker in the village agreed to make mine and I had chosen a cheerful rose-pink crepe. The ceremony was held in the small church in Bad Rothenfelde. For this special occasion, the farmer-owner had dusted off his carriages and brushed his shining horses. The day was cold and windy. Mother worried that our young bride might catch pneumonia sitting in the open carriage.

"Take your warm winter coat along," she urged Herta. Even for picture taking, the sun refused to come out, but Herta's happy face made up for the missing sunshine. She had married the man she loved. As the tradition in the area dictated, the women of the farmer's household took charge of the cooking, baking, and serving. This arrangement permitted Mrs. Berger to enjoy fully the wedding celebration of her son. Although the year of mourning for her deceased husband had passed long since, she still wore a black dress which added an air of elegance to her slender appearance. In her quiet way, she smiled, showing that she was happy with the bride and groom on their most important day.

At the dinner table, Laura's husband acted as the master of ceremony and read the many letters and telegrams, after which he invited the guests to toast the new pair. Throughout the day, especially during the time of dancing, I realized that again East and West Germans had come a step closer.

Mother, reflecting on the wedding later, commented that she had enjoyed the subdued music and was glad that drinking had not gone out of control. When Ursula criticized Albert for not having learned a trade, Mother defended Herta's choice and Maria winked at me in approval.

"Did you hear the surprised comments of the farm women when they inspected Herta's new living quarters?" Maria asked and Mother agreed, saying that their astonishment had amused her. As the gifts from our family had been practical, and Herta had purchased a beautiful bedroom set instead of splurging on a gown, her brand new household in the *Berger-Kotten* was well established.

As Aschendorf was a small village, even the Niemeyers talked about Herta's and Albert's wedding. A refugee had married an Aschendorfer; they were surprised. A week later, however, the gossip had worn off.

The two youngest Niemeyer children, Ernst, Jr. and Greta, spent a lot of time with me in the stockroom. They seemed to prefer my company to that of their strict housekeeper because I would permit them to play make-believe train in the big cardboard boxes and let them roam around unrestricted. The two had such fun kneeling inside the boxes and, pushing themselves forward on their pudgy little hands, huffing and puffing like a train, each one trying to arrive first at their imagined destination. Often Mr. Niemeyer watched them from his office, a smile of amusement on his face. I loved the two children. They shared with me their secrets, their thoughts, their fears, their fanciful imaginations, and asked endless questions. Ernst, a true tomboy, was full of surprises. When spring arrived and he had to start the disciplined life of school, he stormed into the stockroom and voiced his disapproval.

"This is a dirty trick! When you go once, they'll keep you there forever! I'm not going to be fooled; I just won't start!" he declared rebelliously, his little hands stemmed against his hips. Eventually, he attended school, much to his consternation. Yet

Ernst had a very tender heart. The day before Mother's Day, he came to me and, short of breath from racing up the stairs, asked a question.

"Can you draw me a heart, Marianne?" waving a sheet of pink paper before me. On my suggestion, he ran to borrow the scissors from the secretary in the office and handed them to me, his eyes shining in expectation. I had to sit down so he could watch me closely as I folded the paper and cut out a huge heart.

"It is beautiful!" he exclaimed. I asked if he wanted to write something inside, now that he knew the letters of the alphabet. In his natural openness, he did not take long to decide.

"I love you, Mother," he blurted out, beaming from ear to ear. Happy and eager to present his heart to his stepmother, he forgot about the scissors and ran downstairs. This was the golden side of Ernst's personality. But he also had another side, several shades in the dark gray. Luckily, it surfaced only rarely. One day, however, he surprised me. The newest fashion in boys' boots was an ornamented brass clasp mounted against the tip of the shoe which protected it from excessive wear and was decorative at the same time. Ernst, visualizing himself as a future football star, loved to give the ball an extra strong kick with his studded shoes.

I don't remember what caused it, perhaps a minor disagreement or a reprimand on my part but, before I knew it, he had casually kicked me in the shin with his brass-studded shoe as if meaning nothing by it. The pain was excruciating. Grabbing him by the scruff of his neck, I slapped him twice and hard. Only then did he fully realize what he had done.

"Now go and tell your father," I suggested angrily. But he and I knew it would guarantee him another heftier thrashing. Therefore, he preferred to sit down on a shoe box in a corner and mull things over. He did not shed a tear and I did not lose any more words over it. He sat in silence for a long time and then quietly stole out of the stockroom. He had watched me examine the bleeding wound and patch it with a big bandaid. For two days Ernst did not come to visit. On the third day, he strolled into the stockroom, pulling a piece of chocolate, wrapped in crumpled tinfoil, out of his pocket.

"Do you want this piece?" he asked almost gruffly. How could I refuse a young soul's peace offering? Happily, I accepted the soft melted chocolate, thanking him and saying it was most delicious. And to my heart, it truly was.

Seeing the two children grow was a pleasure. Greta, having had a serious accident several years before when I was still working downstairs in the factory, was getting better. Her scalp had been ripped off as she had reached for an empty spool in the sewing department. In a split second, her blond curly braid had caught on a screw hooked to the rotation apparatus of the machinery. Mr. Niemeyer, standing near her and watching this accident in terror, had pulled her out of her entanglement and rushed her to the hospital. As the critical half hour had passed for the scalp to be sewn back on, her little body had rejected it and she needed a skin transplant from her mother to cover her head. For years Greta's head had been bandaged but now, finally, the wound was healing and the bandage was coming off.

"My bumped head is better," she proclaimed in her sweet, innocent way. Having lost her own beautiful hair, she was taken to a wig maker who promised to make one matching her own, a narrow strip at the nape of her neck having remained. When she proudly presented herself a few weeks later, I was amazed at the expert workmanship. The two curly blond braids resembled her own closely and the curly strands covered the scars on the side of her pretty face where the screws of the machine had dug in and left ugly red marks. Yet Greta was a happy little tot, dancing on her tiptoes across the stockroom, completely disregarding her handicap. Why did this angelic soul have to suffer through so many years of pain? What was the cause? Why did God permit this to happen? I asked myself questions but could not find the answers.

While I was puzzled over the reason for Greta's accident, I had one myself. It happened so quickly that I could not even reconstruct what had led to it. Being accustomed to working rapidly when finishing shoes or filling orders, I had developed a system. During the morning hours I finished the shoes needed to complete certain orders. Then I packed them, handing the orders in to the office, where the accounting clerk typed the bill and the shipping papers. Following this pattern, the work flowed easily and I did not have to handle a heavy load at the end of the day.

It was before lunchtime. I rushed to get the papers of the filled orders to the office for billing. Storming out of the door to the landing, I slipped with both feet on the newly waxed linoleum floor and, with a crash, landed on the bottom of my spine. My feet were caught in the banister at the top of the stairs. Caught by surprise and in excruciating pain, I was unable to move for a moment. The crashing noise had drawn Lieselotte, the secretary, and Knopf, our bookkeeper, to the scene.

"How did you manage to do this?" asked Knopf in his dry sense of humor, both pulling me from my awkward position. A stabbing, burning pain shot up from the lower part of my spine but, embarrassed by the whole scene, I forced my tears down. As I cautiously tried to sit down, it felt as if I were broken in two pieces.

"Shall I call a doctor?" asked Lieselotte worriedly, but I brushed off her suggestions, reasoning that anyone could fall on his rear end and the pain would eventually subside. At least, I hoped so. Blaming myself for my constant rushing, I refused to see a doctor to have an x-ray taken. The procedure would be too embarrassing. So I suffered. Telling Mother about my bad fall, she urged me to see a doctor. Still I refused.

Several months later when I finally was able to sit comfortably on a chair again, I developed severe pains in my legs. As a result of this problem, I consented to see a doctor. As the pains in my legs were much worse than in my lower back, I neglected to tell him about my fall several months previously.

"It's rheumatism, very unusual for one so young," the doctor diagnosed the pain in my legs and handed me a bottle of pain-killing medication to ease my suffering. As long as I took the pills, I was able to handle the hard work in the stockroom, but once I withdrew from them, I could hardly lift the heavy boxes with shoes. My back was weak and my legs hurt. Going back to the doctor, he exchanged the pills for another brand of pain-killers, shaking his head in disbelief.

"I refuse to become an invalid," I reasoned with God, asking earnestly where I had sinned. Unfortunately, I could not find my error, could not recall having committed a crime. The heavy work schedule, however, demanded all my attention, concentration, and strength, leaving me no time to question things that could not be changed. I was not to learn the real cause of my condition until much later.

* * * * * *

Life went on and time marched quickly. The calendar registered the year 1953. I had been working at the Niemeyer factory for over seven years, a long time although it did not seem that way.

Observing the growing and maturing of the three older Niemeyer children confirmed that time had passed rapidly. The oldest son, Manfred, heir of the firm, had completed middle school in Dissen and worked in his father's office, learning the trade and its business aspects. Manfred was tall and slender. His dark wavy hair and his deep brown eyes resembled those of his father, Mr. Ernst Niemeyer. Contrary to the other children, especially the two youngest ones, he was extremely shy. He never lingered in the stockroom for conversation. The second son, Herbert, several years younger than Manfred, still attended middle school and had ambitions to improve production and quality of the merchandise in his father's shoe business after completing his education. Herbert was compactly built and had ashblond hair and blue eyes. Inga Niemeyer, the third in line, was a beautiful teenager, maturely built for her age and, in whatever clothes she wore, a very attractive young lady. Her open smile revealed a set of pearly white teeth and her thick blond hair and blue eyes added to her natural winning charm. Her inadequate education in the village school of Aschendorf was the reason she was not admitted to middle school in Dissen. Mrs. Niemeyer, seeing the children grow and the household chores increase, suggested that Inga spend a year working at home. Later she would attend a private school for homemakers in Germany or Switzerland.

The villa, now having been returned to its owners, was undergoing an extensive remodelling and painting job. Equal efforts were spent to rebuild the old house in which they had lived for several years.

After the carpenters had completed their work, the painters moved in and I observed that Inga spent a lot of time with me in the stockroom. I liked her friendly company and one day she bubbled over in conversation.

"Arnold has invited me to a dance at the Kurhaus," she told me happily, giving a detailed description of the pretty gown she would wear. Although she felt that her mother was not pleased that she dated someone beneath her social status, obviously Mrs. Niemeyer did not want to spoil Inga's first date. She had her hair cut short to give the low V-neckline of her new dress the best possible effect. The fondness in her eyes revealed that Inga liked Arnold and, having recently completed a course in ballroom dancing, she looked forward to her big date.

"Who is he?" I asked, curious as to which of the many young painters was the lucky one. She described Arnold as the tall young man with very curly blond hair with a slight tinge of red in it. Having spoken to him only once, I did not recall my impression, but I was certain that Inga with her outgoing charm would attract only someone equally nice.

"I hope Mama and Papa will like him," she said thoughtfully, indicating that Arnold had captured all of her attention. I assured Inga that everything would work out in her favor. Her father, loving her dearly, was definitely on her side. Inga promised to tell me the next day how the evening had gone. With this remark, Mr. Niemeyer entered the stockroom and, as it was close to lunchtime,

Inga lovingly hooked her arm in his and, with a disarming, queenlike gesture, led him down the stairs to the villa.

When I picked up my work after lunch, I noticed that Manfred lingered a while and watched me apply finish to a row of paired shoes. Obviously in his shyness, he did not know how to make conversation, so I simply explained to him the fastest way to finish shoes, demonstrating how to paste in soles without smearing the lining and how to lace them properly. Evidently, he appreciated my casual conversation and volunteered to try his hand with a few pairs.

"I still have a lot to learn," he openly admitted, telling me that he liked the practical side of the business better than the theoretical. Manfred was nineteen now and realized that years later, he would be required to step into his father's shoes and carry on the business. Therefore, he was determined to learn every phase and live out the promise he had made to his grandfather before he had died: that the firm he had founded, Manfred would carry on in his name and industrious spirit.

Slowly, Manfred was overcoming his shyness, although I still had to initiate any conversation. Now it seemed to be less troublesome for him to talk and even Lieselotte, Mr. Niemeyer's longtime secretary, mentioned that Manfred was more relaxed at the office. He enjoyed calculating and typing bills for outgoing merchandise and was especially proud to accompany the firm's truck driver with a heavy load to the post office or the freight station.

The months went on and one day I evaluated my life, questioning myself whether I intended to continue to work at this factory until the end of my days. My answer was a decided "No." Although our work week had been reduced from sixty hours to forty-eight, it still did not allow me sufficient time to attend night school. The one-hour trip to Osnabrueck and, worse yet, one hour back home late at night presented a problem. "We are truly stuck at the end of the world," I sighed in resignation. Father, however, was now making this trip by train to Osnabrueck every day since he had located a job in the heavy steel industry during the summer of 1951. He got up at 4:30 in the morning, used his bike to get to the Dissen station, and continued his trip by train to Osnabrueck to be on the job by 7:00 a.m. In rain, sleet, or snow he travelled, never missing a day. It was a hard job but he never complained.

One day as I was busy finishing shoes, "Uncle Henry" stormed into the stockroom, leaving the door wide open.

"The *Berger-Kotten* is on fire!" he shouted. I knew that Herta was alone in the house. Albert's mother having died and his sister having married. Albert was working in the margarine factory in Dissen.

"Oh, my God!" I gasped, ripping the dirty apron from my dress. Flying down the stairs, I followed the men who were running down the narrow road leading from the factory to the *Kotten*. Thoughts raced through my mind. Herta was pregnant Was she alive? She could not rely on help from the woman who lived with them, a tenant family from the Ruhr area. Would her new furniture be destroyed, the animals be killed? On my arrival at the scene, I saw Herta standing a safe distance from the house and next to her the furniture scattered in the grass. She and Mother were anxiously watching the men battle the blaze.

"How did this happen?" I shouted, still out of breath from running. Excitedly Herta told me that the tenant woman had thrown glimmering ashes on the compost pile close to the house. The strong wind had blown the sparks under the roof and ignited the straw in the loft. Thank God, Herta was all right, and her furniture, linens, and clothes were saved. One small calf, however, had died in the flames and Herta cried about it, being very attached to her animals. When the fire engine arrived, the roof and the front of the house had burnt. Only the living quarters were standing and the water had ruined everything that was still inside.

Once the fire was put out, I glanced at the crowd. At least forty people had helped, neighbors and all the men of the Niemeyer factory. I was amazed and I was grateful. When Albert reached home, covering the distance from the factory in Dissen in minutes, he looked as pale as a ghost. Only when Herta assured him that almost everything valuable had been saved did he recover from his shock and regain his speech.

"God, what will we do? Where will we stay?" he moaned, sick with despair. Mrs. Ahrend, the neighbor who owned the village grocery store, opened her heart in compassion and offered Herta and Albert shelter, one room in her house until they decided what to do. Quickly the men moved the furniture into the Ahrend house and, although the room was congested, at least the two had a roof over their heads. After that, the crowd dispersed.

The next morning on my way to work, I passed the ruins of the old *Kotten*. The smell of burnt wood was still in the air. One of the men of the owner-farm had kept night watch in case the fire flared up again. It was a miracle that no one had been hurt in the fire and nothing lost or damaged except the house itself. I thanked God for His protection, wondering in which direction He would now lead Herta and Albert.

On my way home from work, I stopped to see Herta. She told

me that the farmer intended to rebuild the house as soon as the fire insurance company had settled his claim. She and Albert, however, had spent the long night soul searching and had finally reached a conclusion.

"We'd like to build our own house," she told me, her voice strong with hope, and I was enthusiastic about their decision. Although both had been saving toward this goal, Herta regretted that their funds were not yet adequate to start such a big project as building a house. When I told Mother and Father about the possibilities at dinner, Father suggested that we join efforts with Herta and Albert. Providing an apartment for our family, would grant them a low cost mortgage which would enable them to build a two-family house. This was in conformity with the new housing law in the country, which required that anyone who built a house had to provide an apartment for a second family. This clause provided for the sorely needed housing for refugees and those families who had lost their homes during the war.

"We will move away from the farm," I shouted, overjoyed. Ursula promised to handle all paper work and legal aspects of the project. At night I prayed happily. My Lord had turned another disaster into our favor! He was providing adequate living quarters for us and relieved Herta and Albert of the contract with the farm. God, in His eternal Wisdom, cared about every detail of our lives. He always handled matters perfectly. Happy and grateful, I fell asleep.

When Frederick, our mason in the family, learned about this decision, he was glad and suggested that Albert contract with Frederick's employer for the construction of the house. Frederick would then persuade his colleagues to put in afterwork hours to keep the cost of labor low. Counting on Father's and Albert's help, he estimated the house could be finished within a year. Now came the biggest decision for the clan.

"Where do we want to build?" With this question, we encountered the first problem. Our family, including Albert and Herta, were anxious to leave Aschendorf but we were not able to purchase any land in either Dissen or Bad Rothenfelde. The only person willing to lease on a lifetime basis was the farmer who owned the *Kotten*. Even he was not willing to sell the small parcel. Inspecting the suggested plot with Albert, Father came home, disappointment written on his face.

"It is sour soil; I can tell from the bushels of cut grass growing on it," he said, projecting into the future, hoping to tend a garden again. But as no other plot was available, and the need was pressing, Herta and Albert decided to build in Aschendorf.

Meantime Ursula, in her efficient manner, had applied for the mortgage, handled the deed and a host of paperwork that the project involved.

When the land was surveyed and the mortgage approved, we had passed the first milestone. Father, Frederick, and Albert spent the first weekend digging the foundation. When the cellar floor was poured and the walls raised to reach over the grass surface, a second milestone was passed. Still, Frederick looked troubled.

"We have an active well under the cellar. The water keeps pushing through the cement foundation," he explained to Father, and the two examined the trouble spot. Determined to get the cellar watertight, Frederick worked the area over and over again. Every night the men labored feverishly, hoping to raise the shell of the house and get the roof in place before the onset of winter. Frederick brought some of his colleagues as extra help on weekends. Mother discovered, however, that their minds focused more on the free beer than on the building of the house.

"Will we ever finish?" she vented her frustration over the slow progress. Meantime the weather changed and there were many days when it was cold and rainy.

At the Niemeyer factory, the men talked about a promised bus trip. Mr. Ernst Niemeyer, after the sudden death of his brother Frederick, was now sole owner of the firm. Manfred told me that his father wanted to take advantage of one of the few beautiful days to take his employees on a day's outing. The destination was kept a secret, but Manfred confided to me that we would stop at a quaint place for dinner where we could dance, then walk home from there as early or as late as each one wished.

"Are you coming?" he asked, telling me that his mother and Lieselotte and Knopf from the office would also join the crowd. Although I was reluctant, Manfred prodded until I agreed to join them on the trip.

"I guarantee that in our company you will have a good time," he assured me.

When the day arrived, the bus was waiting at the entrance and, although it was only seven in the morning, a crowd had already gathered. Giving the sky a quizzical look, Manfred assured us that the weather would be sunny. The crowd, used to getting up early, arrived on time and when Mr. and Mrs. Niemeyer joined us, the count indicated that we were ready to leave. Mr. Niemeyer looked rather sporty in his light linen jacket, although lately he had developed a sizable round middle. Mrs. Niemeyer wore a casual print dress for the occasion to assure herself a comfortable ride. Manfred wore his dark green corduroy jacket which he loved and had not parted with for the last month. It looked good on him. I wore my multicolored "Dirndl" dress with a black velvet vest and a pair of comfortable light gray walking shoes, the pair "Uncle Henry" had specially made for me.

Boarding the bus, I picked a window seat and Manfred sat down next to me, whereas Lieselotte and Knopf chose the two seats in front of us.

Once everybody had settled, Mr. Niemeyer gave the driver directions and announced that our trip would take us to the Hermann's Monument. I was delighted. It was a favorite sightseeing spot east of the city of Bielefeld. From its high tower in the mountains, one could view the beautiful surrounding landscape.

"I told you that you would like it," said Manfred, and I was glad he had persuaded me to come, especially as I had never seen the monument. Once the bus left the sleeping village of Aschendorf behind, one of the men in the back started to sing, and soon the crowd joined him in his wanderlust. While I was still trying to wake up, I was surprised to hear Manfred sing along, slightly off key, but to his heart's content. He had lost his shyness. The bus driver explained the sights we were passing, small towns, and villages and the time moved quickly. Manfred and Knopf made their own comments, calling to Lieselotte's and my attention the firm's customers in the area, those paying timely and those lagging behind. Knopf, with his dry sense of humor, was at his best and entertained us with witty remarks.

Soon the bus made a sharp turn and Manfred pointed toward the high monument on the mountain. We had arrived. Glad to stretch our legs, we jumped off the bus and walked slowly up the narrow path to the top of the hill. It was a steep climb but everyone managed, although most of the crowd was lagging far behind the four of us. Disregarding our puffing, we were determined to be first to ascend the old stone steps to the monument. Knopf remembered his history lessons well. With a wide sweep of his arms, he proclaimed:

"Here fought the famous Teuton, Hermann the Cherusker." Lieselotte jokingly answered: "You have failed your calling. Instead of being a bookkeeper, you should have become an actor." Bowing to her, silently acknowledging her compliment, Knopf continued his speech, giving us a full account of the history of the area, mingling with it his own imagination. The laughter hampered our climb considerably, but we scrambled up the stairs. When we stepped out on the square walkway, Knopf recited a long piece of poetry and then bowed ceremoniously. Even strangers chuckled. Meeting the rest of the people on our way down, Knopf discouraged them.

"Don't bother going up; we left nothing for you to see." Not convinced, they climbed upward, big smiles on their faces. Later, Mr. Niemeyer was approached by a photographer and all the people assembled on a wide open staircase for a group picture. Manfred and Knopf, however, were more interested in food. It was past lunchtime and even Lieselotte and I were glad when the bus stopped at the nearby restaurant for a light lunch. While we were eating, Manfred announced a surprise for us.

"We have made reservations for dinner at the Waldhof Restaurant." Owned by Lieselotte's relatives, it was close to Aschendorf and in walking distance of home. After lunch, having replenished our energies, we visited the Extern Steine. This ancient shrine, constructed of gigantic natural rocks, was known to have served as a place of worship. The assembly of rocks, most of them ten to twelve feet high, was set in a circle. The one facing east had a huge round hole cut in its upper portion, allowing the rising sun to shine through it, hitting the ancient sun dial carved into polished, flat rock on the ground. A walkway, built of similar sized rocks, flanking it on either side, crossed over a deep, narrow stream. Knopf convinced us that it had served as an entrance to the circular shrine. This ancient place of worship intrigued me and I was pleased that our tour included this side trip, this surprise.

Slowly the crowd dribbled back and Lieselotte, complaining about a blister on her heel, was first to climb back into her seat. The sun was close to setting and, as the bus rolled homeward, the crowd again started to sing. After an hour's drive, it turned dark. As the bus passed street lights, I saw that Lieselotte had dozed off; even Knopf was quiet. Yet Manfred did not seem tired. He asked me if I would later on, after dinner, teach him to dance the Samba. This was the newest step and popular on dance floors. Manfred confided:

"I feel so self-conscious about dancing; therefore, I never took lessons." Talking with him, I realized that he had lost his shyness. Obviously enjoying our conversation, he asked about my special interests and I told him that I loved photography as a hobby and enjoyed travelling.

"May I join you on your trips?" he asked enthusiastically and I consented laughingly, knowing that usually Lisa Gander, Maria, or Frederick would travel with me.

Shortly after, the bus turned off the road and Manfred announced that we had arrived at the Waldhof. Jovially, he slapped Knopf on his knee.

"Wake up, old man, we're here!" and, with a jerk, Knopf jumped up. Rubbing his sleepy eyes, he made a profound statement.

"Now this man is ready for food and drink," he addressed Lieselotte, who had wakened from the commotion. Knopf permitted her to drink all she wanted because he would gallantly take her home. His comment roused great laughter on the bus because, firstly, Lieselotte lived on the premises and, secondly, everyone knew she was not fond of drinking. Goodhumoredly, however, she assured Knopf:

"I promise I will not create a social problem for you!" The crowd climbed off the bus rather lamely but, when the aroma of cooked food rose into their nostrils, they quickly found a seat at a table, ready to be served.

Manfred had eyed a table in a comfortable corner and motioned the three of us to follow him. I was surprised and pleased with the seating arrangements for four instead of the usual long table set up for a group. While the waiters were busy serving food, Knopf got up, raised his wine glass, and in his deep drawl, addressed a long and philosophical toast across the room to Mr. and Mrs. Niemeyer.

"May the gods reward you for your generosity and hospitality," and, addressing Mrs. Niemeyer, he bowed and continued, "and may the goddess of charm and beauty rain upon you showers of rose petals, perfume of violets, and bestow you with a long life filled with laughter and happiness." Everyone applauded and cheered. The trip had been a success—in spite of Lieselotte's blisters. While I relished the food, sipping the wine carefully from my glass, Manfred reminded me of my promise.

"You will teach me the Samba, remember," he said and appreciated that the tables were cleared and the band switched from dinner music to dance tunes. In honor of the day, Mr. and Mrs. Niemeyer danced the first waltz and, finishing their round, invited the crowd to join them, obviously not much caring for a solo. Manfred closely watched the dancing feet. He looked confused.

"I can't do this; it is too fast. I'll wait for the Samba." As if the musicians had read his mind, the next dance was a Samba. The crowd changed. As the older people took their seats, the younger ones took over the floor. Manfred, seeing enough couples dancing so he could hide in the crowd, finally mustered all his courage.

"Come on; let's try it," and he whisked me off to a corner where we tried the Samba. Realizing that he was stiff and awkward, I joked around and instructed him how to do the steps.

When the tune came to a close, he had finally gotten it; now he only had to lose his stiffness. Triumphantly, he announced to Knopf that he could dance the Samba. Knopf's comment, however, was very dry.

"With half a bottle of wine poured behind his tie, anyone can dance the Samba." He had a unique way of saying things and we laughed. Manfred was proud of his achievement, knowing that his parents were watching him closely.

As the hour passed eleven, I told the three that it was time for my departure. Manfred insisted on walking me home. We both had enjoyed the day and, bidding me goodnight at the Mueller entrance, he squeezed my hand, inviting me to the *Schuetzenfest*, a hunters' ball, next weekend.

"I have to practice my new dance steps," he said with a wink in his eye. Laughingly, I agreed and, as he left, I noticed a gingerness in his usually slow steps.

* * * * * *

Saturday arrived quickly and my brother Frederick, heading for the same place, escorted me to the tents in Bad Rothenfelde which had been set up for the occasion. Entering the grounds, Manfred had spotted us and came to greet me. The grounds were crowded with young people and "Schuetzen," hunters, who appeared to be more interested in the beer than the deer. Manfred, in good spirits, headed for the dance floor where a brass band was doing its best to keep a tune. The next piece was a Samba and Manfred carefully folded my coat and put it on a bench, bidding me to dance with him. He remembered his steps well; he even dared to continue our conversation without getting his feet mixed up. Herbert, his younger brother, was also at the dance. When I questioned Manfred if Herbert was here to keep an eye on us, he shrugged off my query, saying he did not need a baby sitter.

We danced for a while, then Manfred took me to the amusement stands where the oldtime hunters practiced shooting. Full of beer, they bragged to the crowd how easily they could hit dead center. I stayed at a safe distance. Judging by their swaying, I was not sure whether they knew the front from their backs. I was not going to risk standing in their way in case one of them accidentally discharged his dangerous toy backwards. Manfred, without any shooting experience, aimed once, hit dead center, and received a huge pink balloon as a prize. The "Bravo" of the bystanders became overwhelming and, when they started to sing noisily, it was time for us to leave.

It was a cool moonlit night and as it was still early, we took a leisurely walk home. Manfred talked freely now. He admitted that often the complexity of business puzzled him and that the prospects of having to shoulder the full responsibility of managing the firm later in life frightened him. I assured him that he would learn in time. To me, the matter seemed simple. As long as he managed the books well, seeing that customers paid their bills, which would enable him to keep the firm's liabilities low, it had to work.

"I don't know if I can handle it. But I promised my grandfather to carry on the business so his name would live on," he said, repeating the touching story he had told me several months ago. Almost unaware of going slightly out of our way, we had passed the factory. Manfred stopped under the doorway to the yard and surprised me with a spontaneous kiss. Although flustered, I let him be. He was a sweet soul. I was happy that he trusted me and cared for me; that he disregarded the fact that I was a refugee and employed in his father's firm. We continued our walk in silence, Manfred casually holding my hand. Then, turning toward me, he asked a question.

"May I call you Maexchen? It suits you better because you are strong and courageous like the famous prize fighter, but sweet and tender at the same time. It is amazing what these small hands have achieved in those years of work," he commented as if to himself. Then, pressing my hand, in a sweep of romance, he bent down to kiss it. Getting to know this gentle and loving side of Manfred's personality, a warm, comfortable feeling filled my heart. Reminding him that I was four years older than he, he asked, with a searching connotation in his voice.

"Does this matter to you?" I assured him that it did not, but I wondered what his parents' reaction would be. Brushing my concern aside, he was happy that I cared for him; he did not want disturbing thoughts to taint this lovely evening. At Mueller's farm door, he embraced me tenderly and kissed me goodnight. I kissed him on his cheek, whispering "Thanks for a lovely evening" into his ear. He parted with a smile.

"Before winter set in, Manfred and I attended another *Schuetzenfest* and had an equally good time. Not skipping one dance, Manfred set an all-time record. He encouraged me to sip of the champagne he had ordered. Although neither of us was tipsy, we set out early on our walk home to enjoy the cool, dry, night air. When we arrived at the Mueller farm, Manfred asked me a simple question.

"Maexchen, will you marry me?" Although I had known him

so many years, I was shocked. I had not expected this sudden proposal. I cared for him, yet I was certain his parents would not welcome me as Manfred's wife. Recovering from my shock, I agreed, especially as Manfred insisted that his parents knew me; that they did not need a long explanation. I hoped to keep our engagement a secret until April when Manfred would be twenty-one, an age that permitted him to make his own decisions. Yet I did not specifically ask him not to mention it to anyone. Not able to contain his happiness, Manfred broke the news of our engagement to his family the following week. Instead of finding enthusiasm and kind understanding, he encountered cold consternation. When Manfred stubbornly insisted on following through with his decision, his father threatened to send him away from home. Although I had expected some difficulty, when Manfred told me about the cold rejection, I was deeply hurt.

Many nights I prayed, asking for an answer, asking for a way to be shown. My Lord, who had been my close Ally and Friend over the years had to see me through this problem. I was positive that He would. If I was to marry Manfred, He would work things out. If it was not to be, He would let me know very soon.

In the meantime, the Christmas season approached and the firm was inundated with orders. Production was stepped up and I worked endless hours of overtime. The mountains of shoes looked overwhelming; they haunted me in my dreams. Occasionally, I had a truckload of packages ready for shipment by noontime. I worked hard and fast. The oversize workload and my troubled, disappointed heart took a toll on my health. Among the factory staff, a bad spell of influenza threw many on their sick bed, and I suffered a severe cold. One man could hardly talk because of a severely infected throat, yet he plugged away polishing shoes at the finishing brushes. Around Christmas, I had developed a fever and looked forward to the rest I would get over the holidays. Maria suffered from the flu and was in bed.

During the Christmas holidays I took sick. Manfred surprised me with a visit one day. His father had hurriedly arranged for a three-year practicum in the shoe metropolis of Pirmasenz. He was ordered to leave immediately. Although he realized that I was very sick, he hoped I would quit my job and leave with him.

"Maexchen, will you come, please?" he asked anxiously. Too sick and too feverish, I was unable to commit myself. I had to recover, to get back on my feet first. In the meantime, the man who had worked at the finishing brushes had died.

"Don't die, please," he pleaded and I promised that I would get better soon. After embracing me tenderly and giving me a long, last glance, Manfred left.

The doctor visited me frequently. He was concerned about my condition, especially as I was vomiting and losing weight. Each week he gave me a different medication, but my condition did not improve. Therefore, he ordered me to be taken to the *Waldkrankenhaus*, a Catholic hospital for observation and tests. Within two weeks I had lost all my strength and could hold a spoon to feed myself only with great effort. My hands were shaking from weakness. Mother, worried about my condition, could hardly wait for the results of the tests. But the only one taken was a cardiogram showing slight irregularities, nothing serious. Repeatedly, I mentioned my adverse reaction to the various medications which caused me to vomit, and my lack of appetite. The attending physician listened absent-mindedly and when he left, I noticed a peculiar smile on his face. It puzzled me. What was on his mind? During the night I lay awake, analyzing my situation. Within the two weeks I had spent here, I had become steadily worse. Nothing was done about it. Then I prayed. Suddenly a thought entered my mind. Was this hospital doctor assuming that I was pregnant? The thought offended me. How could a virgin be pregnant? Why did he not take any further tests? My stomach had been pumped out, without showing results. Something was wrong.

When my own house doctor visited me later, I had made a decision. I demanded to be released the next day.

"I don't intend to die from neglect in this place," I told him to emphasize my point. It would be at my own risk, the doctor pointed out, but I had nothing to lose; therefore, I readily agreed. The next day I signed the release papers and dragged myself down the corridor to call Knopf. He promised to pick me up.

Mother received me back with great anxiety. Tomorrow we would have to see a homeopath if I would be strong enough to make the bus trip to Osnabrueck. Sheer determination kept me going. The next day, sitting in the overcrowded waiting room of the doctor's office, Mother eyed me worriedly. I assured her that I was strong enough to wait for my turn. Patients, having waited for hours, praised the doctor's understanding, ability and devotion. One woman came out of the office crying.

"Why could not my own doctor diagnose my case as tuberculosis? He has treated me for years," she sobbed, but the homeopath accompanied her out the door, assuring her full recovery after a stay at the sanatorium. Hearing this encouraging statement, my spirits lifted.

Finally, it was my turn. Sitting in the doctor's office, he

moved his chair close in front of me and asked me to keep my eyes steady, looking straight into the pencil-like apparatus, he called the "Lupe." The intense light at the end was blinding me, but he explained that the light was focusing on a microscopic lens, which enabled him, by searching through a patient's pupils, to view the entire organism of the body. His examination was thorough, going over the right and the left side by looking through my right and left eye and pausing over my right eye, the right side that had been troubling me.

"You have had a severe fall. How long ago did this happen?" he asked. I did not recall.

"Not recently," he said, "this is an old break. The coccyx was broken, but has healed together crookedly. I can see it clearly. It must have happened several years ago." Then I remembered my accident, crashing on the waxed floor at Niemeyers, and I confirmed his diagnosis. He scolded me for my negligence in not having consulted a doctor at that time. This neglected problem was now causing the severe pains in my legs, because during my fall, the main nerve leading down through the legs, was impinged between two lower vertebrae.

"In the fall, you did not only break the tip of your spine, but the lower vetebrae jammed close together, they are much closer than normal. As a result, the pain from the broken coccyx has constricted the lower back muscles, and this is the reason for your stiffness, the pain and weakness in your back." He still had not taken his pencil-like search light away from my eye, he was still examining my body.

"You would have had four more weeks to live in this present condition. You are suffering also from a severe medicine poisoning and your body has spent all its reserves. You don't have even an ounce of fat left in your body. All the organs, especially your liver and kidneys are laying bare, the usual fat cushion, protecting them, has disappeared, has been used up. As a result of the medicine poisoning, causing you to vomit every time you put food in to your stomach, you are suffering from a severe case of malnutrition as well."

I was shocked, hearing the famous doctor's analysis. Yet I felt that his diagnosis was correct. When I told him that I had been treated for rheumatism and had been given a whole gamut of medication to relieve the pain, he shook his head in disbelief. Explaining that from the prescription he gave me now, I would vomit one more time, guaranteeing me that it would be my last time, he dismissed me, patting me encouragingly on the shoulder.

"Once the pain has disappeared, try to do light exercises,

stretching, bending your neck and the lower back. It will help relax the muscles, ease the tension," he suggested.

"And eat, eat, eat. I'll see you when you feel stronger." With this encouraging comment, he led me out the door. Mother's eyes were all anxiety. But my smile and the doctor's calmness quickly assured her that I would be all right. We picked up the medication in the drugstore across the street and took the bus back. At home Mother curiously examined the label on the bottle to inspect the doctor's "miracle" medicine.

"It contains arsenic; that's poisonous!" she cried but, confidently, I counted out the prescribed number of drops, willing to play the guinea pig. As predicted, I threw up violently. But shortly after, I wanted to eat. I was famished. Watching me in disbelief, Mother heated a bowl of soup. It did not satisfy my hunger and Mother hurriedly prepared a sandwich. I devoured it in minutes and asked for more. Mother was overjoyed, my stomach was accepting food again!

For several days she was busy preparing food for me. It seemed as if I could not stop eating. A week later my knees had steadied and my hollow cheeks had filled out. My shaking hands had regained their strength, and I felt like myself again. Overjoyed, I thanked my Lord for His help and miraculous healing. He had given me new life again.

Once I felt strong enough to carry a suitcase, I decided to visit Aunt Ina. She and Uncle Oskar had moved to the Black Forest where Uncle Oskar had opened a modest business again, selling radios, phonographs, and bicycles. Aunt Ina was happy to see me when they picked me up at the station.

Aunt Ina's excellent cooking helped me gain some pounds fast. The rest caused my back to relax, the pain in my legs had vanished. Discussing with her my dilemma over the secret engagement to Manfred, she made a very sober suggestion.

"Find yourself another boy. It is not worth the trouble." Her advice sounded so easy, yet my heart still held on, unable to let go. Surrounded by Aunt Ina's care and light-hearted spirit, and talking to my Lord at night, I finally reached a decision. On my return home, I would find another job and then resign from Niemeyers. The day before I left to travel back to Aschendorf, I wrote Manfred a long letter to nullify our engagement, and to tell him that he should consider himself free.

At first, Manfred refused to accept my offer and wrote to me frequently, congratulating me on my decision to change jobs. He was happy and interested to learn that I was taking night courses in typing and brushing up on the stenography I had learned in middle school. He was proud of me. Still, I confirmed my former decision, cancelling our engagement, especially as I did not want him to sacrifice his birthright of becoming owner of the firm. His father had threatened to disown him if he married me. I had nothing to promise but my love and loyalty. Besides, I had the peculiar feeling that God had something else planned for me, something that was less troublesome, something that would make me happy instead of causing me heartache. Therefore, I willingly let Manfred go.

* * * * * *

When I reported back to work at Niemeyers after approximately two months of sick leave, few things had changed. A young man from the production line had been trained to fill my job while I had been away. Mr. Niemeyer briefly explained that the man would stay on the job because I obviously needed help. At home each night I studied the want ads in the local newspaper. Ursula had located a girl in the village who taught advanced stenography and I signed up for a private course. Also, using every spare moment, I practiced my typing, determined to improve my accuracy and speed.

The construction of the house was progressing steadily and it would be only a matter of weeks until we could move in. This was the greatest news—that our family would live in a house again, a house that provided decent, adequate living quarters. It would remove the seal with which we had been stamped: second-class citizens.

One Saturday I spotted an advertisement in the paper offering a position as a secretary-bookkeeper in a small firm in Bad Rothenfelde. I telephoned from Ursula's office and was given a date for an interview. The small knitting mill was housed in a long wooden barrack at the southern end of Bad Rothenfelde. It was also within walking distance. A young man in his thirties interviewed me and, during the course of our conversation, I learned that he was Mr. Rohn, Jr., son of the owner, Mr. Alfred Rohn.

"We have been in partnership with the plastic manufacturer across the yard, but we intend to become an independent firm again. This requires that we separate our books," he explained, giving me the reason for the job opening. The Rohns had owned a large business in the province of Sachsen but were disowned once the Russians occupied their city. Here, in these primitive quarters they had started a modest business again, producing highly fashioned ladies' sweaters. Mr. Rohn mentioned that they kept up their number one goal: high quality.

"Now we need a secretary who can also handle the books," Mr. Rohn said, explaining that the business was small and one girl could easily handle the job. I was honest with him. I admitted this was my first job as a secretary and I had no experience; of accounting, I had no knowledge at all. Taking note of this fact, Mr. Rohn said he would discuss our interview with his father and brother. He would contact me after he had interviewed the second applicant. Having been honest with the man regarding my abilities, I walked home gingerly. I felt good.

Two days later, a girl from the village stopped by to tell me that Mr. Rohn wished to see me again. When he continued his interview the next day, he dictated a letter for me to take in shorthand, then asked me to transcribe it on the typewriter. I was nervous and, not prepared for this surprise, I made several typing mistakes, leaving one sentence out altogether. Defeatedly, I thought I had failed. But Mr. Rohn did not mind my errors, coming right to the point of the matter.

"If you promise to take accounting lessons immediately, you have the job. The girl who claimed to be a bookkeeper knew no more than you." With Knopf in mind as my private tutor, I assured Mr. Rohn that I would start my lessons as soon as possible. Passing Ursula's office, I dropped in to tell her of my triumphant success: I was hired as a secretary-bookkeeper. She was very happy. So was the whole family. It was enough reason for a small celebration.

As I had hoped, Knopf agreed to tutor me in accounting. As a matter of fact, he crammed a two-year course into me in six weeks.

Meantime, we had started to move into the new house. A lot of packing had to be done because we were able to carry small boxes the short distance up the road.

The day after Mr. Rohn hired me, I told Mr. Niemeyer that I had found a new job and, to my amazement, his face turned white. His curious inquiry where I would be working, made me realize that he feared I might move to Pirmasenz to marry Manfred. When I told him my new job was in Bad Rothenfelde, he visibly relaxed.

"I don't like to lose you, but I understand your move. Your ambitions reach beyond a dirty job in our factory," he said, groping for words, painfully avoiding mentioning Manfred's name.

When I finished my last day at Niemeyers, I had worked for them over eight years. Yet Mr. and Mrs. Niemeyer regarded me as a total stranger.

At night, finishing a chapter of my life with a prayer of thanksgiving to my Lord, I closed with a happy note: "Lord, forgive them, for they know not what they do." My Lord and I loved them still, in spite of their limitations.

Chapter XIV

Freed to Serve

Our move into the new house was finally completed. Herta let me have a room downstairs. Now I had my own domain. After being cramped into the tiny, gray, and depressing quarters at the Mueller farm, I could stretch, pursue my hobbies, and read to my heart's content. The room was sunny, spacious, and comfortable and I shared it with Maria. The new, complete bedroom set, which I had ordered after Manfred had asked me to marry him, gave us ample room. Maria and I enjoyed the luxury of having a bed to ourselves. The big double window, covering almost the entire wall, faced south and on a clear day the sun shone through the white, lacy curtains, making the room a sheer delight.

On the wide window sills, I lined up my collection of cacti, which I had started from the culture Aunt Ina had given me. On a tile, stool-type stand in the corner, I nursed my ear cactus. It seemed to enjoy its new location because, happily, it was growing two earlike extensions. Maria and I had chosen wallpaper in a very light color with a free style design loosely scattered across the panels to give the room an open, spacious effect. The small, multicolored, floral carpet blended with the light and airiness of the room, adding to it a sense of warmth and comfort. Now Maria and I had a place we could again call home.

"Once I'm finished with sewing the bedspread, we are settled," said Maria, giving the room her keen appraisal, insisting that she sew the bedspread herself. She had selected a pattern which harmonized with the color scheme of the room.

My new job at Rohns demanded my full attention and Knopf came to the house twice a week to tutor me in accounting. Therefore, I had little time to think about Manfred. I still received letters from him, yet less frequently now. He encouraged me to move to Pirmasenz, to marry him. But I was fully aware that his father paid his tuition and board. How could we get married? Confident, however, that I could have been able to support myself, I did not intend to start my life with him on such a difficult basis. Furthermore, I could not accept Manfred's suggestion that we marry in secrecy behind the back of his parents. I did not feel right about having to hide my actions. It was against my sense of honesty. Besides, I felt it was against the will of God. My Lord would never have wanted me to live my life in hiding. I had not committed a crime. That I was a refugee was unfortunate. In due time, however, God would offer me a chance to make up for my losses, for my setbacks, for my sacrificed time. Therefore, I preferred to remain free, to be ready when He called. Meantime, I felt that my Lord was preparing me for something greater, something more important. My job at Rohns was part of this preparation. So far I was not sure of my destination, but I knew in time my Lord would show it to me.

It was difficult to convey my philosophy, my convictions, in a letter to Manfred. But as I prayed that my Lord might help him understand, his letters arrived less frequently, and then stopped. We had made the break.

Knopf taught me with devotion and persistence, insisting stubbornly that I complete the mountain of homework he gave me at every session. At first I had difficulty understanding the technical material, but when Mr. Rohn's part-time bookkeeper explained the practical side of it to me in the evenings after work, accounting made sense. I enjoyed posting bills and cash receipts and within six months I was able to close the books on my own. I had become a full-fledged secretary-bookkeeper. Mr. Rohn, Sr., proud of my achievement, had the auditor check the books and, finding them in order, discontinued the part-time bookkeeper's services.

Everyone in my family congratulated me on this step forward. On Sundays when our entire family sat together at the dinner table, we engaged in serious discussions. During one of these sessions, I suggested again that our family emigrate to the United States. Having mentioned this matter repeatedly over the years, especially during our difficult years at the Mueller farm, Father realized that I was serious about my suggestion. He considered my idea unreasonable.

"We own the house in Gumbinnen, in East Prussia. Some day we will return to it. It would be impractical to move so far away. Do you realize that America is an ocean and a continent away?" he pointed out. Trying to persuade him, I argued that the Russians would never give up East Prussia. It was aginst Communist tactics to move out of gained territory. It was against their idea because Stalin, like Hitler, promised that Communism would conquer the world. Neither Father nor Mother could be convinced that East Prussia had to be written off; it was lost. We would never again live in our house in Gumbinnen. They could not understand the reason why I wanted to leave Germany, venture out to a foreign country.

"So many Germans have migrated to Canada and America; why can't we go?" I argued. But Father brought up a valid point: we had no relatives in either country. Karl Gander, our neighbor from Gumbinnen, had relatives in Canada and had migrated to Toronto. I envied him and his young bride. Secretely I also envied those German girls who had gone to England on a contract basis to serve a year in a British household. This direct exposure to the new language enabled them to increase their vocabulary, to attain fluency in pronunciation, to speak English correctly. Even Maria, usually adventurous, discouraged me, saying she had no intentions of leaving Germany.

"If I only had a chance," I told them, "I would go." I regretted that my correspondence with the Methvens, my Scottish friends for whom I had worked as a baby-sitter during previous years, had not been continued. Mr. Methven had been stationed with the British Air Force in Bad Rothenfelde and occupied one of the houses which was assigned to Father for maintenance. On nights when Mr. and Mrs. Methven attended Club functions, I stayed with Helen, their eight-year-old daughter. Because Helen could not pronounce my name, Marianne, she simply called me Madge. As I liked the new version of my name, Maria and Andreas also called me by my Scottish name. Helen and I had become friends and we had corresponded for several years. Unfortunately, I lost contact with them after Mr. Methven had been transferred to a different post.

During leisure hours on Sundays, I leafed through old copies of the *National Geographic Magazine*, which Mr. Methven had given to Father. The photographs of the United States were captivating. To me, the continent was the most scenic, the most beautiful. I felt drawn to it. Although Father had collected these copies because of their outstanding photography, he did not have the desire to live in America.

"Helen has seen the world," I told Father enviously. At the age of seven, she had seen Germany, had attended school in Bad Rothenfelde. Later the Methvens had moved to Guetersloh, where I had visited them. "Where did they live now?" I wondered. "Why did Herta and Albert have to build in Aschendorf?" I asked myself. It was the most Godforsaken place. Maria at least agreed with me on this point. She also dreaded the long, dreary winter months with rain, sleet, and snow, when the icy winds whipped the countryside. With nothing to do on weekends, it was desolate. Neither she nor I attended the dances because of the inclement weather. We had to search for a substitute of entertainment to prevent our minds from going stale.

One Saturday Maria brought home a few magazines, something interesting for us to read in the evening. She suggested that we retire early. It had been a gray day, conducive to reading. While I was struggling to complete a difficult crossword puzzle, Maria interrupted, reading something from a magazine to me.

"Listen Madge, this one is for you. Blond, 5'8", architect, serious-minded; desires to meet intelligent girl for purposes of marriage. Write to Box 1234." At first I was confused, not knowing to what she was referring.

"Are you all right?" I asked, giving her a puzzled look. She held the page under my nose, pointing to an ad she had just read.

"If you don't like this one, I'll find another for you; just give me a minute," she continued with a wistful smile. I laughed, realizing that she meant well and I had to read the ad whether I liked it or not. The magazine carried columns with a variety of advertisements—people searching for a marriage partner, for a companion, for a pen-pal. Having captured my attention, Maria had persuaded me to examine the possibilities. We both agreed that we would never reply to an ad where a man was trying to find a wife, the pen-pal idea did strike our fancy. It added a touch of adventure to our desolate social world during the winter months. Studying these columns carefully, I noticed several ads with foreign addresses, indicating that these German men were living in far away places: Australia, Asia, South and North America, Canada. It was understandable that they desired to marry girls of their own nationality, hoping to find one with a great deal of courage to respond and join them in a life on a distant continent. The more I thought about it, the more the pen-pal idea intrigued me. I had not been able to complete my middle school education. Here was my chance to correspond with someone in English. In the process, I would expand my knowledge, gain fluency in the language. At least Maria approved of this promising adventure.

"I'll buy the magazine every week. Just promise you won't move away," she said, but I did not commit myself. For several months we scrutinized the ads in the *Constanze*, our favorite magazine. Occasionally Maria read an ad in the marriage section to me, hoping it would capture my attention. Finally, when I suggested she find a husband for herself, she gave up. I was not interested. So far I had been unable to find an interesting ad in the pen-pal section. Consequently, I put the magazine aside for a while and concentrated on reading my beloved books again. Maria continued to interrupt me with ads, reading the ones to me that appealed to her. She considered the advertising pages fun reading. One evening she read a long ad to me, emphasizing each word. As I reached for the paper, she grinned.

"That one is not listed; I just made up the ad," she joked. Calling her a clown, I was about to throw the magazine across the bed when, at a glance, I caught a name. Did I read right? It was East Prussian. I recognized it immediately—Richard Serkau. The ad listed the man's full address in the Middle East, giving a box number in Bagdad, Iraq. I ripped out the page; Maria eyed me suspiciously. I folded the page and handed her back the magazine. She implored me, begging to know what had struck me like lightning.

"Secret," I mumbled, turning to my book again. Maria stole the folded page from me and scrutinized every ad, asking me over and over again."

"Is it this one?" Getting tired of her continued interruptions, I pointed out the ad and let her read it. She gasped.

"Madge, you must be kidding; you don't ever intend to live in Bagdad! Where in the world is that?" As I did not volunteer any information, she was determined to find it in the Atlas. Barefoot and in her nightgown, she ran upstairs to get the big Atlas. Giving me a scolding look, she settled back in bed. Finally she located Bagdad in Iraq, in the Middle East.

"This is insane! Bagdad is hundreds of kilometers away from Germany!" By now, I regretted having shown her the ad. In our family nothing was private. I had visions of Mother protesting against such an adventure, even writing to the man. I pressed Maria to keep it a secret, and she agreed.

It took me several weeks to muster enough courage to draft a letter to this unknown man in Bagdad, a man with an East Prussian name. In my brief note, I inquired why he had chosen this out-of-the-way place as his residence. Somehow I did not expect to receive a reply. In my mind, I envisioned this stranger being flooded with a deluge of mail. The thought made me laugh. One of those letters, a straggler, so to speak, came from me.

Many weeks later, having almost forgotten about my writing adventure, Mother handed me an airmail letter. Her face expressed a big question mark. I was as surprised as she. The letter was postmarked in Bagdad. Then I remembered the advertisement in the *Constancze*. In the meantime, I had forgotten under which category the ad had been listed, marriage or pen-pal. Now I appreciated the honor system regarding mail in our family. No one opened anyone else's letters and no one asked questions about the contents. Whatever was volunteered, however, was received with great interest, if not outright curiosity.

After lunch I read the letter and, as expected, Mr. Serkau was from East Prussia, from Insterburg, the next big city west of Gumbinnen. In typical East Prussian simplicity, he wrote that due to the war he had lost his parents and his home. One married sister lived in Philadelphia in the United States. Searching for work, after being released from the liquidated German army, he found a job in Iraq researching and drilling the Iraqi soil for oil. His position was that of a surveyor and in his Volkswagen he had traveled from Bagdad as far as the Turkish border, testing the ground. During the scattered correspondence of the following months, we exchanged snapshots. The one photograph I received revealed the man out of 1001-nights to be at least six feet tall, slender, and sober looking. His writing was clear-cut and easily legible.

Mother was under the impression that Mr. Serkau was a pen-pal and, having explained to her that he was East Prussian, she never criticized my adventure. It helped make the dreary winter months pass quickly. When I met Knopf one day at the post office and he told me that Manfred had gotten engaged to a girl in Pirmasenz, I took it matter-of-factly, surprising myself.

Many months later Mr. Serkau wrote that he planned to visit Germany during his vacation. Would I allow him to stop by and introduce himself. Perhaps, if I was interested, we could marry and I could drive back with him and live in Bagdad. I was nervous, also very excited, and told myself that I could take my time in making a decision. After meeting "Pete," as I secretly called him, I would know what to do. When Father learned of this possibility, he gave me a long lecture. In no uncertain terms, he pointed out that it was dangerous to live in the Middle East and, to frighten me, he claimed that it was known for its still flourishing slave trade. Neither Father nor I believed this rumor to be a fact nor did he need to have worried because, shortly thereafter, King Feisal of Iraq was assassinated. During this time of political upheaval in

Iraq, I lost contact with Mr. Serkau and never heard from him again. Father was greatly relieved. Quietly I filed the experience under the department of adventures to be fondly remembered.

In early spring when Mr. Rohn, Jr. assembled a new collection of spring sweaters, he asked me to model his new creations for the buyers of his customers. It thrilled me to try on one pretty sweater after another, watching the buyers order great quantities, commenting on the chic fit, the beautiful pastel colors, the modern design. The girls at the factory could never produce enough, keeping the expensive machinery running day and night. Occasionally one of the sample sweaters Mr. Rohn designed did not sell. If the sample fit me, he would sell it to me at cost price. As a result, I owned an assortment of sweaters in the latest styles and prettiest colors. I also kept our entire family supplied. I considered it much more fun to work with beautiful sweaters and cardigans than with men's work shoes. I was glad I had changed my job.

* * * * * *

Time passed quickly and I had completed my third year working at Rohn's Knitting Factory. Although I held a respectable position, I was not satisfied with my achievements. Something was tugging at me, urging me to move on. Should I go to England, I asked myself. The condition to serve as a housekeeper for one or two years did not appeal to me. I had a too strong-minded and independent character to make a good maid. When I mentioned the subject at the dinner table, Father disapproved.

"The British barely manage to feed themselves. Under their economic system, with your experiences and qualifications, you would not earn enough money to support yourself," he reasoned. Although not appreciating Father's rebuff, I did not stress my point, especially as it was only an idea. Besides, Father might be right. My adventure would lose its excitement if I had to return home, admitting that it had been a failure. The idea of leaving the country, at least on a temporary basis, appealed to me more and more. Thinking about the possibility of emigration, I realized that it had to be an English-speaking country because this was the only foreign language I knew. Therefore, logically, I decided to emigrate to the United States. By now, I was aware that I would meet stern criticism, if not outright discouragement, if I shared my plan with anyone in the family. If I wanted to succeed, I had to work on my project in secrecy, telling absolutely no one, including Maria. This tactic had another advantage. If my plan did not work out, it would not require lengthy explanations to anyone. The more I thought about my project, the more I liked the idea.

Somewhere on the big continent called North America, I would live some day. Although our family had neither relatives nor friends in the United States, I had to find a contact. As I had done so often in the past, I summoned my Lord in prayer, asking Him to work this plan out with me and, as my close Friend and Ally, go to America with me. Our family, each member being on his way to establish his life, to grow self-sufficient, did not need my services any more. That night, in silence, I renewed my pledge to God: I will serve Thee and Thine creation.

Now I was happy and excited about my decision. I felt as if I had received my Lord's approval and blessing on the project. The first step in my adventure was to find a sponsor; everything else would follow in chronological order. My Ally gave me the idea as to how I might locate a sponsor: via an address in the United States. Remembering my correspondence with Mr. Serkau, I bought a copy of the *Constanze* and scrutinized the ads for a complete name and address in America. In most issues, the ads from the United States were listed under a box number. This meant the time was not right, that I had to wait. With the Lord as my Friend, this adventure had to result in success.

Then one weekend, I almost let out a cry of joy. Listed under the marriage ads, I found a full name, giving a New York address. This was my contact! Explaining my plans for immigration, I wrote to the man, stressing the fact that I had no intentions of marrying him. In my politest German, I asked him to name the most widely read newspaper in New York, giving me its address, as I intended to place a "Want Ad" asking for a sponsor and a job. Having clipped out the ad, I typed the letter explaining my intentions, thanked him for a reply, and then I sealed it. The next day I dropped it into the mail box at the post office, blessing it silently, and sped it on its way. To my amazement, I did not have to wait long. Two weeks later, Mother handed me an airmail letter at lunchtime, eyeing me curiously, but did not ask questions.

After lunch I flew over the letter downstairs in my room. It was several pages long and was worded in this vein: I warn you not to come to this country if you have any preconceived notions. The work is hard. Any person of an unstable character might land in the gutter. But at the end of his long-winded moralizing speech, he had phrased a pro forma ad in English and suggested that I place it in the *New York Times*, assuring me that it was the most widely read newspaper in the city. He urged me to place it in the Sunday issue and, for this purpose, he enclosed a rate schedule for my use. This was exactly what I needed. Blessing the man, I sped off a note of thanks to him. The following day I rephrased the ad, calculated my bill, and purchased a money order from the local bank in U.S. dollars, which I enclosed and mailed to the *New York Times*.

In the meantime, I sat tight and prayed hard, anxious to receive a reply. Who of the many millions in New York would read my ad? Would I receive a reply at all? But—I reminded myself—the Lord was on my side. The first letter was correspondence from the newspaper itself. Confirming the receipt of my letter, the Advertising Department of *The New York Times* wrote that I had missed one deadline but my ad would appear in the following Sunday issue. Although I was tempted to make a bus trip to Osnabrueck to purchase this particular issue, I could not spare the time.

Nevertheless, proof that my ad had been in the paper arrived a week later. I received two responses. One letter came from a German-Hungarian couple in their sixties, offering me a housekeeper's position, but they apologized for being unable to sponsor me. In a footnote, however, they invited me to visit them once I was in the country. Realizing I would need friends in the States, I answered them promptly and kept their letter in a safe place. The second letter contained what I needed—the offer of a sponsorship and a job. It came from a Mr. James Hobart and was postmarked in the town of Teaneck, New Jersey. In a fluent but almost illegible handwriting, he gave me the following data. He managed a small real estate business in Teaneck and worked with his married son and one salesman. He was divorced and lived in an apartment adjacent to the office. He needed someone to prepare lunch for him and the men, someone who would also be competent to cover the phones at the office while he and his staff were out. The position paid $50 a week and he was willing to sponsor me.

As these were the only two answers to my ad, I had no difficulty deciding which job to accept. It was the Gal-Friday position including light cooking for $50 a week. The only factor that disturbed me in the deal was that Mr. Hobart was divorced. I consulted Pastor Baring in Dissen on the matter. He promised to keep our discussion a secret and, after hearing me out, offered his help, shaking his head in disbelief. My good Pastor knew a German minister in New York whom he would contact, requesting that his colleague get in touch with Mr. Hobart to form an opinion on my sponsor's moral outlook and intentions. In a sense, I appreciated the fact that no one in our family read English because the divorce clause would have definitely disqualified Mr. Hobart as my sponsor and future boss. It was assuring to know that I had made a pact with my Lord. He was able to look into the hearts and minds of Man. Being in charge of our project, my Lord had searched out this man. Therefore, it was all right to accept the offer, and I did. While Pastor Baring rushed off a letter to his German colleague in New York, I requested application papers for emigration from the German Consulate in Hamburg. I was curious as to how long it would take to receive my visa.

Mother had seen my letters from the United States arrive in the mail and, under the impression that I had started another pen-pal correspondence, made a few comments but, thank God, did not ask questions. I could not have lied to her, but it was simpler not to be plagued with questions about my project. My Partner upstairs was handling every detail with the utmost perfection.

When the heavy envelope with a yard-long questionnaire arrived from the Consulate, I was happy. Things were moving and my sponsor, Mr. Hobart, agreed to locate a rented room for me in Teaneck. His next letter stated that the German minister had telephoned him, asking a string of questions, to which Mr. Hobart did not seem to object. Close to seventy years of age, he had been married twice and had nine children of whom several were still under twenty-one. Now divorced, he lived in an apartment adjacent to his office.

The following week Pastor Baring told me that his colleague in New York had confirmed Mr. Hobart's divorce but he felt, if I insisted on renting a room in the neighborhood, I should have no problem. To this request, Mr. Hobart had already agreed, advising that a short distance away a German couple would be glad to rent me a room. This was an acceptable arrangement and I answered my sponsor expressing my thanks for his thoughtfulness.

Having carefully completed the questionnaire, I took a day off from work. Applications for emigration to the United States had to be filed in person at the Consulate. The minimum waiting period for German emigrants was half a year. If I was lucky, my registration number could fall into the next quota. I smiled, giving thanks for the perfect timing. After spending the entire morning at the Consulate answering questions, taking fingerprints, undergoing a brief medical examination, I hurried through a late lunch and then jumped on the next train to Aunt Erna's. Inviting me to spend the night with her, she bombarded me with questions.

"How does your mother feel about your adventure?" she asked excitedly. But I could not give her Mother's opinion because she had not yet voiced any. Mother had only glanced at me in disbelief when I told her of my trip to the Consulate.

Returning home the next day, Maria started to question me seriously. For the last few weeks she had watched me study English, read English literature, and write a lot of letters. It could not be just another fancy of mine. I answered her briefly without volunteering details. To some questions, I myself did not know the answer.

"Mother does not believe that you would emigrate to the States alone," she told me, evidently voicing her own opinion as well. When I invited Maria to come with me or join me later, she turned down my offer with a flat "No." She shared Mother's hope that I would change my mind. From her quiet, subdued spirit, however, I sensed that she was worried. Although everyone in the family now knew of my intentions, and as I did not volunteer information, no one asked curious questions.

This freedom of being undisturbed was very convenient because it permitted me to concentrate on my studies, brushing up on English, reading, writing, and typing. Reading presented no difficulty, but typing in English made me feel as if I had two left hands. My mind could spell the words but my fingers could not find the right keys on the typewriter. Nevertheless, every night I clanked away with determination, disturbing the quietness of the house. To my amazement, no one complained although an air of suspense hung around the dinner table.

* * * * * *

In late summer of 1958, my sponsor, Mr. Hobart, wrote that he planned to visit Europe and intended to meet me in Aschendorf to discuss any questions I might possibly have. When I announced the news to Mother, she was visibly nervous and asked: "How will we communicate with the man?" I was the only one in the family who could speak English, but I assured her that I would manage to carry on a conversation. Father was aware that I had been working on my emigration to America and realized why I kept my project a secret. This time, I did not permit him to interfere with my plans, to discourage me again. He did not know, however, that the Lord was my Partner in this adventure. Nevertheless, Father surprised me with a positive reaction to Mr. Hobart's proposed visit.

"At least I'll have a chance to meet the man into whose hands you trust yourself," he said. In my next letter I sent directions to Mr. Hobart, instructing him of the shortest travel route from Koeln to Aschendorf. He planned to rent a car at the airport.

"His visit will stir up a great deal of gossip in the village," said Mother with concern, but Herta laughed, answering, "It will give the gossipy farmers something interesting to talk about." Herta offered to cook for the day, mentioning that Mother would be too nervous and would ruin the food.

Mr. Hobart arrived around noontime on the agreed day. Watching him slam the door casually of the beige, rented Mercedes and straighten out his coat, I knew I could trust him. Mother and Father met him at the door and I introduced the members of my family. He was a tall, slightly overweight man and spoke with a deep, slow drawl. His blue eyes, framed by a ray of wrinkles, indicated boyish curiosity. Settling relaxed and comfortably at the dinner table, he looked around and smiled, complimenting the cook. Mother was pleased to see him eat heartily and I was busy translating the conversation. It was fun.

To my amazement, even Father enjoyed the day. Digging out the few words of English he had learned during his stay in Egypt, Father carried on an animated conversation with Mr. Hobart and both managed well in understanding each other. It was obvious that our guest enjoyed his visit as much as we did. Late in the afternoon, Mr. Hobart inquired about a hotel where he could stay overnight. He had agreed that he would drive to Hamburg with me and help me speed up procedures for my emigration. Ursula phoned the owner of a small hotel in Bad Rothenfelde, who was delighted to accommodate our guest from the States for the night. For the traditional afternoon coffee, Herta had baked a fruit pie and a buttercreme torte. It was a delight to watch Mr. Hobart enjoy his pieces. He sheepishly commented, patting his round stomach, "They do my expanded middle no favor." After a quick tour of the house, he confirmed that he would pick me up in the morning and then drove off to his hotel.

It had been a very exciting day and my impression was favorable. Father seemed more relaxed about my adventure.

"He is all right," he commented with a smile, reflecting on his conversation with Mr. Hobart, in which both had displayed a sense of humor. Mother still worried.

"How will you ever understand the man?" she asked, in spite of the fact that she had seen me manage very well. Herta's response to our visitor was enthusiastic.

"If I did not have a house and family, I would go with you." Her comment made me happy. I had gained another ally.

After the excitement of the day, I slept amazingly well and got up early to meet Mr. Hobart. He arrived on time and we set out on our two-hour drive to Hamburg. Giving him directions, I taught him the meaning of the various German traffic signs. He talked about his business in Teaneck and told me that his parents were of Hungarian descent. Both were deceased now. The deep drawl in his voice and the fluency of his sentences demanded all my concentration to follow his conversation. The American English was so different from the distinctly clipped London English which I had been taught in school. Yet it was entirely different again from the Scottish English that the Methvens spoke. But I was determined to master the language and was glad Mr. Hobart had no difficulty understanding me. My vocabulary at this time was rather limited, yet Mr. Hobart complimented me on my clear pronunciation.

"You speak well and your grammar is correct. Your vocabulary will expand once you are in the States," he encouraged me. When we reached the outskirts of Hamburg, I had to ask for directions several times. It was a sunny day and the area around the Consulate was the most beautiful and undestroyed section of Hamburg. Passing the *Rathaus* and then crossing one of the Alster-bridges, Mr. Hobart expressed his delight.

"I'm glad you suggested this trip. Hamburg is a beautiful city," he said enthusiastically. The sunshine made the city look its very best.

At the Consulate, a clerk told me that the waiting period of six months could not be reduced. It counted from the day I filed my application and I could expect to receive my visa in early December. Mr. Hobart, pleased to see me happy, invited me to a late luncheon. He asked me to recommend a quality hotel and I remembered that Ursula had mentioned the Hotel Vier Jahreszeiten as the best in Hamburg. Therefore, I suggested it to Mr. Hobart for his overnight stay. At the entrance he handed the car over to a liveried driver and two porters eagerly helped him with his baggage. Another porter showed us to the dining room and the maitre d'hotel motioned us gallantly to a table. It was the plushest hotel I had ever seen. As soon as we were seated, four waiters were at our elbows, anxious to serve us. Even Mr. Hobart was surprised. Fully enjoying the attention, he ordered oysters and a three-course luncheon as a celebration of the day.

"Even in Monte Carlo, I have not seen such service," he commented in amusement, encouraging me to order something special. But I stayed on safer ground with meat, vegetables, and potatoes. A glass of champagne topped the celebration of the day. During lunch, Mr. Hobart again confirmed that he would pay me $50 a week and told me that the room up the street in Teaneck would be available for me. When we finished, I wished my sponsor a pleasant vacation and took the train to Aunt Erna's.

Mr. Hobart's visit had proved to be a success. I was glad to have had the opportunity to meet him. We had agreed that I would send him a telegram, notifying him of the day of my arrival, and he had promised to meet me at Idlewild Airport in New York. My Lord and Partner had made perfect arrangements in choosing a man I could trust.

When I arrived at Aunt Erna's apartment, she greeted me excitedly.

"I still can't believe that you are going to America," she exclaimed and proceeded to ask me hundreds of questions. "Why do you have to go so far away?" "Wouldn't England be a better idea?" "Will you not get homesick?" "Who will be your friends?" She finally stopped when my cousin Gerd came home from work and happily congratulated me on my adventure.

"I'm proud of you, Madge," he said, slapping me on my shoulder.

"Some day I will venture out too, but it will be Spanish-speaking country," he admitted, desiring to become fluent in the language he was now studying. In Gerd I had gained a third partner. We talked late into the night and finally went to bed.

Before boarding the train homeward to Dissen the next morning, I picked up a copy of *Reader's Digest* in its original English issue. My two hours of traveling time would permit me to take a refresher course in English. I carefully used all of my spare time familiarizing myself with the English language, the language which would soon become the substitute for my own, the German I had spoken all my life. Systematically and thoroughly, I read every sentence, pronouncing the words in my mind, and underlining those that were unknown to me. Later I would check that vocabulary in my dictionary. When I had finished the first story, I counted the words I did not know. A rough calculation indicated that I understood forty per cent of the text, was able to guess another twenty per cent, but that the rest was unknown to me. I was optimistic about my analysis, especially since my last English lesson had been fifteen years ago in middle school. I was determined to learn this language and to pronounce it correctly. When I jumped off the train at the station in Dissen, I had an intensive self-taught, two-hour English course behind me, a very practical investment of my time.

At home, Herta whispered to me that Mother still did not believe I would go to America.

"She thinks you are not serious," she said, explaining that she had trouble convincing her. Gingerly, I stepped into my room, happy and light-hearted. I thanked my Lord and Partner for joining me in this venture, for going with me. Mother had heard me return and waited at the top of the stairs, eyeing me curiously.

"How will you manage to live on such a big continent all alone?" she asked worriedly. But she did not know of my Ally, my Partner in this undertaking. Trying to explain it to her was useless; she would not have understood. Over the years, especially during our last evacuation from Dievenow, God had become very close, very real to me. I considered Him a personal friend, available at all times, under any circumstances, any place. He was definitely not limited to a continent, to a language. My Lord was in charge of the Universe, in control of our planet, our solar system. He was Almighty. Therefore, I did not need to worry. As He had proven to me countless times that He cared for me, He had arranged for my emigration even to the minutest detail, I loved Him; I trusted Him unconditionally. My promise to serve Him and His Creation was out of gratitude that He loved me, that He took time to provide for everything I needed and more; that in the process He had blessed me with insight, with understanding. He had helped me to overcome my resentment toward the Hitlerjugend, toward the Muellers, toward the Niemeyers, by showing me that these experiences were necessary and part of His over-all plan for me, to take me to America, His own country. My experiences served as a school, preparing me for some special task He had in store for me. He had freed me of my limited Self, the fearful, intimidated, resentful Self and, in the process, had made me free. Now, instead of wasting my energies in negative self-absorption, I had learned to serve silently, to give, to bless, to love. These feelings and insights were sacred to me. I could not discuss these with anyone in the family. Instead, I told Mother that my visit to the Consulate had been successful and that I expected to receive my visa in early December.

"You will not leave before Christmas?" she asked anxiously and, to change the subject, I told her that Aunt Erna sent regards. But she stubbornly pursued her train of thought.

"How long do you intent to stay in America?" To ease her mind, I told her of my plans.

"A year or two, depending on how well I like it." Now she regretted that Father had discouraged me from going to England. The British Isles would have been closer than America. Nevertheless, I appreciated that Father had discouraged me. The United States held greater promises, greater opportunities for me than England. Mother, in another feeble attempt to change my mind, suggested that I should move to Hamburg if I did not like to live in Aschendorf. She did not understand. I was not tied to Germany, one country. I was free! Free to go as far as my Lord desired to take me. I was excited about going.

Since the traditional landing of the "Mayflower" with her first brave load of pilgrims arrived on the shores of America, millions of others had been drawn to the Land of the Free. I considered myself one more soul drawn by the spirit of Freedom to the shores of the Free, guided by the Hand of my Lord, the Creator of us all. The One who had breathed life into me knew my feelings. He did not need an explanation. It was very simple.

* * * * * *

The next day at work, I calculated my net earnings until December, subtracting my living expenses. By converting my savings into U.S. currency, I had sufficient money in reserve for a round-trip ticket—just in case, and over one hundred dollars in spending money for the first weeks after my arrival. Even from the financial point of view, I was adequately supplied.

Mr. Rohn knew of my intentions to leave Germany and had hired a young girl to be trained for my position. His father, Mr. Rohn, Sr., was enthusiastic about my adventure and reflected on his life as a young man. For many years he had lived in the United States and, returning to Germany to get married, had found the opportunity to buy a knitting mill in Sachsen, where he settled with his young wife. Reflecting on his years in America, he assured me that I would like the country.

"The soil and her people are very generous," he said, remembering his experiences fondly.

My nights after work I spent in sorting out things, separating the clothes and items I intended to take with me to New York. Planning to travel the fastest way possible, once I received my visa, I planned to fly with Lufthansa, the German airline, on the first available flight. Therefore, my luggage had to be ready so I could leave without delay. My bedroom set I intended to give to Andreas, positive that he would marry some day. Frederick, who had married in the meantime, had purchased his own furniture. Maria, whenever she married, would like to buy a different style. Her taste and mine were not the same. All other furniture I divided among Mother, Ursula, and Herta. The closet full of linens and silverware, Herta offered to keep in an airtight container until further notice. She, as well as I, knew intuitively that I would not return soon. Consequently, I planned to leave everything in perfect order.

Maria, who had shared the room with me over the years, had grown quiet, realizing that I was serious about my decision. But my offer for her to join me in the States, even at a later date, she flatly rejected.

"I don't feel right about leaving the country," she said without giving me any further explanation. Many nights when I arrived home late from a course, I found her sound asleep in the kitchen, her head on the table. Could she be frightened to go to bed by herself, to sleep alone in our room downstairs? Not wanting to embarrass her, I did not ask questions. She surprised me with a statement a few weeks later.

"After you have left, I will also leave Aschendorf," she told me, mentioning that her work was too far away, requiring two hours of traveling time each way. Why did she turn down my offer? I asked myself. I did not understand. But I did not want to prod into her mind. I wondered. Could she possibly be thinking seriously about Lothar, the boy from our study group in Dissen? She had been dating him occasionally.

After completing her apprenticeship with the tailor in Dissen, she had been employed as a cutter in a factory manufacturing bathrobes and towels. Although her earnings were substantially larger, her trip to Steinhagen, by bike and by train, was very tiring, leaving her almost no spare time to pursue her own interests. Before accepting this job, Mother had urged her to open her own tailoring business, but Maria had explained that tailoring men's suits and coats was a man's job. It would be too impractical for her, a girl.

My replacement at the office was learning fast. The girl proved to be a much more accurate and speedier typist than I. She also enjoyed the accounting aspect of the job, keeping the postings in the ledger up to date. The auditor promised to teach her how to close the books at the end of the month.

In the village of Aschendorf, the news of my emigration to the United States spread like wildfire. I was positive the Niemeyers knew about my plans. It did not matter because Manfred was now engaged, possibly to be married soon. As it was the last day of November, I expected my visa to arrive any day. Mother worried.

"I hope you will not leave before Christmas," she said, indicating that she dreaded the thought of my departure. Wisely, I had not mentioned to Mother that Mr. Hobart had given me the option in his last letter to postpone my trip until after the holidays because real estate business was slow at this time of the year. Fearing he might change his mind about the sponsorship, I confirmed to him that I would come to Teaneck as soon as I had received my visa.

The next day, the first of December, I found my visa in the mail. Overjoyed, I told Mother that I would call Lufthansa in the afternoon to book the first available flight. My baggage was ready except for the last few minute details. Gobbling down my food, totally unaware of what I was eating, my mind was traveling ahead, already arriving in New York. I rushed back to the office. Dialing Lufthansa reservations, I was told that an evening flight for the third of December was available, arriving in New York the next morning at ten. I booked. In three days I would be in New York! Hurrah! When Mr. Rohn, Jr. returned from lunch, I announced the news.

"Tomorrow will be my last day," I said happily. Although he had known I would be leaving, he was surprised that it happened so quickly. Upon my request, he dictated a reference, confirming my employment with the firm, adding that he had been satisfied with the performance of my work, my attendance, my attitude. His new secretary typed the letter for me. Only a few last-minute details needed an explanation. My competent replacement could easily handle routine matters. In the evening I raced to the post office in Bad Rothenfelde to speed off a telegram to Mr. Hobart, notifying him of the flight number and the date and time of my arrival at Idlewild Airport. The postal clerk at the window, having known me for several years, gave me a quizzical look, realizing that the text of the telegram was in English.

"What does this mean?" he asked curiously and, smiling happily, I told him that I would be in New York in two days. Shaking his head in disbelief, he went off to send the telegram.

On my way out, through the big glass door, I recognized Niemeyers' blue delivery truck pulling into the driveway. A feeling like lightning struck me when I recognized Manfred at the wheel. He must have had the same reaction because the truck stopped with an abrupt jerk. Manfred jumped out, telling the driver to take care of the load of packages and, lifting me down the three big steps, gave me a big kiss. Words bubbled out of me like a stream and, with a happy smile, I told him I had posted a telegram a minute ago to my sponsor, notifying him of my arrival in New York two days hence. Manfred turned white, holding on to the iron banister. Touching his forehead with one hand, he stammered:

"Oh, my God! Now I know why!" Realizing that my leaving the country was shocking news to him, I explained why I had made my decision, but his mind seemed to be elsewhere. His mind only vaguely seemed to grasp my words. He sat down on the side of the stoop as if in despair, holding my hand.

"Do you have to go to the States, Maexchen?" he asked. But I was determined to follow my plans, knowing that he was engaged to someone else. When I softly reminded him of this fact, he turned his eyes to me and said sadly:

"But we broke the engagement." Collecting himself, he stood in front of me, holding me by the lapels of my coat, explaining to me:

"Listen, Maexchen, I arrived here only yesterday upon Papa's strict order to return. Now I realize the reason for it. He knew you were leaving. Neither he nor Mama told me about this." Now I understood his shock and despair. I tried to help him understand his parents' limitations, their fears, telling him that everything would work out for the best, once he was in charge of the firm.

"The firm," he laughed bitterly, "is going downhill and has been going in that direction since the day you left. Why did this calamity have to happen? Why did we not get married?" he asked, imploring me. He had left a well-paying and prestigeous position to return to Aschendorf, a place that held no promise for him. Yet I assured him that God would find a place for him as He had for me, and some day we would both be happy, each one in his own little niche. Begging him not to harbor any resentments against his parents, I kissed him softly, then departed.

"God bless you, Maexchen," he whispered, knowing that I had made the break, that I was on my way to a new life.

I was glad to walk the long stretch home alone and I appreciated the darkness, hiding the trickle of tears rolling down my cheeks. My Lord had even permitted me a final goodbye from Manfred, explaining to him my reasons for leaving the country. Praying for the one I had loved, I was confident that in the care of a loving Lord, he would overcome the resentment he now held against his parents. My Lord, my Partner, had helped me grow so that even now, this very day, I loved them still, every one of the Niemeyers, including "Mama." I realized that she had been one of God's instruments, speeding me on the way to greater things, to a happier life.

* * * * * *

The next day flew with office work and last-minute preparations. Maria insisted on traveling with me to Duesseldorf, to see me off at the airport. Frederick was to drive us to the station in Dissen. We went to bed early to be refreshed in the morning. Before retiring, Father looked straight at me, saying: "Once you live in America, you will meet many Jews. Promise me, that you will never hate them." I promised, not fully understanding the meaning of Father's request.

Amazingly, I slept well. Hardly anything in life was able to rob me of my sleep. Only for a moment I wakened when Father stepped into the room at 5:00 a.m. to kiss me goodbye, to whisper a blessing. As I turned over, I heard muffled sobs coming from Maria's bed. But within minutes I was fast asleep again to wake only by the sound of the alarm, telling us that it was time to get up.

The room was cold but a glance out the window assured me that it would be a clear day once the thin fog had dissipated. As noiselessly as possible, I went upstairs to be first in the bathroom. But the creaking door had wakened Maria and she got up immediately. On the landing, passing my parents' bedroom, I could hear that Mother had also gotten up. Having laid out my clothes the night before, I dressed quickly. When I walked into the kitchen, Mother had started a fire in the stove. Maria joined us moments later and, while the three of us ate breakfast, one after the other scrambled in. Because most of us were still sleepy, we had breakfast in silence, each one following his own train of thought. Excusing myself, I checked my papers and locked the tightly packed suitcase. When Frederick honked the horn outside, I was ready. Maria came flying down the stairs to get into her coat.

I quietly embraced each one, noticing tears in Mother's eyes but, not giving in to emotions, I joked, saying, "Here goes your pioneer," and quickly turned toward the car, taking my seat next to Maria. Frederick started the motor and off we went. I waved to Mother, Ursula, Andreas, Herta, Albert and their young son through the rear window. Passing the Niemeyer villa, I noticed someone standing at the window behind the white curtains, slightly moving them. I waved in that direction and then, turning my eyes on the road, left Aschendorf.

At the station Frederick unloaded my baggage and helped us on the train. He embraced me, wishing me luck, and then got off. He waved until the rolling train moved around the bend. Maria, sitting in the corner, looked sad and depressed. I tried to snap her out of her melancholy mood by focusing on lighter matters.

"We had no chance to notify Aunt Tina in Duesseldorf. What will we do if she's not at home?" I asked jokingly. Maria replied dryly, "We will have to sit on the stoop and wait until she returns." The thought was funny and made me smile, glad to know that Maria had overcome her spell of sadness. Several years ago our cousin Christa had finally located Aunt Tina and Trude in East Germany where they had been transported by the Russians from Koenigsberg. Uncle Anton had been arrested and eyewitnesses re-

279

ported that he had been shot. From East Germany Christa had taken the two to Duesseldorf, where Trude had remarried, finding a husband and a father for her young son. It was miraculous that Aunt Tina and Trude had survived the Russian occupation in Koenigsberg where Trude had been forced to learn a trade as a house painter. In their own home town, they had been dispossessed and had suffered from hunger and deprivation. Mother had suggested that Maria stay with Aunt Tina overnight and return to Aschendorf the next day.

I talked enthusiastically to Maria about the possibilities and opportunities America would have for me and promised to keep her current on any developments. Our train ride was rather uneventful as we met the connecting schedules on time. When we arrived in Duesseldorf, one of the major cities in the Ruhr district, I was amazed not to find even a trace of the ravages and destruction of the war. The city was booming. New, modern buildings were springing up everywhere; construction was in full swing. We took a taxi to Aunt Tina's apartment and, as I had feared, she was not at home. We dropped the heavy suitcase in the hall and sat down on the stoop next to the apartment door. Maria looked disappointed, but I laughed. How many more times in my life did I have to beg for shelter? This time, it struck me as being funny.

We must have sat in the hall for over an hour while neighbors, going up and down the stairs, gave us quizzical looks, very much to my amusement. Finally, I heard Aunt Tina's voice downstairs and I called over the banister to her:

"Surprise!" She did not believe her eyes or the story I told her moments later, but she recovered quickly and prepared something for us to eat. As we still had a few hours left before departure, we sat and talked about my new adventure. Trude, her husband, and her teenage son insisted that they see me off at the airport. I was pleased because the happy troupe would help Maria overcome her sadness.

We broke off early as I did not like last-minute rushes and hailed a cab to take us to the airport. Weaving our way through heavy traffic, I breathed a sigh of relief when we arrived. I checked my suitcase at the counter. At the same time I received my boarding pass and, looking at it happily, I noticed that Maria had become very quiet. Neither Aunt Tina's quiet, gentle conversation nor Trude's son's enthusiasm could snap her out of it. She cried bitterly when I kissed her goodbye and boarded the plane. They will take her home and console her, I assured myself, feeling sorry for my little sister. On the ramp to the plane, I waved once more and then followed the smiling stewardess to my seat. I had a window seat and visualized that my Lord took the seat next to me. Thanking Him for bringing me this far, right on schedule, I envisioned that we now were taking this flight together.

The sudden roar of the engine switched my attention from the inside to the outside and I watched the plane roll slowly into position on the landing strip. The stewardess quickly checked our seat belts. The engines roared full blast. The plane gained speed and, after a few minutes, the rattle of the airplane subsided. We were airborne, heading for New York! Over the wings I could see the city of Duesseldorf left behind down below. Once the plane had nosed through the cloud cover, I saw the blazing disc of the setting sun. What splendor! Soon dinner was served, demanding my attention for a while.

Finally, after the clatter of dishes stopped and the stewardesses pointed out the pillows and blankets overhead, I had time to think. In the meantime, it had turned dark and, from my reclining position, my head resting on the small, white pillow, I could see the crescent of the moon rising in a deep azure sky. What a clear, beautiful night!

My thoughts returned to Gumbinnen, to the time when I was a child. God must have known my destination when He sent my soul forth to be born. He must have persuaded Mother to call me by my middle name, Marianne, instead of Erika, my harsh sounding first name, because He knew that Marianne would be an international name, needing no change, once I arrived in America. As the only member of our family, He sent me to middle school where I learned to speak English, providing the background for the language I would adopt later in life. As a young traveler, spending time with Oma as a baby and, later, many years with Aunt Ina, I was conditioned to be happy in many different places. My Lord had moved me around at a young age, preventing me from ever getting homesick, preparing me to be flexible and not to become too attached to people, places, belongings—material things which He knew I would have to sacrifice later. God had been with me from the beginning, from the beginning of time. Therefore, I was certain He was with me at this moment, guiding me toward a life that He had planned for me. I was happy and curious to find out what my Ally and Friend had in store for me in America, His country, a country that proudly proclaimed: IN GOD WE TRUST. I was certain He already knew the pattern of my entire life, guiding and tutoring me along the way, revealing to me as much each day as He knew I could handle. I was excited about my life, wondering how many more surprises God held in store for me.

Then I tried to visualize Idlewild Airport but, not having seen a photograph of it, no picture came to my mind and I let it go. For a second, I wondered whether Mr. Hobart would be at the airport. But, realizing Who was on this flight with me, I was certain my sponsor would be waiting at the airport early in the morning, expecting me. Soon I fell into a light sleep. Even the roar of the engines seemed to fade away and, as the plane crossed varying air currents, its light swaying gave me the impression that I was in a huge cradle, my beloved Lord rocking it gently.

Although the trip was scheduled to take eight hours, time seemed to vanish. Now and then I stirred, watching a passenger move down the aisle in the almost dark plane. Most of them were sound asleep. It seemed only moments later when I noticed a light, pinkish haze over the eastern horizon and, as the color increased, it got lighter. A new dawn, a new day had started, holding for me a new life on a new continent. Craning my neck, I watched the sun rise slowly out of the clouds that resembled a cover of fluffy white snow. With the increasing daylight, the sleeping passengers stirred and one by one wakened.

Then the pilot announced over the speaker system that we were flying over Newfoundland and after breakfast would approach New York within a few hours. He confirmed local New York time to be 7:30 a.m. After washing the sleep out of my eyes in the tiny cubicle of the lavatory, I was ready for breakfast, which several stewardesses served in a very efficient manner. The aroma of freshly brewed coffee wakened the last sleepers and bits of conversation started here and there.

The business man, who had taken the aisle seat in my row, had buried himself in his paper at take-off and had been snoring loudly during the night.

"It will be a clear and sunny day in New York," he commented optimistically. Explaining to him that this was my first trip to the United States and that I was an emigrant, he made a motion like tipping his hat, and said:

"Good luck to you." I thanked him, smiling. After breakfast, I noticed that the plane was gradually dropping in altitude and soon the sign to fasten our seat belts flashed overhead. The pilot announced that we were approaching New York and that the weather was good. As the plane dropped through a layer of thin clouds, I could see the blue ocean below and a coastline. My neighbor explained that this was part of Long Island. Then, with tipped wings, the plane made a sharp curve and dropped down foot by foot. At one point I had seen high square buildings in the distance and realized this was the skyline of New York. The brakes at the wings went up as we approached the landing strip at tree-top level. With a gentle bump, I felt the wheels touch the ground and I was overwhelmed at the size of the airport, the vastness of land surrounding it.

Idlewild, its name meant lazy wilderness, lying idle. The land before me did not impress me as a winderness, but the endless miles of flat, white open space fascinated me. When the plane had come to a stop, I took my flight bag and moved with the crowd to the door. The early morning sun, the crispness in the air, the vastness of space, filled my heart with joy. Slowly stepping down the stairs, I glanced around. Very far away I could see the horizon, the sky touching land, and, to the other side, the water.

When my feet touched the ground, although it was cool outside, a feeling of warmth surged through me. I had the peculiar feeling of homecoming, a feeling I had not had since I had lived in Gumbinnen, my home town. Had it not been for the disembarking crowd, I would have thrown my arms up into the air. I felt so happy! I felt so free! It was the morning of December 4, 1958.

I had come to the Land of the Free: To Serve Thee.

EPILOGUE

Today, more than eighteen years after my arrival at Idlewild (now Kennedy) Airport, I feel that I am closer to God, my silent Ally and Friend, than to anyone else.

For His own peculiar reason, my Lord has promoted "Stinker's" problem math student from Assistant Bookkeeper to Full-Charge Bookkeeper, from Junior Staff Accountant to Senior Staff Accountant. If "Stinker" knew that I am earning my living by working with figures, he would be shocked but pleased to see he managed to hammer a sufficient amount of mathematics into one of his students. Now that God has given me adequate training in accounting, He has presented to me another opportunity: writing.

The strict disciplines of accounting are advantageous to the occupation of writing, because in both professions accuracy and productivity are highly rated. If Miss Zahn, my former homeroom teacher, were alive, she would be proud that her prediction has come true. When I was ten years old she had mentioned: some day you might become a writer, just keep this possibility in mind.

In taking night courses at BMCC (Borough of Manhattan Community College), a branch of the City University of New York, I try to catch up on my lost education, with the subjects of English and Creative Writing as my major focal points. My goal is to become a professional writer and move out of New York to a smaller city, to a city approximately the size of my hometown, Gumbinnen.

Father has long since reconciled to the fact that one of his daughters has become an American citizen. He had persuaded

Mother to pack their suitcase and visit me after I had enthusiastically written him about the weekend house I had recently purchased, a house nestled away in the village of Hillsdale, in upstate New York. My description of the clear creek meandering its way through the far end of the property had caught the angler's attention: where there is water, there must be fish! Father reasoned. He had to come.

The size of New York City did not impress either Mother or Father, except for its unusual opportunities. Our visit to the Frick Museum delighted Father, where he admired original masterpieces by the famous artists Rembrandt van Ryn and Franz Hals among numerous others. On our visit to Chinatown, Mother was amazed to see the sizable and elaborate collection of intricate hand-carvings, carvings in ivory, jade, rose quartz, teak wood and mother-of-pearl. How much talent, artistry and patience had gone into the creation of each piece!

At my house in Hillsdale, Mother and Father felt very much at home. The long row of strong scented silky pines bordering the three-acre lot brought back memories of Gumbinnen, of Fichtenwalde. Father loved the stillness at night, the song of birds at sunrise and Mother had never seen such colorful foliage at the onset of fall. While Father helped me turn over the soil in the sizable organic vegetable garden that I had fenced in, Father was amazed at the strength of my back. I explained to him that I had been fortunate to locate a Bavarian masseuse in New York, a lady in her late sixties, displaying the strength of a bull, who had examined the set of X-rays of my spine, which I had obtained from a hospital. Administering regular steam baths, massages and osteopathic adjustments to my tense back, she had stretched and aligned the spine over a six months period, after which my muscles had relaxed and the entire body had grown stronger. For the first time, after my accident at the Niemeyer factory, I was free of back pains. Mother called it a miracle.

On a brief shopping trip to Great Barrington, Massachusetts, Mother commented that it felt like being in Bad Rothenfelde; the town was similar in size, people looked and dressed the same, and if it were not for the difference in language, she would think she was at home.

Our day trip to the Adirondacks was gift of God; it was a sunny, clear and comfortably warm day. Equipped with rubber boots, fishing rod and a New York State fishing permit, Father was impressed with the size of Lake George and happy about his angler's luck: he caught several fish. Later, at our picnic-lunch at Lake Champlain, Father let his eyes wander over the deep blue water below and said: "It is easy to imagine Indians around this area. How much they must have loved this beautiful lake." He could hardly tear himself away. Lake Placid, located in the center of the Adirondack Mountains, was our destination, where I turned the car around to take a different route back. In early evening we stopped at Cascade Lakes, where Father once more shouldered his rod and asked permission to go down to the lake alone. Mother and I gladly agreed and got engrossed in conversation. Noticing the onset of dusk, Mother looked at her watch and told me to go and bring Father back before dark. How many times had I done this routine in Gumbinnen, run down the Beethovenstrasse to the large pond, where I would find Father hidden behind high reeds watching his rod, forgetting all about time? Reluctantly Father parted from the lake and on our trip home, after a long period of silence, said: "It is not fair that this country is blessed with so many beautiful lakes, whereas in Aschendorf we have no lake, no river, not even a creek. America is truly God's country."

Could Father, now passed the age of seventy-five, have regretted not having emigrated to the United States thirty years earlier? I did not ask the question, but before taking Mother back home to Germany, he made me promise that I would keep his fishing rod and rubber boots—just in case he might decide to come back.

Meeting one of my friends at my apartment in New York, Mother and Father were given a surprise trip to the West of America via a slide presentation, narrated by Dana, a native of Ohio and a descendant of the famous Indian Chief, Sitting Bull. I acted as the interpreter. The majestic, snowcapped mountains of Colorado, the deep, purple tinted gorges of the Grand Canyon, the crystal clear mountain lakes and the blue sky over the rugged terrain, captured Father's imagination. His eyes were shining. He had glimpsed America's West through the eyes of an "Indian," as he called my friend, an expert photographer with the God-given talent to capture through her lens the soul of nature.

Although Mother had enjoyed her visit to the United States, she was glad to return to Aschendorf, to be close to her children and grandchildren. Father regretted that the limited time had not permitted him the opportunity to meet my little Jewish Godchild, Keri, a precious tot, daughter of a long time girlfriend. Telling him that her mother and I had vowed to teach Keri about the God of the Hebrews, but also expose her to the Christian teachings, Father was pleased, saying: "Christ came especially to the Israelites and He will return to them, His chosen people; so that they may be Christed also."

Father, after more than ten years of retirement, is busier than ever. Having helped four members of the family build houses, he occasionally takes out his brushes to work on an oil painting. His favorite themes are landscapes, floral bouquets, Indian heads and the moose. Again, he has supplied the entire family with his masterpieces. From one oil painting, however, he promised not to part: the Indian Chief, Sitting Bull, in color. From a small black and white photograph, Father had copied the famous Indian. Mother mentioned, that although an art dealer had offered Father a sizable sum of money, Father would not part from the painting. He loved the Indian.

Before boarding the plane, Mother reminded me of their new address: they lived in Ursula's new house.

In 1974, the men in the family had joined Frederick in his efforts and built a two-family brick house for Ursula in Aschendorf, located very close to the Niemeyer villa. Ursula, working for over twenty years with the government, is unmarried and has persuaded Mother and Father to live with her.

Frederick, the mason in the family, has built a three-family brick house in the small town of Dissen for his wife and three teen-age children. He rents out the two spacious upstairs apartments. Employed as a foreman with a large contractor, he has supervised Father and his two brothers-in-law in brick laying. In teamwork the men have built four houses. Herta's house, the first result of their efforts, is now over twenty years old and presently being remodeled. Herta and Albert Berger, married over twenty-five years, are the proud parents of two adult sons, the oldest planning to marry shortly. Herta and Mother keep in touch with several East Prussian families, who either live in East Germany or the southern part of East Prussia, the part of our province now under Polish occupation. Both women consider it their duty and it is a family project to send packages with food and clothing, especially before Christmas, to these German people less fortunate than we.

Although Herta has not been in touch with Gertrud Seefeld recently, she recalls from their earlier correspondence, that Gertrud's parents were chased off their farm in Lautern by the occupying Russians. Mr. Seefeld was separated from his family and was deported to the Ukraine, where he reportedly died. Mrs. Seefeld and her young daughter were shipped to East Germany, where Mrs. Seefeld died several years later. The last news Herta received from Gertrud mentioned that her young sister has become a nurse and is working at a hospital in East Berlin.

In 1972 Father helped Frederick to build a modern brick

ranch for Maria and her husband, who live with their three children in Steinhagen, near the city of Bielefeld. Maria's husband earns his livelihood as a draftsman and illustrator for a publishing house in Bielefeld. Maria, after having mustered all her courage, learned to drive and is now busy shuttling the children to and from school.

Andreas, the youngest brother in the family, has established himself in Hamburg. His wife, a very calm, content and happy personality, is from our hometown, Gumbinnen, and teaches her two children, by means of recordings, to understand and speak the East Prussian dialect. Andreas, after having learned the building trade, switched jobs and has recently completed several years of special education, hoping to advance to the position of Inspector with the Custom House in Hamburg, where he has been employed for over ten years.

Oma, Father's mother and the heart of the Schmeling-clan, celebrated her 100th birthday on May 12, 1976 and enjoyed the army of visitors: her children, grandchildren and great-grandchildren. Shortly thereafter, however, she had an accident and a few months later, as a result of her injuries, died peacefully in her sleep.

Aunt Ina and Uncle Oskar decided to sell their small business in the Black Forest and move in with their son, Hans, who lives in the village of Grossenwiehe, near the city of Flensburg, located in the northernmost part of the province of Holstein. Shortly after their move, Uncle Oskar died suddenly. Although Aunt Ina is still unreconciled to the loss of her husband and unreconciled to the cold, stormy climate of the North, she lives in an apartment in her son's house, enjoying the liveliness of her four adult grandchildren. Hans, my favorite cousin, has stepped into Uncle Oskar's shoes: he is a radio mechanic and owns a small business, selling and repairing radios, record-players and television sets, building antennas for customers upon request. His wife, a very industrious woman, sells clocks and serves the many customers in their modern village store.

Aunt Maria, Father's aunt, had evacuated at the last minute from the Mozartstrasse in Gumbinnen and lives now in Bad Oldesloe, a spa located in the southern part of the province of Holstein. Erwin, her son, after having safely returned from the navy, completed his studies to become a doctor of science in the field of chemistry. He built a brick ranch for his mother in Bad Oldesloe, so that his sister, Waltraud, living with her family in Hamburg, could visit her frequently. Although holding an important position in one of the gold mines in Johannesburg,

South Africa, a city to which he has moved his family, Erwin keeps in close telephone contact with his mother and cares lovingly for her.

My cousin, Gerd, Aunt Erna's son, has made his earlier vision come true. After holding a manager's position for several years with one of the leading firms in Hamburg, he was offered the opportunity, because of his fluency in the Spanish language, to establish an overseas branch office, serving the Lufthansa and Hapag Lloyd in the South American cities of Cali and Medellin, Colombia. After the expiration of his three-year contract, he and his wife moved back to Hamburg, where he purchased a house and shortly thereafter welcomed the arrival of twins.

The Niemeyer villa has turned into a quiet place. Mrs. Niemeyer lives alone in the house, the children have flown out. Mr. Ernst Niemeyer, unable to reconcile to the fact that the shoe factory, his father's and his own life's work, went bankrupt, died of heart failure.

Manfred, having foreseen the dilemma of the firm, accepted a manager's position in a shoe factory located near the city of Hamburg, in a company owned by one of his student friends he met in Pirmasenz. Manfred, very fond of children, experienced heartache when he lost his only daughter in a premature death. Manfred's brother, Herbert, is married and lives and works in Wuppertal, one of the cluster of cities in the industrial Ruhr area. Charming Inga, Martin's sister, happily married to Arnold, the painter, is mother of two sons.

Although Greta and Ernst Niemeyer, Jr. are still unmarried, both have left Aschendorf. Greta holds a secretarial position with a firm in West Berlin and hopes to visit the United States on her next vacation. Ernst, Jr., employed as a board mechanic with the German Merchant Marines, has seen many parts of the world. Nevertheless, the village of Aschendorf is home to him and he enjoys spending his vacations with "Mama," his dear stepmother.

The village of Aschendorf has recently been incorporated into its neighboring spa and is now part of Bad Rothenfelde.

Often friends and members of my family ask me questions, questions like this: After living in the United States over eighteen years, do you still believe that it is the ideal place to live? In view of the high crime rate, ever increasing taxes, rapidly rising prices, the steady climb of unemployment, and the ousting of a president, have you ever entertained the thought of returning to Germany? Isn't America sliding downhill? Are the American people really free?

I am fully aware of the sad statistics but, contrary to the

popular attitude, I contribute my share to stem the downhill trend by using the powerful tool of prayer. I pray for our country, I pray for our president, and, most important, I pray for peace.

Reflecting upon my own life, I am convinced that prayer is man's most powerful tool. Through earnest and diligent prayer, I have come to know this stranger, I call Self. In getting to know myself, I became very familiar with God, with the Law under which the Universe operates. My first commandment was, that I had to become pure in the eyes of my Maker. Having helped me to cast out the debris of fear, hatred and resentment from my mind, God made me grow strong, daring; daring to pray not only for myself and friends, but daring to pray for our crime ridden cities, for the addicted, for our troubled country, for our confused civilization, for our planet which is violently reacting to the turmoil.

If we as Americans demand that our representatives in government be honest, we will have to become honest citizens ourselves, citizens who abhor the thought of filing an incorrect tax return. The responsibility for honest government lies in the hands of its people. The leader we elect fully represents the consciousness of us, the people. It is time, therefore, that each citizen shoulders responsibility, lives his life frugally, contributes his fair share of labor, thinks honorably, because apathy, criticism and rebellion will breed characters like Hitler, characters who are anxious to strip the masses of their power.

Then let us pray together, and in prayer invoke the Love and Power of the Almighty to set our country straight again.

Whenever anyone poses the question to me, if I ever regretted having emigrated to the United States, I have only one answer: I regret not having come sooner, to America, God's country.

Acknowledgments

I would like to acknowledge my gratitude to all my friends who have been influential in germinating the idea for this book.

I am grateful to Professor Abraham Kupersmith for his encouragement to write down these ideas, and for his tireless effort in his structural assistance with this work.

Furthermore, I want to express my humble gratitude to my dear friend, Professor Maye C. Hylton, for her great devotion to the creation of this book in spending endless hours in typing and retyping the manuscript.

Finally, I like to express my thanks to Reverend Paul Solomon for his kind help and guidance along the way.

The Unilaw Library Series

Unilaw Library is a line of inspirational, metaphysical and religious books which demonstrate the basic compatability of classic religious principles with ancient and modern metaphysical cosmology. The line will include fiction, children's books and practical, self-help applications. The purpose of Unilaw Library is to draw from all disciplines which contribute to the evolution of human thought, from the latest scientific discoveries to the use of intuitive process in creativity, and to contribute to the re-thinking of old dogmas and attitudes which will lead humanity to the truth about the nature of life and the universe.